CLEAN AND WHITE

Clean and White

A History of Environmental Racism in the United States

Carl A. Zimring

NEW YORK UNIVERSITY PRESS

New York and London

NEW YORK UNIVERSITY PRESS
New York and London
www.nyupress.org

References to Internet websites (URLs) were accurate at the time of writing.
Neither the author nor New York University Press is responsible for URLs
that may have expired or changed since the manuscript was prepared.

ISBN: 978-1-4798-2694-0

For Library of Congress Cataloging-in-Publication data, please contact the
Library of Congress.

New York University Press books are printed on acid-free paper,
and their binding materials are chosen for strength and durability.
We strive to use environmentally responsible suppliers and materials
to the greatest extent possible in publishing our books.

Manufactured in the United States of America

10 9 8 7 6 5 4 3 2 1

Also available as an ebook

To Jen, with love

CONTENTS

ACKNOWLEDGMENTS

Many hands made this book possible, not least hands from several libraries and archives. I am grateful for the help of Fath Davis Ruffins and Archives Center staff at the National Museum of American History; the authors of the Integrated Public Use Microdata Series, including Steven Ruggles, J. Trent Alexander (who introduced me to the Integrated Public Use Microdata Series many years ago), Katie Genadek, Ronald Goeken, Matthew B. Schroeder, and Matthew Sobek; Ed Frank and the staff at the University of Memphis Library; the New York Public Library; the New-York Historical Society; the Library of Congress; and Deborah Rice and the staff at the archives of the Walter Reuther Library at Wayne State University.

For financial and institutional support, thanks to the American Society for Environmental History for its Samuel P. Hays Fellowship. Thanks to Roosevelt University for a faculty development grant and sabbatical support. Thanks to Carol Lasser and the staff at Oberlin College's Department of History and Library for research access.

I have been fortunate to teach at supportive schools. Roosevelt University proved a nurturing interdisciplinary home with engaged colleagues; warm thanks to Mike Bryson, Brad Hunt, John Cicero, Amanda Putnam, Gary Wolfe, Greg Buckley, Julian Kerbis Peterhans, and all in the College of Professional Studies and to Chris Chulos, Sandra Frink, Erik Gellman, and Margie Rung in the Department of History and Philosophy.

Midway through writing this book, I moved to the Pratt Institute's Department of Social Science and Cultural Studies. Pratt is an invigorating interdisciplinary place to call home. Thanks to my colleagues, including (but not limited to) Cisco Bradley, Ric Brown, Josiah Brownell, Lisabeth During, Ann Holder, Gregg Horowitz, May Joseph, and Uzma Rizvi. Thanks as well to my students at both Roosevelt and Pratt, as they provided thoughtful discussions of this work in our seminars.

Steve Corey, Alexandra Filindra, Jim Longhurst, Chris Wells, and two anonymous reviewers gave careful readings and constructive feedback on drafts. Jennifer Hammer at NYU Press was a supportive and rigorous editor. In addition to Jennifer, Constance Grady and Dorothea Stillman Halliday have been invaluable in bringing this book to publication. I am grateful to all.

Feedback in public talks was a great help during the writing process. I thank audiences at the Labor and Working Class History Association meeting in Chicago, the Social Science History Association meeting in Chicago, the New York Metro American Studies Association "Dirt" meeting in Manhattan, the American Historical Association meeting in Chicago, the Race and Justice Symposium at Middlebury College (with particular thanks to Susan Burch and Kathryn Morse for their hospitality), and forums at Roosevelt University, DePaul University, and the Pratt Institute. You have helped me strengthen this book; any oversights or errors within are mine alone.

Jen Potter has lived with this book (and my attention to this book) for longer than anyone else. She has indulged my work habits with great cheer, and I cannot thank her enough. The dedication of the book to her is for those reasons and in no way due to the subject matter herein.

Introduction

The Biopolitics of Waste

Waste is a social process. We usually consider waste as material we discard, relying on public and private systems to remove unwanted materials from our homes, neighborhoods, and workplaces. These practices are consequences of our decisions to classify particular materials as waste, employ people to handle those materials, and develop systems to dispose of them. Waste informs the construction of our social and cultural values. In her 1966 study, *Purity and Danger*, anthropologist Mary Douglas defined dirt as "matter that is out of place," threatening the social order. Dirt and other waste matter derive their power not simply through being waste or having a kind of negative value. Rather, as "matter out of place," things deemed dirty, spoiled, or noxious carry polluting effects, by touching. In the introduction to the 2002 edition of *Purity and Danger*, Douglas remarked that classifying dirty things "reduces intellectual and social disorder . . . The concept of dirt makes a bridge between our own contemporary culture and those other cultures where behaviour that blurs the great classifications of the universe is tabooed. We denounce it by calling it dirty and dangerous; they taboo it."[1]

The social dimensions of waste are visible in recent American history. The Environmental Justice movement emerged in the 1980s as a response to hazardous waste siting in or near communities of color across the United States. The term "environmental racism" entered widespread use after the Reverend Benjamin Chavis used it to discuss the results of *Toxic Wastes and Race in the United States*, a national study of hazardous waste siting that the United Church of Christ published in 1987. Chavis defined environmental racism in 1992 as "racial discrimination in environmental policy-making and the enforcement of regulations and laws, the deliberate targeting of people of color communities for toxic waste facilities, the official sanctioning of the life-threatening presence of poisons and pollutants in our communities, and the history of excluding people of color from leadership in the environmental movement."[2]

Chavis expanded on his definition in a 1993 *Ebony* interview celebrating his appointment as executive director of the National Association for the Advancement of Colored People: "It is the deliberate targeting of people-of-color communities for hazardous waste facilities, such as landfills and incinerators. One of the responsibilities of the Civil Rights Movement is to define the postmodern manifestations of racism. We must not only point to overt forms of racism, but also to institutionalized racism."[3]

In the three decades since the *Toxic Wastes and Race* report identified a strong link between race and hazardous waste siting, identification of environmental racism has produced actions in urban and rural locations across the United States. A defining characteristic of these actions is the battle against exposing vulnerable peoples to hazardous wastes in nearby land, air, and water. Even in attempts to broaden the definition of "environmental justice," activists note that much of their work relates to battles against waste siting. "Waste facility siting battles are but one aspect of the movement for environmental justice," Luke W. Cole and Sheila R. Foster argued in 2001. That one aspect, however, "is the arena in which a great deal of grassroots action takes place."[4] The United Church of Christ recognized that the dimensions of environmental racism predated Chavis's use of the term. United Church of Christ Environmental Justice Program member Carlos J. Correa Bernier noted: "People of color, individually and collectively, have waged war against environmental injustices that predate the first Earth Day in 1970."[5]

Historians have responded with assessments of environmental inequalities evident between the mid-nineteenth century and the end of the twentieth century. These studies include monographs about African American experiences in Northern and Southern cities, African American fights against rural waste dumping in the South, indigenous protests against radioactive waste siting in the interior West, and Hispanic demonstrations against polluted agricultural lands in the West. These studies provide valuable understandings of how environmental racism affected the lives of particular communities at particular times.[6]

Less well understood are the historical factors shaping environmental racism in the United States. Too often histories of environmental inequalities treat race and ethnicity as static constructs. A binary construction of race serves to determine inequalities, leaving unconsidered the dynamics of race and racism. Considering changing constructions of race allows for a greater understanding of how environmental racism has evolved over time. Studies of whiteness in the United States have focused on the roles of the law, economics, literature, and science in the changing social construction of race over time,[7] but little attention has been paid to how environmental factors have shaped perceptions of race. One notable exception is Conevery Bolton Valenčius's work on how frontier settlers in the nineteenth century considered frontier life as transforming perceived racial characteristics,[8] but beyond this study little attention has been paid to theories of public health as they relate to racial constructs in American history.[9]

Historical analysis of environmental racism should consider how boundaries between the body and environment need to become foci for our historical inquiry. This book presents a history of environmental racism in the United States, using the lens of dirt. In doing so, it proposes the following: Although racism has been a structuring factor in creating environmental inequalities concerning waste, American constructions of race, of waste, and of their interactions have evolved since the nation's founding. Increasing scientific definitions of waste as hazard and of racial categories in the immediate antebellum period established a foundation for later racist constructions that posited that white people were somehow cleaner than non-white people. This assumption defined white supremacist thinking. Its evolution shaped environmental inequalities that endure in the twenty-first century, including in the marketing of cleaning products, the organization of labor markets handling wastes, and the spatial organization of waste management and residential segregation in the United States.[10]

By focusing on whiteness, this book aims to examine not only how people of color have been exposed to environmental dangers but also how contested minorities such as Southern and Eastern Europeans successfully adopted American notions of hygiene to achieve white identity in the twentieth century even as African Americans who engaged in rigorous hygienic practices were denied white privilege. Attending to hygiene and waste is central not only to understanding environmental inequalities in communities of color but also to understanding modern constructions of whiteness. White identity's conflation with cleanliness has a long and largely unexamined history. Understanding the dynamic relationship of whiteness and hygiene is crucial for understanding environmental racism in the nation's past and present.

This book examines the social and cultural constructions of race and hygiene in American life from the age of Thomas Jefferson to the Memphis Public Works Strike of 1968. Over this long history, eight developments are evident:

1. *American anxieties about race and dirt in the early years of the republic reflect contradictory impulses about slavery and urbanism.* Thomas Jefferson's ideals valued pastoralism and egalitarianism yet also depended upon slavery and urban trade. The inherent tensions are reflected in the Constitution, in the policies of the nascent federal government, and in Jefferson's own life.

2. *Justifications for slavery after 1820 relied more upon scientific racism and definitions of purity.* Threatened by the end of the international slave trade and growing calls for abolition within the United States, slaveholders used the language of scientific racism to explain the legitimacy of both slavery and white supremacy. The language used to justify racism at times resembled the language of the emerging public sanitation field.

3. *Although the Civil War marked the abolition of slavery and great advances in sanitation, insecurities about race and dirt endured.* The postbellum period has been described as a search for order amid an era of tumult, and this search is evident in the ways Americans described race and sanitary concerns. The most infamous insecurities involved "redeemers" of white supremacy, such as the Ku Klux Klan attempting to reassert white dominance through intimidation and violence, but a wide spectrum of society used references to pollution to define racial purity.

4. *Between 1865 and 1930, new constructions of waste and race redefined white people as innately cleaner than any non-white peoples.* Equating non-white skin with dirt, these constructions

(apparent in popular culture, academic discourse, and repeated tropes in advertising) marked new, emerging constructions of environmental racism.

5. *The new constructions of environmental racism had material consequences in the emerging occupational structures to manage wastes between 1870 and 1930.* New European immigrants, Asian immigrants, and African Americans participated in "dirty" jobs such as laundry, waste hauling, scrap recycling, and other sanitary services in numbers far above their representations in the general population.

6. *The new constructions of environmental racism had material consequences in the spatial organization of residences and of waste handling businesses between 1870 and 1960.* Racial residential segregation intensified in the twentieth century, and waste handling and disposal businesses clustered in non-white residential areas. Spatial environmental inequalities emerged by 1960.

7. *Some Americans assimilated into white society after World War II by abandoning dirty work and dirty neighborhoods.* Many Jews and Italians successfully moved into more reputable jobs and more prestigious residential suburbs. The power of white identity to inform environmental burdens endured; burdens on Hispanics and African Americans in the workplace and in residential neighborhoods intensified in the postwar era.

8. *Environmental inequalities produced a new rhetoric of resistance in 1968.* The Memphis Public Works Strike of 1968 marked both a culmination of growing environmental inequalities and an articulated resistance to those inequalities that defined the work of waste management as a civil rights issue. The response in Memphis was an important precedent to Chavis's definition of environmental racism and foundational for the Environmental Justice movement.

These consequences are a product of the changing racial constructions of the eighteenth and nineteenth centuries. Racial subjugation existed in the Americas well before the War of Independence, though the language of that subjugation did not use the categories that would become common by the mid-nineteenth century. Power in the English colonies initially rested with those who identified themselves as

Christian. This differentiated them from "savages" and "heathens," classifications used to enslave or kill. During the international debate over the morality of slavery between the mid-eighteenth and mid-nineteenth centuries, the historian Nancy Shoemaker has observed, the marker of superiority switched from "Christian" to "white." Whiteness denoted not only pale skin but also a certain moral superiority that voiced itself in increasingly strident tones by slaveholders as the peculiar institution became harder to justify. By focusing on the most visible aspect of the body, self-defined white people wore their status on their faces and on their hands.[11]

Skin in the United States became (to use Michel Foucault's term) a technology of power, a marker connoting any number of traits from intelligence to virtue to sexuality, depending on the insecurities and fears of those seeking to gain power from racial superiority. The biopolitics of the nineteenth century had skin color emerge as marker of purity and pollution. In the first half of the century, skin color marked boundaries between freedom and slavery, with heightened emphasis on whiteness as strength. After abolition, color did not wane in importance; instead, it actually increased during the struggle for a new social order. In a period of great social insecurity, white identity gained increased significance, attaching itself to another great concern of the era, cleanliness.[12]

This cultural shift has a history, one that is less obvious than contemporary perspectives on race might assume. In nineteenth-century constructions of race, white supremacists stained Native Americans, Asian Americans, and African Americans with assumptions that their skin, bodies, and behaviors were somehow dirtier than the skin, bodies, and behaviors of "white" people. Similar pejoratives were used against Jews, Slavs, Italians, Hungarians, and a host of people Americans now uncritically identify as being white. These were people who were entrusted to keep American society clean; these were the people who got their hands dirty to do so. When Americans of Southern and Eastern European heritage began to become identified as white ethnics in the twentieth century, they did so as they left sanitary occupations to African American and Hispanic workers. Understanding the historical dynamics that produced these inequalities requires examining the ideals on which the United States was founded.

PART I

Antebellum Roots

1

Thomas Jefferson's Ideal

Few Americans embodied the tensions of the new republic quite like Thomas Jefferson. An Enlightenment scholar who held slaves, and a champion of rural farm life whose presidency saw unprecedented industrial urbanism in the United States, Jefferson's thoughts and actions reflected his country's growing concerns about science, race, public health, and the role of government in the lives of the citizenry.

Although he died so destitute that his fellow Virginians raised money for him via lottery, Jefferson spent his final days on his beloved plantation, Monticello. It was there he drew his final breath at fifty minutes past noon on July 4, 1826, as the nation celebrated its fiftieth birthday. His final public utterance took stock of the nation he helped build, declaring it an enlightened land of liberty: "All eyes are opened or opening to the rights of man. The general spread of the light of science has already laid open to every view the palpable truth, that the mass of mankind has not been born with saddles on their backs, nor a favored few, booted and spurred, ready to ride them legitimately, by the grace of God. These are grounds of hope for others; for ourselves, let the annual return of this day forever refreshed our recollections of these rights, and an undiminished devotion to them."[1]

Jefferson's desire to live and die at Monticello reflected his vision of the young country he helped build. He was as worldly as any American of his time, an educated man and educator who took such pride in letters that the script he chose for his tombstone identified him as author of the declaration of American independence, founder of the state of Virginia for religious freedom, and, ultimately, father of the University of Virginia. Independence, religious freedom, and education were more important to the man in his dying days than the title he held as third president of the United States of America.[2]

Jefferson chose to spend his final days on his plantation, a choice consistent with the values he had espoused for more than half a century.

He saw himself as a farmer and his country as a society of farmers working together in a nation where none are king and all are learned equals. For Jefferson, the American farm was a symbol of self-reliance and egalitarian democracy, an "equilibrium of agriculture, manufactures and commerce. . . . essential to our independence." Cultivating the land produced people of "substantial and genuine virtue" while those involved in manufacture risked "subservience and venality." In contrast, he found the great cities of Europe as "pestilential to the morals, the health and the liberties of man" and felt that health and virtue could only thrive away from the polluted, impoverished urban slums. Far from the corruption of Europe, free people working the land had built a rugged, independent nation.[3]

Long after Jefferson's death, his ideas continued to shape the nation he helped found. Most obviously, this was true in the laws he crafted, but his ideal of a democracy of farmers independent from Europe became one of the most enduring American values. One reason for the power of this idea is what it grew in reaction against. Jefferson worried that developments in Europe were counterproductive to enlightened society, and he hoped to spare the United States the mistakes of European society. The dangers of monarchy involved accidents of birth determining political power rather than demonstrated ability among a national of equals. America, however, was a grand experiment. Jefferson's ideal sought to preserve some ideas and privileges of European society in an uncorrupted land where merit reigned supreme.[4]

The Dirty Cities

Although Jefferson valued the European statesmen and scholars he befriended in Paris, he hated much of what he saw in France's largest city. Industry belched smoke into the air and chewed up the bodies of the many to make profits for the few. The poverty and filth of large cities disgusted him when he traveled in Europe, and that distain stayed with him when he returned to America.[5] Even as he grudgingly accepted during his presidency that urban industry was beneficial to the young republic's economy, he never warmed to love cities.[6] Three years before his death, Jefferson opined that city life was an invitation to "vice and wretchedness."[7]

Jefferson's utopia was a farmer's paradise where all farmers owned land and shared comparable shares of wealth, political power, and stewardship over thriving natural wonders. Land for Jefferson was meant to be tilled, not turned into city blocks and settings for great buildings or large factories. In Paris he mused about the possibility of avoiding manufacturing industries altogether in his native land, relying instead on imported manufactures from Europe as Americans focused on the business of farming the fertile, wild lands. A nation of farmers, Jefferson argued, lacked the degradation and inequality Jefferson found in Paris and London. For Jefferson, rural Monticello represented exceptional American values.[8]

Urban grime was matter out of place; rural soil, conversely, was part of the natural order. On American farms, Jefferson believed, men interacted with the soil in ways that invigorated both. For the Virginian farmer, soil was the essence of his labor, and rich Virginian soil was capable of "elaboration into animal nutriment" and produced "rich fruits and grains."[9] Jefferson contrasted the fertile New World soil with those parts of Europe where "the poverty of the soil, or poverty of the owner, reduces [European domestic animals] to the same scanty subsistence."[10]

Jefferson explicitly categorized farm work as orderly and natural in his contrast with manufactures:

> Those who labour in the earth are the chosen people of God, if ever he had a chosen people, whose breasts he has made his peculiar deposit for substantial and genuine virtue. It is the focus in which he keeps alive that sacred fire, which otherwise might escape from the face of the earth. Corruption of morals in the mass of cultivators is a phaenomenon of which no age nor nation has furnished an example. It is the mark set on those, who not looking up to heaven, to their own soil and industry, as does the husbandman, for their subsistence, depend for it on the casualties and caprice of customers.

In this language, soil is not chaotic nor dangerous; it is as natural to the farmer as his own air and work.[11]

In the small, agricultural communities of his ideal, he boasted: "You will seldom meet a beggar [whereas in] the larger towns indeed they sometimes present themselves. These are usually foreigners, who have never obtained a settlement in any parish. I never yet saw a native American begging in the streets or highways." To be clear, the native Americans Jefferson referenced were colonists of European origin.[12]

By the time Jefferson took the oath of office as president in 1801, his ideal was already giving way to the ills he feared. American industry grew in the early nineteenth century, and with it, American cities grew, and grew quickly. When he died in 1826, New York's population had well exceeded 100,000, was fast on its way to the 202,589 enumerated in the 1830 Census, and would continue its growth into the kind of metropolis Jefferson had despaired of on his European visits. At the dawn of the U.S. Civil War, more than a million people lived within the boundaries of what we presently know as New York City, and well over 100,000 people lived in each of Philadelphia, Boston, Baltimore, New Orleans, Cincinnati, St. Louis, and Chicago (the latter of which was not incorporated until 1833). The United States under President Jefferson's watch urbanized quickly, transforming the nation.[13]

As American cities grew, so did the inequality, degradation, and diseases Jefferson feared would come of industrial cities. If Jefferson had a dour opinion of European cities, what he saw at home could hardly change his mind. The historian Suellen Hoy characterizes the colonial cities as "conspicuously unclean."[14] Philadelphia, Boston, and New York City were small compared to London or Paris, but they, too, were plagued with disease and dirt. Little in the way of sanitary infrastructure served these urban populations. Available drinking water was limited; Philadelphia in 1771 had only 120 public wells to draw water for drinking and firefighting. Philadelphians were at risk of contaminated water, and a series of yellow fever epidemics led to the development of a more extensive public water system in the 1790s. This, too, proved inadequate for the growing population; at no time in Thomas Jefferson's life could the people of America's largest city be free of worry about their water. Similarly, ad hoc water systems served the people of Boston and New York City. Mains of hollow pine logs served (when they didn't rot) the few hundred Bostonians that could afford to pay $10 a year. Most residents relied on wells dug where excrement and other filth could contaminate the water.

American cities experienced dangerously unsanitary conditions that produced regular epidemics of yellow fever, typhoid, cholera, and other infectious diseases. Part of the problem was population growth overwhelming the local environment's capacity to supply clean drinking water. Residents of the three largest cities, New York, Boston, and Philadelphia, relied on wells they dug in their increasingly congested neighborhoods. Writing of Philadelphia in 1798, the architect of the U.S. Capitol Benjamin Henry Latrobe found obvious links between poor water sanitation, overcrowding, and regular outbreaks of yellow fever. "The houses being much crowded, and the situation flat, without subterraneous sewers to carry off the filth, every house has its privy and its drains which lodge their supplies in one boghole sunk into the ground at different depths." Thousands drew their drinking water from this environment, as urban families pumped from wells close to the polluted streets, risking all manner of infectious diseases.[15]

Yellow fever epidemics were common. An outbreak killed 5,000 Philadelphians in 1793, and another killed more than 1,600 in New York City five years later. The conditions Latrobe described forced civic leaders to install a public water system, but it failed to keep up with population growth and civic needs. It would be half a century before Philadelphians could enjoy safe, dependable water on a regular basis.[16]

The risks of human waste from households contaminating water were joined by waste from other sources. Nuisance trades such as soapmaking, animal slaughter, and tanneries produced noxious odors, sounds, and runoff. Horses were abundant owing to their use to haul goods and people across town; the animals left thousands of tons of manure in the streets and, after dropping dead from overwork, their carcasses contributed to the solid waste problem. Chickens, goats, and hogs were kept for food, dogs and cats were kept as pets; excrement from all contaminated streets and water supplies.

The mounting sanitary challenges facing American cities threatened to replicate the ills Jefferson witnessed in Paris. The Paris Jefferson knew in the 1780s had a population of over half a million people, or more than twenty times the population of any contemporary American settlement. When Jefferson was elected president in 1800, the United States, like most of the world at the time, was primarily rural. The largest urban area was New York City; the Census that year measured its population (totaling Manhattan) at 60,515. If we consider all areas that would become the present five boroughs, that population would be 79,216.

Ten years later, New York's population had jumped to 96,373 (119,734 for current boundaries). Compared to Paris, these smaller, newer cities had fewer sanitation problems. The public health historian John Duffy argues that if we compare colonial cities with similar British and European towns "nearly all Europeans visiting the colonies in the eighteenth century commented upon the spaciousness, orderliness, and relative cleanliness of American towns." Still, American cities had more problems finding and consuming clean drinking water than did the smaller villages in the countryside. Life in Monticello was safer than life in New York City.[17]

During Jefferson's lifetime, Americans who lived in cities were the minority. Most Americans enumerated in the nation's Census of Population between 1790 and 1910 were rural and not directly concerned with the uncertainty of urban water supplies. Changing population patterns, however, made more Americans vulnerable to the dangers of the cities. In the 1820s, cities multiplied and expanded, greatly increasing outbreaks of cholera and yellow fever. Jefferson died at a time when urban residency was a greater threat to Americans' health than ever before.

All Men Are Created Equal

If Jefferson worried about urban health and poverty, race was the great divide cleaving Americans in his lifetime. The question of slavery was among the most vexing for the authors of the Constitution of the United States because slavery was such an enduring and troubling institution in the colonies. It undermined the Enlightenment creed Jefferson embraced that all men are equal under God.[18]

Jefferson's pastoral democracy is an ideal, a strong and alluring vision that provides Americans with romantic views of men living happily and empowered in nature. Land ownership remains a core definition of wealth in America, an ideal that has long shaped the laws of the land and that by the middle of the twentieth century shaped policies that produced mass opportunities for economic upward mobility for homeowners. The idea of a government of equals, in which resourcefulness and wisdom wins out over family name and station, is especially powerful. Jefferson's vision of meritocracy remains a defining part of the American character.

In practice, the United States of Jefferson's time was more complicated than his ideal. Though his vision of a body politic of citizens instead of royalty emerged, the political system could not be said to universally enfranchise all living in America. A full half of adults living in the country had no vote or easy access to landowning because of sex; the new democracy was a democracy of men, as were all the democracies in the Western world until New Zealand extended the vote to women in 1893.

Many men in the new republic were also denied the full measure of citizenship. These included the indigenous men of the land, seen as savage forces to be controlled rather than fellow Americans. Wars between the European settlers and indigenous peoples were regular elements of the colonial period and continued throughout Jefferson's life. Citizenship was reserved for those deemed sufficiently civilized to enjoy its rights and privileges. The criteria for citizenship included racial identity; in its first statement concerning citizenship, the U.S. Congress reserved the right to naturalization of foreign-born individuals to "white persons."[19]

Jefferson knew well the other Americans denied citizenship, for he lived among them and, as he brokered the compromises that enabled a diverse collection of colonies to form a political union in the late eighteenth century, codified a legal code that marginalized these Americans. During Jefferson's entire life, slaves provided the labor for many of the thriving farms in his pastoral vision, including Jefferson's own Monticello.

Where the slaves came from mattered. Slavery had existed for centuries, a tool the Romans used over conquered peoples in expanding their empire. Peoples in the Mediterranean and Europe had lived as slaves in many periods; a central facet of the story of Judaism is Moses leading his people to emerge out of bondage in Egypt. The experience of slavery in Southeastern Europe was sufficiently central that the people of the land are still named "Slavs" centuries after slavery ended there. Slavery was once a common facet of the human experience, and many peoples of many physical appearances were put into bondage over human history.

Between the sixteenth and nineteenth centuries, however, the form of slavery used in the Americas relied upon forcibly importing people from Africa. During this period, economic and political tensions within Africa encouraged the capture and sale of conquered peoples. Landowners in the Americas, especially plantation and mine owners in the Caribbean and South America, desired captive labor from Africa for a variety of reasons. Attempts to enslave indigenous Americans failed, in part because diseases such as influenza, the cold, and small-pox devastated peoples who had not built immunities to them in the pre-Columbian period and also because natives of the land had more knowledge of and access to escape paths than newly imported labor-ers did. Conversely, people in Africa shared a similar disease pool and similar immunities as people in Europe. For three hundred years, the economies of the New World increasingly depended upon the toils of enslaved people from Africa.

Over these long three centuries, slavery shaped the history of the Western world. All manner of riches—including silver from Venezu-elan mines, sugar from Haitian fields, tobacco from Virginian farms, and cotton grown throughout the southern region of the new United States of America—was extracted from the New World. Slave labor enriched plantation owners, traders, and merchants on both sides of the Atlantic. Manufacturing industries were not immune to the influ-ence of slave labor as several colonial industries used slaves in factory settings. Indirectly, textile operations in the United Kingdom and New England relied upon cotton harvested by slaves. Even if the people working the looms were wage laborers, those looms would be empty without the work of slaves. The economies of the Americas were built upon African slavery.[20]

The social structure of the Americas required the continuing enslave-ment of Africans and the peoples of African origin who were the chil-dren and grandchildren of those forced to leave their native lands to work in bondage. A complicating factor during this time was the exten-sion of the Enlightenment ideals that shaped Jefferson's view of the world. The growing influence of Protestant Christian theology posited that all human souls were equal before God regardless of station in life. Though interpretations of this idea varied greatly, one strand of thought that gained widespread support in the eighteenth and nineteenth cen-turies was that slavery was incompatible with this ideal. Abolitionist movements grew in both Europe and the Americas, leading to a cessa-tion of the international slave trade before Jefferson's death.

The tensions over the moral question of slavery inspired a powerful reaction among the peoples most dependent on the institution. Justifications emerged, among them a dichotomy between "Christians" and "savages." The historian Nancy Shoemaker observes that Indians and Europeans did not remark upon skin color until the middle of the eighteenth century. Obsession with color as understood in the United States appears to have started with the transatlantic slave trade, as references to "Negroes" or "blacks" to describe slaves from Africa became common. Few of European descent referred to themselves as "white"; instead, pioneers and pilgrims from Europe to the Americas differentiated themselves from the natives and slaves by identifying as "Christian." To be Christian was to be civilized, enlightened, and morally advanced; to be otherwise was to be savage and debased.[21]

This divide first became associated with color where slavery had become established. Eighteenth-century Carolina colonists (some who emigrated from Barbados, where concern about color was already evident) differentiated between "white, black, & Indians," not yet associating indigenous Americans with a color but keeping them distinct from whites. This nomenclature took a while to reach the northern colonies, whose residents of European descent called themselves Christians until the middle of the eighteenth century. The term "white" began appearing in records in the 1730s but did not supplant "Christian" as a dominant label for some time.[22]

During Thomas Jefferson's life, the term "*white*" was regularly but not exclusively used to identify American colonists of European origin. By the War of Independence, the mix of color and religion as significant markers was striking in New York City, where people of European and African heritages lived close together, and "Negroes" were perceived as godless savages who were as one English settler warned, "black and polluted." Moral associations had begun their journey from Christian individuals to white individuals.[23]

Jefferson's own history is entangled with the facts of slavery. He owned slaves, and although the declaration of independence he authored asserted that all men are created equal, he served in a government that guaranteed that slaveholding states would retain their economic and political power while preserving slavery. Dissension over how to treat enslaved peoples led to a tortuous compromise in the Constitution claiming that each slave counted as three-fifths of a man for the purposes of congressional apportionment while otherwise being treated like cattle owned by citizens. How to justify treating fellow humans in this matter involved great ambivalence for men subscribing to egalitarian philosophy. Jefferson's views on categorizing non-European residents of America reflected the nation's contradictions.

Heritage mattered greatly to Jefferson, who saw Americans as descending from Saxons through England. An inveterate collector of books, he amassed the nation's largest collection of Anglo-Saxon and Old English documents. He wrote *Essay on the Anglo-Saxon Language* in 1798, equating language with biological descent, emphasizing the myth of blood purity of the Saxon people from Roman times to the present day.[24]

Distinguishing Saxons from other peoples remained important in the New World. Writing from Paris in 1785, Jefferson gave François Jean de Beauvoir, Marquis de Chastellux (who Jefferson had met when the Frenchman served as a major general for the French military aiding the colonists during the War of Independence), his views of red and black men in America. He started by defending "the lower class of people in America" from charges that they were less informed and had less of a capacity to learn than their European counterparts. Moving from class to race, Jefferson then defended "the aboriginal man of America" from the opinion that he had "an inferiority of genius." Jefferson went on to describe a state of affairs in which environment and education mattered more than biology in considering the intellectual potential of humans:

I am safe in affirming, that the proofs of genius given by the Indians of North America, place them on a level with whites in the same uncultivated state. The North of Europe furnishes subjects enough for comparison with them, and for a proof of their equality. I have seen some thousands myself, and conversed much with them, and have found in them a masculine, sound understanding. I have had much information from men who had lived among them, and whose veracity and good sense were so far known to me, as to establish a reliance on their information. They have all agreed in bearing witness in favor of the genius of this people. As to their bodily strength, their manners rendering it disgraceful to labor, those muscles employed in labor will be weaker with them, than with the European laborer; but those which are exerted in the chase, and those faculties which are employed in the tracing an enemy or a wild beast, in contriving ambuscades for him, and in carrying them through their execution, are much stronger than with us, because they are more exercised. I believe the Indian, then, to be, in body and mind, equal to the white man. I have supposed the black man, in his present state, might not be so; but it would be hazardous to affirm, that, equally cultivated for a few generations, he would not become so.[25]

Here Jefferson acknowledged his prejudice toward biological inferiority of black men. He supposed they were not equal to him yet openly admitted that there may be an environmental reason for what he observed as inferiority and that, in time, any gaps could possibly be bridged. Jefferson both articulated white supremacy in the existing social order and offered hope it could be transcended.

Such a transcendence would have to happen at a later time for America and for Jefferson. The plantations Jefferson championed relied upon slavery. Jefferson considered people of African heritage naturally servile. Not all American farmers could afford land; many were impoverished. Furthermore, the fruits of the land did not simply go back into the local village to promote self-sufficiency. Tobacco, foods, and especially cotton had become commodities feeding the growth of industrial production on both sides of the Atlantic. Jefferson's Monticello, far from an isolated rural idyll, was very much part of the industrializing world he criticized in 1784.

The contradictions of slavery in a free republic were not lost to Jefferson. His own thoughts on slavery were, to understate matters, complex. Jefferson perceived "the races of black and of red men" as intellectual and cultural inferiors to whites: "This unfortunate difference of colour, and perhaps of faculty, is a powerful obstacle to the emancipation of these people. . . . The slave, when made free, might mix with, without staining the blood of his master. But with us a second is necessary, unknown to history. When freed, he is to be removed beyond the reach of mixture."[26]

In the late eighteenth century, one of the most enlightened political thinkers of the New World thought that intermarriage between European and African (or, for that matter, between European and indigenous American) was a pollutant, a stain upon the European's blood. He stated this opinion using the terminology of color to define separate races of "white," "black," and "red" men.

If Jefferson valued purity in his history of Saxon heritage, he showed little concern with staining that heritage via sexual relations. That Jefferson engaged in a long-standing, child-producing relationship with his slave Sally Hemings is a contradiction between stated value and action that was by no means unique to the founding father. Despite his union with an African American woman, Jefferson extended his ideas of white superiority beyond purity of blood to included supposed intellectual capabilities. Writing of black men, he concluded: "Comparing them by their faculties of memory, reason, and imagination, it appears to me, that in memory they are equal to the whites; in reason much inferior, as I think one could scarcely be found capable of tracing and comprehending the investigations of Euclid; and that in imagination they are dull, tasteless, and anomalous."[27]

Far from believing that all men were created equal, Jefferson engaged in racial classification. Doing so put him squarely in the mainstream of American ideas of race in the late eighteenth century. White identity was already crucial to Americans at the founding of the Republic. Congress initiated its discussion of citizenship in 1790 by restricting naturalization to "white persons."[28] Jefferson upheld this notion of racial purity in his office and his writings, if not his sexual behavior.

In *Notes on the State of Virginia*, Jefferson articulated moral concerns about what slavery had already done to society in the young United States. He was pessimistic about racial equality because of the corrosive effect a heritage of bondage had had on both slaves and masters. "Why not retain and incorporate the blacks into the state," he asked, "and thus save the expense of supplying, by importation of white settlers, the vacancies they will leave?" The answer was that irrevocable damage had already been done. "Deep rooted prejudices entertained by the whites; ten thousand recollections, by the blacks, of the injuries they have sustained. . . ." These, along with new provocations and many other circumstances, will "produce convulsions, which will probably never end but in the extermination of the one or the other race."[29]

The political impossibility of an integrated nation, Jefferson then reasoned, was matched by purportedly physical and moral barriers. Skin color struck Jefferson as profoundly significant in asserting the superiority of those with European ancestry over those of African or indigenous American ancestry. "Whether the black of the Negro resides in the reticular membrane between the skin and scarf-skin, or in the scarf-skin itself; whether it proceeds from the colour of the blood, the colour of the bile, or from that of some other secretion, *the difference is fixed in nature, and is as real as if its seat and cause were better known to us.*"[30] While Jefferson admitted to no definitive scientific knowledge for what produced different gradations of color in different people's skins, he asserted that it was an inarguable product of nature that differentiated different races from one another.

Not only did skin color differentiate races, Jefferson argued, but it also created a hierarchy among the races. Having identified the significance of skin color in demarcating races, Jefferson asked, "Is it not the foundation of a greater or less share of beauty in the two races? Are not the fine mixtures of red and white, the expressions of every passion by greater or less suffusions of colour in the one, preferable to that eternal monotony, which reigns in the countenances, that immovable veil of black which covers all the emotions of the other race?" Not content with his conclusions on skin color, Jefferson invoked a series of secondary physical characteristics that supported white superiority: "Add to these, flowing hair, a more elegant symmetry of form, their own judgment in favour of the whites, declared by their preference of them, as uniformly as is the preference of the Oranootan for the black women over those of his own species. The circumstance of Superior beauty, is thought worthy attention in the propagation of our horses, dogs, and other domestic animals; why not in that of man?"[31]

Aside from visual markers of difference, Jefferson appealed to the other senses to distinguish between white and black. Smell was significant. He described Africans as people who "secrete less by the kidnies, and more by the glands of the skin, which gives them a very strong and disagreeable odour." The smell resulted from a natural advantage, as Jefferson claimed such sweat "renders them more tolerant of heat, and less so of cold, than the whites." With the logic of an animal breeder, Jefferson argued that European humans were the prize lineage in the New World.[32]

Which is not to say that Jefferson was an unabashed supporter of enslaving people of African heritage. Slavery ran counter to the idea that all human souls were equal, and Jefferson worried about the effects it had on his nation. He asked, "Can the liberties of a nation be thought secure when we have removed their only firm basis, a conviction in the minds of the people that these liberties are of the gift of God? That they are not to be violated but with his wrath?" Jefferson concluded that Americans violated these prized liberties. "Indeed I tremble for my country when I reflect that God is just: that his justice cannot sleep for ever." Whether this justice came in the form of successful slave revolts or other acts of provenance, it would be terrible. Jefferson expressed optimism that slavery would ultimately be a temporary condition in the United States, and he hoped, "under the auspices of heaven, for a total emancipation" eventually. This might be through freeing slaves within the United States or, as Jefferson opined would be more likely, repatriating the descendants of Africans to Africa. Either way, Jefferson believed that slavery in the United States would end at some point in the future.[33]

That point would not fall under his watch. After losing the 1796 presidential election, Jefferson denounced the Federalist administration of President John Adams for its expansion of national power. Facing Adams again in 1800, Jefferson defeated the incumbent with the strong backing of Southerners concerned about the future of state sovereignty (and with it, the institution of slavery). Jefferson received 82 percent of the South's electoral votes compared with only 27 percent of the North's electoral votes. Jefferson's Republican supporters won a majority in the House of Representatives with Southern support, and Virginia's representatives accounted for more than a quarter of Republicans in that body in 1801.

Both a product of Virginia and attentive to the desires of the constituents that elected him, President Jefferson's stance on slavery was to preserve the status quo. Whatever Enlightenment values might guide abolition, he argued that "no more must be attempted than the nation can bear."[34]

Re-election in 1804 did not move the president to interfere with slavery. Writing in early January of 1805, Jefferson noted that the moral inconsistency of slavery was increasing and that "interest is really moving over to the side of morality. The value of the slave is every day lessening; his burden on his master daily increasing." Yet despite this moral argument, Jefferson noted he had "long since given up the expectation of any early provision for the extinguishment of slavery among us." The moral argument may proceed, he reasoned, but without federal action to hasten abolition.[35]

Jefferson's optimism on the slave's burden to his master neglected changes occurring in the structure of slavery and agricultural production. Demand for cotton on both sides of the Atlantic Ocean and the proliferation of Eli Whitney's cotton gin after 1793 allowed for more intensive production of short-staple cotton, and the warm climate of the South allowed for intensive production of the cash crop. Prioritizing cotton production produced vast growth in size of plantations across the South in the early nineteenth century and, with that growth, vast increases in the number of slaves working individual plantations.

Interest in the side of morality was certainly increasing at the time of Jefferson's letter. Abolition spread through the Northern states after the War of Independence, and anti-slavery laws covered all states north of the Ohio River and Mason-Dixon line by the end of Jefferson's first term. In 1810, more than three-quarters of all African Americans in the North were free.

European moral disapproval of slavery led to the abolition of the international slave trade in 1808, and on Jefferson's recommendation, Congress in March 1807 outlawed the import slave trade effective January 1, 1808 (the first year the Federal Constitution allowed a ban). By the time President Jefferson left the White House, sentiment for abolition extended through most of what he regarded as the civilized world.

The exception was his home region. In Virginia and across the South, slavery deepened its hold on the economy, social order, and politics of the region. With the international slave trade curtailed, the internal slave trade of the region grew. It continued to grow until the 1860s, when the slave population of the United States was four million. Indeed, the international ban proved profitable to domestic slaveholders who could now sell their property at increased prices. Demand increased with time, as cotton production moved west from the Carolinas into Georgia, Alabama, Mississippi, Louisiana, and Texas. With the geographic expansion of cotton came increased demand for slave labor.[36]

Virginians felt the demand was crucial to maintaining the order within their home state. The historian Alan Taylor argues that Virginians believed that only with a vibrant interstate slave trade and an untrammelled expansion by slaveholders could they "vent" enough slaves annually to release the demographic pressure that threatened an inevitable race war. Ex-president Jefferson felt this way in 1820, declaring that the Missouri crisis was "like a fire bell in the night, [which] awakened and filled me with terror." The symbolism of a fire bell, rung during slave revolts, was deliberate, and Jefferson's understanding of the terrible cost of slavery to Virginia was as acute in 1820 as it was more than thirty years earlier. "As it is, we have the wolf by the ears, and we can neither hold him, nor safely let him go. Justice is in one scale, and self-preservation in the other." Jefferson rationalized that the interstate slave trade would be good for both slaveholding Virginians and the slaves themselves, claiming that the passage of slaves from one state to another would produce "a diffusion over a greater surface [that] would make them individually happier, and proportionally facilitate the accomplishment of their emancipation." Expanding slavery westward would diffuse tensions of slavery.[37]

The elderly Jefferson was pessimistic over the strife that slavery has caused his nation. "I regret," he remarked in 1820, "that I am now to die in the belief, that the useless sacrifice of themselves by the generation of 1776, to acquire self-government and happiness to their country, is to be thrown away by the unwise and unworthy passions of their sons, and that my only consolation is to be, that I live not to weep over it."[38]

Jefferson's notions of racial inequality were contradicted by his actions, and his ideal community also diverged with reality over the course of his lifetime. A nation composed of small villages, each composed of equal, landed farmers who engaged in democratic governance over their affairs, required an absence of industry. Industry, for Jefferson, brought social and economic inequities and upset the balance of a working democracy. He argued:

> "For the general operations of manufacture, let our work-shops remain in Europe. It is better to carry provisions and materials to workmen there, than bring them to the provisions and materials, and with them their manners and principles. The loss by the transportation of commodities

across the Atlantic will be made up in happiness and permanence of government. The mobs of great cities add just so much to the support of pure government, as sores do to the strength of the human body. It is the manners and spirit of a people which preserve a republic in vigour. A degeneracy in these is a canker which soon eats to the heart of its laws and constitution.[39]

Although Jefferson lived and studied in Paris, he considered he was "savage enough to prefer the woods, the wilds, and the independence of Monticello, to all the brilliant pleasures of this gay Capital." He longed to return to Virginia, "for though there is less wealth there, there is more freedom, more ease, and less misery."[40]

But increasing wealth was a goal of the newly independent nation. The president realized that the United States needed to increase manufacturing capacity if it was to survive. In his message to Congress in November 1808, the president noted a justification for domestic manufacturing—autonomy from England when diplomatic relations between the two nations were tenuous. The United States's foreign commerce was suspended. "The situation into which we have thus been forced, has impelled us to apply a portion of our industry and capital to internal manufactures and improvements. The extent of this conversion is daily increasing, and little doubt remains that the establishments formed and forming will—under the auspices of cheaper materials and subsistence, the freedom of labor from taxation with us, and of protecting duties and prohibitions—become permanent."[41]

These words of the outgoing president were prophetic. American industry grew in the years after he left office, and with it, American cities and their sanitary problems rapidly expanded. Social inequality in the cities was matched by enduring slavery on plantations. The rural, egalitarian nation Jefferson founded had more in common with the messy societies of Europe than he cared to admit.

The Contradictions of Thomas Jefferson

A lover of Enlightenment philosophy who held slaves, an educated man who preferred the backwoods of Virginia to the salons of Paris, and a fervent believer in agrarian society who advocated expanding industrial productivity at the end of his president, Thomas Jefferson reflected in his life and values the contradictions of the nation he helped found.

If Jefferson prized agrarian life over industrial urbanism, he still recognized the need for domestic manufactures and valued friendships with urbanites like Benjamin Franklin. While Jefferson's views and actions on race preserved a social structure privileging whites, he did not associate whiteness with superior hygiene. He associated whiteness with more advanced civilization, but that had no explicit connection with dirt at a time when sanitation services were primitive. Jefferson could characterize himself as a soil-tilling savage, muddling the social constructions Europeans and settlers of European heritage had established to separate themselves from peoples of American and African heritage. Moreover, Jefferson's racial hierarchy allowed for the possibility that red and black men could one day achieve the same level of civilization as whites. This indefinite deferment of equality allowed him to preserve the existing order while still championing Enlightenment values. Yet, just as the man who wrote that all men were created equal kept slaves and left the question of slavery in his nation unresolved at his death, his government pursued economic policies that encouraged the growth of the cities he despised.

Away from the cities, Jefferson died in his rural idyll. But that idyll was an illusion, representing only a small part of the American experience in 1826. As Jefferson lay dying, cities in the North and South grew alike. With them grew economic inequality, sanitation problems, and epidemic disease. Although Monticello remained small and rural, its economy continued to rely on the perpetuation of slavery even as the international slave trade had been dismantled. Concerns about health, hygiene, and race present since the colonial era intensified and intertwined in the years after Jefferson's death.

2

The Decay of the Old

Thomas Jefferson died as his country continued to grapple with the complexities of urban development and deepening divisions over slavery. In the years after Jefferson's death, the openness of his white countrymen to the possibility that black and white men were equals diminished. But the same Enlightenment thinking that produced the ideas of the French and American revolutions also boosted the ideas of abolition. If all men were equal in the eyes of God, how could one man enslave another? That question would be repeated over and over, on both sides of the Atlantic, in the years after American independence. The transatlantic slave trade was banned during Jefferson's presidency. Slavery throughout Europe and Latin America also was abolished. By 1830, the United States stood increasingly isolated as a nation with slaves. Although President John Quincy Adams, son of Jefferson's rival and friend, boasted of the virtues of the "representative democracy" of the United States, it was a democracy that included slaves only as fractions by which to determine representation, not as citizens with rights to vote, to go to court, or to own land.[1]

Slavery not only continued in the United States, it intensified. Cotton plantations grew beyond the imagination of farmers working when Jefferson established Monticello in the late eighteenth century. Demand by the mills of New England, the mills of South Carolina, and the mills of London led to vast expanses of land in Virginia, North Carolina, South Carolina, and Georgia and moving west through Alabama and Mississippi becoming devoted to giant cotton plantations.

These plantations had devastating effects on the ecology of the South, exhausting soil and leaving crops vulnerable to pestilence. The plantations also demanded huge labor forces. Continuing the pattern of the smaller plantations, the workers used were slaves of African heritage to such an extent that the term "Black Belt" began to be used to describe the agricultural region of the South in the nineteenth century. As the rest of the Western world abolished slavery, the United States increased its reliance upon the peculiar institution. Though abolition took hold in Northern states, Northern industry continued to rely indirectly upon the toils of slaves. Southern cotton became clothing fashioned in Lowell and Lynn in Massachusetts and in Philadelphia. The United States remained a nation with an economy powered by human bondage.

These problems in many respects were caused by the abundance of opportunity in the United States. Transportation within the nation improved, particularly after the Erie Canal opened trade west of the Atlantic coast. A series of canals and, later, railroads, integrated vast tracts of land into a network of commerce by 1860. This network spurred industrial development, which in turn fueled population growth in existing cities and sparked the growth of new cities by major rivers and lakes. Westward expansion into new territories caused migration away from the Atlantic seaboard across the continent, though without resolving existing political and social tensions. America in 1860 was far more productive than it had been when President Jefferson urged the United States to expand manufacturing in 1808, but this productivity came at the cost of industrial pollution, public health crises, heightened racial animosity, and, ultimately, a nation fractured over the question of slavery.[2]

The economic inequalities and filth Jefferson saw in European cities came to America as poverty became unavoidable on the streets of Boston and New York and was eminently visible. In contrast to the bracing vigor of rural life, the image of urban life was disease ridden and filthy. So, too, was the image of urban residents, especially the waves of immigrants who came from Ireland and Germany in the wake of European political and economic upheaval at mid-century. Often lacking literacy or English verbal skills, these newcomers might have been stigmatized on racial grounds. Indeed, the Catholicism of many immigrants was remarked upon by Protestant native-born people who disdained the newcomers to their cities. Boston and New York City saw regular political and occasionally physical struggles over access to land, water, and political power based upon religious identity. Antipathy toward Irish Catholic and German Catholic immigrants led to successful nativist campaigns for Congress in New York and Pennsylvania in the 1840s and a spreading "Know Nothing" movement among Northern working-class Protestants in the mid-1850s with the growth of the Fraternal Order of the Star Spangled Banner. In 1854, a chapter opened in San Francisco in opposition to the growing number of Chinese immigrants in that city; the party's candidate Stephen P. Webb won the mayoral election that year. By 1856, more than one hundred congressmen had taken the order's anti-immigrant oath. The movement ultimately split over the question of slavery but had consensus that immigrants threatened the economic and social stability of its members.[3]

If race was remarked upon in a more heterogeneous society, it was not automatically associated with the growing problems of urban sanitation. Although new urban residents were blamed with spreading disease in antebellum cities, this blame was not based on their racial identity so much as it was based on their economic station. In the words of the historian John Duffy, the 1830s brought the perception of a dangerous underclass characterized as the dirty, immoral, and dissolute poor.[4]

Deadly Cities

Thomas Jefferson would have been sickened by the sight of American cities in the 1850s. Aside from strong evidence of economic inequality, New York City, Philadelphia, and Boston now had slums as filthy and dangerous as any in Great Britain or France. Urban residents were plagued by periodic epidemics that seemed to grow worse after waves of immigration increased in the 1840s and 1850s. Within ten years of Jefferson's death, urban sanitation deteriorated faster and more dramatically than it had done during his life. Population continued to outpace urban infrastructure in straining the water supplies and streets. Organic waste from livestock accumulated in the streets. With them came the excrement of humans, either from overflowing privy vaults or simply a bucket thrown into the street. The streets were dirt. In wet weather, they would mix with the filth to form muddy bogs. In dry weather, fecal matter and rotting carcasses would turn to dust, blowing in the eyes, noses, and mouths of all around the street.

Cholera struck regularly and without mercy, usually affecting the poorest urban residents the most. In 1830, middle-class observers attributed the high mortality rates of the poor to shortcomings in their character and moral temperament. If the poor fell ill and died in greater

numbers, it was due to personal faults. The Renaissance and the Protestant Reformation had ended the association of sanctity with poverty;
acquiring wealth had become a Christian virtue well before the War of
Independence. By the early nineteenth century this view led logically to
the assumption that poverty, rather than being a sign of holiness and of
Christian virtues, instead represented weak moral character.[5]

Most affluent Americans in 1850 believed that poverty and immoral-
ity went hand in hand and that cleanliness was next to godliness. The
laws of nature and of God were the same, and those who deviated from
them paid the price in poverty, disease, and death. The wealthier classes
observed that the immigrants pouring into Boston, New York, and other
port cities lived crowded together in filth and were intemperate in their
drinking and eating. Those same people also suffered exceedingly high
rates of sickness and death as cholera, typhoid, and yellow fever struck
them down. Disparaging the sick as immoral, lazy, and dirty was largely
a function of class, as statements in North and South using those terms
were applied to Irish immigrants, African Americans, Indians, and poor
Southern whites alike.[6]

This attitude was challenged by the growing hazards of city life. Filth
accumulated, giving off foul odors. Flies and rats flocked to the stench,
causing urban residents to connect odor with outbreaks of cholera,
typhoid, and yellow fever. Outbreaks that killed dozens of people were
frequent, and occasionally far more lethal outbreaks occurred. An 1853
yellow fever epidemic killed about 9,000 people in New Orleans. Disease on this scale was not limited to threatening the poor but to all who
lived in the compact, congested cities.

Some chose escape or longed for it. Discontent with the city led many
urbanities to set out for rural areas, either permanently or seasonally.
The mid-nineteenth century is peppered with literature and art reflecting this quest, ranging from Thomas Cole and the Hudson School's
romanticized paintings of unblemished nature in the 1840s to Henry
David Thoreau's descriptions of Walden one decade later. A unifying
thread through all of this work was that it was made by people who had
spent considerable time in cities and longed for a pristine alternative
found in the countryside.[7]

This longing was not far removed from Jefferson's pastoral ideal,
although by mid-century it was due to revulsion of industrial cities

within the United States instead of across the Atlantic. It influenced the design of new city parks and the early suburban subdivisions of Frederick Law Olmsted. As more of the United States became urban between 1800 and 1850, more urbanites despaired of the loud, dirty, disease-ridden cities that affected their health and well-being. More longed to be someplace cleaner, quieter, and safer. It was an impulse that would not soon die.

Rise of the Sanitarians

Others chose to better the conditions of the filthy cities. Long after independence, American and British scientists faced very similar problems of public health, concluding that a relationship between malodorous wastes and communicable disease was apparent. The British sanitarian Edwin Chadwick used this connection to advocate for new sanitation laws in the 1840s to remove miasmas. His efforts influenced American public health offices to adopt similar measures in order to prevent disease. Early American sanitarians gravitated to the largest cities of the East Coast. Two, John H. Griscom of New York and Lemuel Shattuck of Boston, demonstrated both the growing threat to public health found in cities and the rapidly evolving theories of who or what was responsible for disease and what measures should be taken to make cities safer.

Griscom delivered a report on the sanitation problems of laborers in New York City at the end of December 1844. He repudiated the moral theory of contagion, observing that wealthy people were hardly noted for their moderate behavior yet they still lived longer and healthier lives than the poor did. Griscom concluded that living in clean surroundings and eating better food improved their lives, and this lesson should be used to improve the environment of all urban residents.[8]

Griscom observed that more than half the patients he observed were foreign born and that probably over 75 percent were either foreign born or the dependent children of immigrants. He attributed their poor health to "the confined spaces in which they dwell, the unwholesome air they breathe, and their filth and degradation," all conditions that caused them to fall ill and miss work, increased the danger to public health, and placed a further burden on public and private charity.[9] Griscom suggested the creation of a "sanitary police" that would teach the poor how to manage their household operations, specifically that "the value of fresh air, ventilation, cleanliness, temperance, &c., would form constant themes for them."[10]

Shattuck did not go as far in dismissing moral causes of disease. A Massachusetts legislator and statistician, he possessed attitudes more typical of his day. Worried about the debilitating effects of Boston's immigrants on the American native-born population, Shattuck and his fellow researchers described unbearable conditions, reporting that the average age of Irish life in Boston did not exceed fourteen years and describing 568 dark, crowded cellars used as dwellings, each occupied by between five and fifteen residents.[11] Asiatic cholera plagued the Irish emigrants who had settled in such conditions.[12]

Shattuck sympathized with the plight of the poor, explicitly stating that "no sanitary system can be adequate to the requirements of the time, or can cure those radical evils which infect the under-framework of society," without improving the social condition of the poor. Shattuck reasoned that if a person lived in "inevitable domestic filth," how could they possibly be expected to maintain adequate standards of personal cleanliness?

Shattuck maintained that any moral shortcomings, "improvidence and recklessness," that the urban poor might have were a result of their social condition rather than personal shortcomings. Any "ignorance and prejudice" the poor might have about proper sanitation could be corrected if the public recognized that the sanitation of the poor was an obligation of society.[13]

In the eyes of more affluent urbanites, the basic problem with the poor lay in their lack of moral fiber. Shattuck and his colleagues agreed but found the situation correctable. If poverty produced filthy people, poverty's ills could be alleviated, altered, or reformed. At mid-century, a dirty person was a person who could be uplifted. Economic condition was not immutable, basic, or secured from birth. No matter how pejorative the descriptions of the poor, these descriptions were in a context that, *if these people were taught good manners and changed their ways*— or, perhaps more paternally, *if those of us who know better would provide a safe environment for these people*—then the poor could be divorced from their dirty status. A function of government was to uplift the morals and sanitation of the urban poor through education. Since hygiene and morality were linked, another function of government was to encourage it through a program of civic cleanliness for public and private spaces. Keeping the poor clean and healthy kept them from starting epidemics that threatened all residents of the city. Shattuck's general plan for improving the public's health was not implemented when he proposed it in 1850, but it would prove valuable to improving health of Union soldiers during the Civil War and formed an important precedent for subsequent municipal sanitation efforts.[14]

If a city was dirty, it was now perceived to be deadly. Dirt was defined especially by smell, and a putrid stench posed a threat. The "miasmatic," or filth, theory of disease shaped American and British responses to public health for half a century. According to the theory, the cause of contagious diseases were vapors produced by wastes. The proper way to prevent epidemics was by draining sewers, ventilating buildings, and otherwise improving the cleanliness of cities.

Environmental sanitation became popular. A program that sought to reduce disease as it improved the aesthetic experience of living in cities was a program that politicians and private citizens were willing to fund. Sanitarians conducted state-funded reports on urban health in the 1850s, leading to the creation of several state boards of health in the 1860s and 1870s and the passage of the New York Metropolitan Health Law in 1860. Sanitarians developed a professional infrastructure, using a coherent theory of disease, to fight the ills of urban society. If cholera had been considered "a scourge of the sinful" in 1830, by the end of the Civil War, sanitarians saw it as "the consequence of remediable faults in sanitation."[15]

Simply because a cause was associated with urban epidemic did not lead to eradication of communicable diseases. Physical infrastructure to handle wastes remained inadequate, in part because municipal governments in rapidly developing cities such as Chicago often opted to charge only those businesses and residents immediately adjacent to a street for its maintenance. Such policies not only produced unequal access to healthy environments based upon ability to pay but were also inadequate to reduce the threat of highly communicable diseases to all who lived near (or had services performed by) vulnerable peoples. Although sanitarians attempted to order and combat the chaos of urban waste in the 1840s, more progress was made in identifying causes of disease than in eradicating them. American cities remained deadly environments.[16]

Maintaining clean cities as well as individual dwellings was more important than ever. Ideas of who would deserve to be clean and who should do the cleaning began to codify. In homes on both sides of the Mason-Dixon line, women bore much of the burden for maintaining household cleanliness, either through marriage or employment. In the latter, class and racial identity already began to shape expectations of who would be hired to clean.

Catharine E. Beecher regarded hygiene as woman's work and categorized the hygienic levels of people based on their national origin. While not explicit in her descriptions of who was unclean, Beecher saw the English as a people "distinguished for systematic housekeeping, and for a great love of order, cleanliness, and comfort."[17]

Other Ango-American women shared this assumption and expressed it in their hiring practices. Eliza Burhans Farnham of Rensselaerville, New York, married the lawyer Thomas Jefferson Farnham in July 1836. The middle-class couple moved west, residing in a small village on the Illinois prairie, absent the civilized amenities of New York. Mrs. Farnham wrote that she was unable to hire "a stout Irish or colored woman" to do the scrubbing, as she probably would have done had she still been living in New York, and unwilling (she wrote) to sit down and cry over the mess, she attacked it head on. Farnham's assumptions reveal expected norms of gender and ethnicity as it related to housework—the labor of first resort were either African American women or women from the most populous current immigrant group—at this time, the Irish.[18]

Cities grew in part owing to migrants from abroad. Between 1821 and 1850, one million Irish came to the United States, with numbers rising at the end of the period because of the Potato Famine. The Irish made homes in the older cities of the Atlantic seaboard as well as in younger Midwestern cities like Pittsburgh and Chicago and in San Francisco on the West Coast. The arrival of Irish immigrants in New York City led to violence and discriminatory exclusion in jobs and housing opportunities. In Boston, mass immigration of Irish Catholics exacerbated political and environmental tensions. Access to the Boston Commons was fiercely contested, with Yankee Protestants worried about immigrants trampling the land with their livestock (something the Yankees themselves had practiced on the same grounds). The historian Suellen Hoy remarks that antebellum nativists argued for exclusion of the Irish from America in part because, they jeered, "the only water the Irishman used consistently was Holy Water."[19]

These insults reflected class divisions and also differences in experience. Many of the Irish had lived in rural villages, where cottages had dirt floors. Upon arrival in congested American cities, their new homes were crowded tenements, often lacking indoor plumbing or adequate ventilation. These living conditions did not prepare Irish women to uphold middle-class standards of household sanitation once they were hired as domestic workers. Stereotypically referred to as "Biddy," Irish servants were sometimes described as "unwashed" and were often said to perform housework "dirtily and shiftlessly."[20]

Cleansing the Frontier

If cities were cauldrons of filth, the frontier represented territory to where unwanted peoples who were considered out of place in the expanding nation could be removed. The federal government used racial designation based on skin color to physically relocate indigenous peoples. During Thomas Jefferson's administration, the president hoped to "civilize" indigenous peoples into rural American society, telling Congress in 1803 that "in leading them to agriculture, to manufactures, and civilization; in bringing together their and our settlements, and in preparing them ultimately to participate in the benefits of our governments, I trust and believe we are acting for their greatest good." Jefferson's sentiments, however much they might have raised the possibility of assimilation, came after more than seventy years of efforts and negotiations to relocate indigenous peoples away from colonial settlements, joined by the president voicing the possibility of using the Louisiana Territory for such relocations.[21]

By 1830, official policy was unambiguous in supporting removal. Racialized descriptions of indigenous people were used to justify a form of social cleansing. Political leaders used "red" for skin color alongside "savage" to both indicate indigenous peoples' differences from colonists of European heritage and classify peoples of diverse tribal heritages under one racial group. These classifications were used, not to assimilate native peoples, but to remove them altogether from lands occupied by settlers of European origin. John C. Calhoun, a South Carolina native whose political career figured strongly in the virulent racism of the period, strongly urged a policy of Indian removal. As secretary of war, Calhoun drafted plans for removal for President James Madison in 1824 that directed moving peoples in the Southern states west.

Upon signing the Indian Removal Act of 1830, which established the relocation of Native Americans from their farms in Virginia, the Carolinas, Georgia, Alabama, and Tennessee to territories unoccupied by colonists west of the Mississippi River, President Andrew Jackson declared: "The waves of population and civilization are rolling to the westward, and we now propose to acquire the countries occupied by the red men of the South and West by a fair exchange, and, at the expense of the United States, to send them to land where their existence may be prolonged and perhaps made perpetual."[22]

What President Jackson perceived as a fair exchange to the "red men" had lethal consequences. Federal policy removed—ostensibly by mutually negotiated treaties that were in fact conducted under great duress—people belonging to the Chickasaw, Choctaw, Cherokee, Creek, and Seminole tribes from the Southeast. In October 1838, the U.S. military forcibly pushed the Cherokee people west of the Mississippi River into what had been designated Indian territory, a journey that killed more than 4,000 people within eight months. The federal government consistently used skin color to differentiate the peoples to be removed over the nineteenth century, ultimately settling many tribes on reservations far away from white settlements.[23]

American Exceptionalism

Tensions over purportedly unwashed immigrants in cities and the policies of Indian removal were joined by disputes over enslaving African Americans that made racism more corrosive and threatened to tear the nation apart. By the 1830s, the American South stood alone in the Western world in its reliance on slaves working ever-larger plantations harvesting cotton. As the rest of the Western world abolished slavery, the United States increased its reliance upon the peculiar institution.

Even as Northern looms used Southern cotton, political thought above the Mason-Dixon line generally agreed with the principles of European nations that slavery was untenable. This exacerbated regional tensions that had been evident even before the first constitutional convention grappled with the question of slavery. John C. Calhoun, already notable as an early advocate of Indian removal, openly discussed the possibility of the South seceding from the Union, arguing that the North could not interfere in the South's way of life.

Calhoun had reached the office of vice president under presidents John Quincy Adams and Andrew Jackson. Less than four years after leaving that office (following protracted disputes with Jackson), he was a sitting senator when abolitionists delivered petitions to the U.S. Senate. In 1836, the international slave trade had been banned, and moral calls for abolition grew louder in the North. These moral appeals only hardened divisions between the slave and free states, divisions Senator Calhoun indicated were irrevocable when he spoke against the petitions on the Senate floor on March 9:

> The relation which now exists between the two races in the slaveholding States has existed for two centuries. It has grown with our growth, and strengthened with our strength. It has entered into and modified all our institutions, civil and political. None other can be substituted. We will not, cannot permit it to be destroyed. If we were base enough to do so, we would be traitors to our section, to ourselves, our families, and to posterity. . . . Come what will, should it cost every drop of blood, and every cent of property, we must defend ourselves; and if compelled, we would stand justified by all laws, human and divine. . . . With these impressions, I ask neither sympathy nor compassion for the slaveholding States. We can take care of ourselves. It is not we, but the Union which is in danger. It is that which demands our care—demands that the agitation of this question shall cease *here*—that you shall refuse to receive this petitions, and decline all jurisdiction over the subject of abolition, in every form and shape. It is only on these terms that the Union can be safe. We cannot remain here in an endless struggle in defence of our character, our property, and institutions.[24]

Calhoun's claim of slavery's vitality made dissolving the Union sound noble and virtuous. Allowing abolition would betray the South, therefore the South could not remain part of a nation bent on abolition. The necessity of racial inequality was that central. Slavery had perverted the values of half the nation; as Calhoun put it, slavery had "entered into and modified all our institutions, civil and political." Far from an isolated voice, he shaped the rhetoric that ultimately led to the creation of the Confederate States of America after Abraham Lincoln defeated Stephen Douglas in a presidential election defined by the question of slavery. The South bound itself to the institution of slavery. The frequency of demeaning blacks as intellectually and morally inferior intensified in remarks by doctors, academics, and especially politicians fighting to preserve slavery.

If the subjugation of the black race was that vital to the preservation of the Union in 1836, its importance grew over the next two decades. Because of the psychological, economic, and political capital invested in maintaining slavery, the biological justifications for bondage would only grow more creative and demeaning over the period.

The science emerging to defend slavery was interwoven with religious justifications that had also supported the institution. Citing the Bible, especially the curse of Ham in the book of Genesis, where Noah curses Canaan to servitude, was a frequent device of Protestant clergy supporting slavery. By the 1850s, educated Southerners devised elaborate justifications for continuing the institution. The South Carolina parson and naturalist John Bachman offered that Africans, though of "our species," were inferior in "intellectual power" and "incapable of self-government."[25]

The Southern physician S. A. Cartwright offered a particularly exaggerated scientific defense of slavery in 1851. He traced the problems of black people to inadequate decarbonization of blood in the lungs, "conjoined with a deficiency of cerebral matter in the cranium . . . that is the true cause of that debasement of mind, which has rendered the people of Africa unable to take care of themselves." The physician invented a disease he called "dysesthesia," a disease of inadequate breathing, in which slaves broke tools, spoiled crops, and were unresponsive to physical punishment not because of conscious resistance but, rather, owing to this disease. Cartwright also thought the problems of slaves attempting to escape was due to a mental disease called "drapetomania," or the insane desire to flee. "Like children, they are constrained by unalterable physiological laws, to love those in authority over them. Hence, from a law of his nature, the Negro can no more help loving a kind master, than the child can help loving her that gives it suck."[26]

Cartwright combined paternalism with medical explanations for abnormal behavior. For him the slave was like a child, or a pet, a creature clearly inferior to the master yet one that bonds with the master in a way that is beneficial to the slave. A slave trying to break that bond would, using this logic, have to be insane.

Cartwright's explanations were preposterous, yet they represented the justifications of the 1850s. Isolated from the rest of the Western world, the slave states intensified their justifications for keeping the institution. These pseudoscientific justifications lived into the Civil War.

If black Americans were blamed and feared by white Southerners for social and physical ills, concerned scientists spent little time actively investigating their lives and troubles. Shattuck's research related the problems of Massachusetts cities to problems elsewhere in the United States. The appendix to an 1850 report by the Massachusetts Sanitary Commission included extracts from the communications of J. D. B. De Bow, Esq., the superintendent of the Bureau of Statistics of the state of Louisiana, with the sanitarian Dr. Edward H. Barton of New Orleans.

De Bow admitted that "we are strikingly deficient in knowledge of the black and colored population, although living among us for nearly three hundred years. Investigations, notwithstanding their importance, have never been made in this field until within a very few years."[27]

Hygienic concerns also were used against people of Scots-Irish heritage in rural Appalachia and the South. Championing white supremacy extended beyond subjugating non-white peoples to also marginalizing white farmers. The phrase "poor white trash" emerged in the 1830s; the historian Matt Wray dates the earliest recorded use to 1833.[28] Exactly how the term originated is unclear; it may have started with black slaves denigrating poor whites or white servants, or whites may have starting used it to insult other whites. The term implied a racial aspect to cleanliness. While whites were ostensibly superior, poor whites joined blacks and Indians in being described as dirty and immoral. Class joined skin color in shaping notions of racial superiority and hygiene.[29]

Views from Abroad

Changes in racial perceptions were likely internalized by most Americans; observers from abroad could see how constructions of whiteness evolved into a more virulent form between 1830 and 1865. If the most famous observation of antebellum American life from a European is the Frenchman Alexis de Tocqueville's *Democracy in America*, it is an observation that appears confused about the racial climate in the country. Writing between 1835 and 1840, de Tocqueville discusses the merits and opportunities of life in the New World but then observes that racism left little opportunity for non-white peoples. The forced suffering of Indians on the Trail of Tears are evils de Tocqueville would find impossible to relate. Slavery and racism, de Tocqueville found, would inevitably spark a great war: "If America ever experiences great revolutions, they will be instigated by the presents of blacks on American soil; that is to say, it will not be the equality of social conditions but rather their inequality which will give rise to them."[30]

Slavery, for de Tocqueville, prevented the Southern states from truly sharing the egalitarian image he had of America; that was reserved for the Northern states, especially New England. That said, however, he engaged in classification as well. In chapter 17 he wrote that, "among these widely differing families of men, the first that attracts attention, the superior in intelligence, in power, and in enjoyment, is the white, or European, the MAN pre-eminently so called, below him appear the Negro and the Indian." He concluded in chapter 18 that "you may set the Negro free, but you cannot make him otherwise than an alien to the European. Nor is this all we scarcely acknowledge the common features of humanity in this stranger whom slavery has brought among us. His physiognomy is to our eyes hideous, his understanding weak, his tastes low; and we are almost inclined to look upon him as a being intermediate between man and the brutes."

Other Europeans found racial animus in all white Americans. Charles Dickens decried virulent American racism in 1852, arguing that white

Americans scorned black Americans whether they be slave or free. In *Household Words*, Dickens wrote,

> however respectable the position earned by a free negro . . . though he be clean of body, neatly dressed, and by the color of his mind a man of sense and honour: there is not a white fellow, black with dirt in his body, and black with rascality in his mind, who would not scorn to sit beside him on an omnibus; there is not a kitchen scullion claiming to be white under his grease and soot, who would not consider it an insult to be told that he must dine at the same table with the negro gentleman.[31]

By 1852, the justifications for slavery had belittled Americans with black skin to such an extent that Dickens found the actual station of slavery irrelevant to how white Americans regarded black Americans. Race had overtaken economic relation.

With race at the forefront of American identity, it also touched upon other concerns. A decade after Dickens lamented American racism, his countryman Anthony Trollope remarked upon the industrial development of Pittsburgh. In his 1862 account *North America* (a series of reflections on travel in the United States), Trollope explicitly linked the soot of western Pennsylvania's central city to skin color. He called the city "without exception the blackest place which I ever saw," and all the soot and grease and dinginess of Great Britain's dirtiest cities could not compare to the pollution he witnessed in Pittsburgh. The mills and factories belching out black coal smoke befouled what he supposed was a picturesque site of mountains and rivers. Whatever colors the landscape or built environment once possessed, now all was black.

Including the people. When he returned to his hotel after touring the city, Trollope found that "everything in the hotel was black; not black to the eye, for the eye teaches itself to discriminate colours even when loaded with dirt, but black to the touch." He did not except himself from the pervasive soot. "On coming out of a tub of water my foot took an impress from the carpet exactly as it would have done had I trod barefooted on a path laid with soot. I thought that I was turning Negro upwards, till I put my wet hand upon the carpet, and found that the result was the same."[32]

Trollope explicitly conflated skin color with soot as he tried to convey the scale of Pittsburgh's pollution. He did not otherwise link race and hygiene or make claims about purity of blood or physiological traits. His casual association of skin and dirt, however, represents a troubling way in which the national concerns of race and hygiene were becoming intertwined.

The Illogic of Racial Categories

Away from the industrial cities, abolitionist threats to slavery hardened notions of white supremacy and political secession in the plantations of South Carolina. These newly virulent constructions of whiteness not only threatened black Americans but also threatened to negate the white identity of poor Scots-Irish farmers. The unpredictable experience of westward migration further threatened settlers' assumptions about race. The illogical assumptions of racial hierarchy were tested when Southern whites settling across the Mississippi Valley experienced floods, droughts, miasma, and harsh conditions. The frontier transformed its inhabitants, altering hygienic practices, skin textures and tones, and the physical health of people considered "white," "black," and "red." De Tocqueville's observation that the frontier crossed with civilization transformed Americans into something quite different than Europeans may be taken further. American-born whites moving to the borderlands saw their own faces and bodies transformed into something quite different from the appearance of their Eastern contemporaries (and, ironically, closer to the appearance of the indigenous peoples being pushed beyond the frontier by the government of white Americans). Their resulting worries, as the historian Conevery Bolton Valenčius observes in reviewing antebellum settlers' accounts of their experiences, exposed the medical and environmental underpinnings of racial anxiety and violence in the western territories. Racial anxiety and violence were abundant in these lands. From the fights over slavery in Bloody Kansas to the subjugation of Mexicans in Texas to the continued forced migration and battles with indigenous American peoples, the expansion westward radicalized the rhetoric and actions of white supremacy between 1830 and 1860.[33]

Toward Civil War

Slavery's hold on the South intensified in the decades after international opinion hardened against the institution. New York State's last slaves were freed in 1827, as large cotton plantations spread across the south. Westward expansion of the United States exacerbated the divide between North and South, and the question of slavery defined American politics between 1840 and 1860.

The political process in Congress did little to resolve American conflicts over slavery, with mutterings of secession by the slaveholding states increasing in the 1830s and inflamed battles over Missouri and Kansas territories over the next two decades. The social effect of America's increasing isolation as a slaveholding Western nation was a more virulent defense of white identity as superior to all other peoples. This manifested in political campaigns, theology, and pseudoscientific claims to white supremacy.

The result of American conflict about slavery was civil war. The Union's victory in the war abolished the institution of slavery but did little to eradicate the constructions of race that slavery begat. The war also underscored the threat of contagion, as disease killed the majority of soldiers fighting on both sides. At the end of the war, public health professionals still viewed hygiene as a primarily economic problem, correctable with proper education. The attitudes regarding racial identity that grew corrosive as the racial hierarchy was challenged had already insinuated race into concepts of purity and danger. During the war, fear of germs and fear of a social order without slavery produced fears that would endure and intertwine.

With Abraham Lincoln's election to the presidency in November 1860, Calhoun's home state of South Carolina enacted his proposal of secession, triggering a rash of secession across the South and the Civil War. Although President Lincoln's stated goal was to preserve the Union rather than abolish slavery, as the war progressed, Emancipation became a step to winning the war as incentive for mobilizing troops and marginalizing the South on the international stage. President Lincoln delivered the preliminary Emancipation Proclamation on September 22, 1863, after the Union victory at Antietam, establishing that a Union victory in the war would not only preserve the nation but also end slavery. African Americans from North and South alike enlisted in the Union Army, totaling more than 186,000.[34]

Racial tensions persisted in the North. Working-class New Yorkers, often first-generation immigrants from Ireland and Germany, blamed African Americans for the war (and the circumstances of the draft). As the Union Army drafted working-class Americans while allowing wealthy men to buy their way out of service, drafted men in 1863 targeted black New Yorkers in resulting riots. Many fled across the water to Brooklyn. Race relations in the North were far from harmonious even if the Union moved to abolish slavery.

As the nation battled over race, it moved to exert control over dirt as longtime concerns of sanitarians helped shape policy during the Civil War. Lemuel Shattuck's 1850 proposal was the first plan for an integrated public health program in the United States, though one that was not enacted before the Civil War. The acute health crises of the military conflict led to implementation of several of Shattuck's plans as relief and aid societies were founded in Northern cities almost immediately after the start of the war. The need for medical personnel overwhelmed the military's capacity; professionals in 1861 estimated the Union would need to recruit at least 1,400 new doctors to attend to the growing army.[35] Sanitarians recognized that battling disease would determine the success of the army; in 1864 Jacob G. Forman wrote that, until the Civil War, "not less than five soldiers usually died of disease for every one killed in battle."[36]

The reverend Henry W. Bellows and Dr. Elisha Harris founded the U.S. Sanitary Commission to employ methods for obtaining clean water, clean clothing, and the separation of refuse and excreta that Shattuck had recommended in military contexts. Initially, the Commission researched the living conditions of the army and advised hospitals of any shortcomings in sanitary conditions. The Commission appointed Frederick Law Olmsted as executive chairman, and he hired sixty inspectors to report on the cooking, sleeping, drinking, and overall hygienic conditions of Union camps. As concerns became acute by 1864, the Commission expanded its responsibilities beyond advising to supplying nurses, clean clothing, bandages, and food to the army, responsibilities that later were transferred to the American Red Cross. Commission representatives instructed soldiers in proper personal hygiene and ordered supplies to make camps and hospitals cleaner.[37]

Sanitarians' concerns rested with the perils of dirt, as disease was linked to soil, mud, and murky water. The miasma theory of disease transmission continued, and the war on dirt was vital to maintaining the health of the troops. Indeed, dirt was identified as the root cause of several physical and moral ills, with one sanitary inspector pronouncing "dirt at one end and cowardice at the other."[38]

Noxious odors were linked to diphtheria, though during the war sanitarians also noted that boiling water could prevent diseases such as cholera and typhoid. Whether shaped by miasma theory or germ theory, these measures proved popular and effective in the war effort. Jacob G. Forman spoke to Sanitary Commission member A. W. Plattenburg, who noted in his travels through Missouri that the commission greatly improved the sanitary conditions of military hospitals, with wounded soldiers wearing clean clothes and lying on clean sheets. Doctors who had found wounded men wearing the soiled clothes they had fought in lying on floors had demanded that the army provide proper supplies. Clean clothing and bedding were crucial in the struggle to limit casualties.[39]

Sanitary conditions had improved such that, instead of five soldiers dying of disease for every one killed in battle, the ratio had narrowed to two to one for Union troops and perhaps an even lower ratio for Confederate troops. The war on dirt elevated public confidence in medical professionals, making nurses such as Florence Nightingale heroic figures and cities more apt to listen to sanitary professionals' recommendations on improving public health.[40]

A Country at the Crossroads

The period between Jefferson's death and the Civil War saw scientific justifications for white supremacy and for eradicating dirt. These two issues both involved notions of purity, albeit ones that were generally distinct outside the racism used to justify the physical removal of native peoples from land coveted by whites. Calhoun's hardened views on race, slavery, and the limits of political compromise demonstrate the heightened tensions about race and waste in American society in the second

quarter of the nineteenth century. For the first time, scientific justifications for subjugating people of African heritage emerged. Furthermore,
those justifications focused on skin color.

Tensions on race and slavery culminated in a war between the states
that appeared to settle the political question of slavery on the side of
abolitionists. The war's horrific toll in casualties forced the Union to
adopt some of the sanitary recommendations proposed over the previous twenty years, beginning the implementation of significant public
health advances. The end of the Civil War, it seemed, brought with it a
great leap forward for the Enlightenment values Jefferson held dear and
an end to many of the justifications for white supremacy that had developed in the nineteenth century. Legally, once the Union had defeated
the Confederacy, race no longer could be used to justify the bondage of
some humans by others. Emancipation removed the legal framework
that white supremacy evolved to support between 1790 and 1860, but
the abolition of slavery could not erase the beliefs and values of white
supremacy that intensified as slavery came under attack.

Just as the war brought change to American race relations, it also
had implications for how Americans viewed dirt and disease. The terrible toll of infectious disease on both sides of the war forced medical
personnel and sanitary professionals to innovate new ways of prevent-
ing and fighting infectious disease. Even away from the battlefield,
sanitary concerns grew. New York City, Philadelphia, and Boston accumulated filth during the war well beyond the ability of their municipal governments to handle it. New York City had welcomed the largest
number of immigrants (especially from Ireland and Germany) of any
American city between 1840 and 1865, and many of these newcomers
were mired in poverty, housed in tenements, and most vulnerable to
epidemic disease.[41]

"White trash" would become a common insult after the Civil War,
but the term's existence in the late antebellum period revealed the growing conflation of race and cleanliness. This conflation grew along with
worries about epidemic disease in cities and insecurities about slavery
and racial hierarchy. Political tensions relating to slavery exploded into
sectarian violence. Attempts to negotiate the question of slavery through
political compromise resulted in bloodshed in the western territories,
and growing calls for secession in the slaveholding South culminated in

a civil war. That war transformed the United States in several ways. The vast carnage—with most battlefield deaths caused by infection rather than arms—required advances in treatment and disease prevention. The enforced abolition of slavery that came with the Union's victory over the Confederacy preserved the Union and banned the institution that had been written into the nation's founding documents.

An industrializing nation finally free of the shackles of slavery had many possibilities ahead of it. The legal basis for white supremacy had, it seemed, been dismantled; social and cultural hierarchies would prove more durable. American concerns about race in the years after the Civil War became enmeshed with ever-growing concerns about waste.

PART II

New Constructions

3

Searching for Order

Attempts to create order require classifying matter as dirt. In 1967, the historian Robert Wiebe characterized the turbulent period between 1877 and 1920 as a search for order as the nation's society, economic system, culture, and politics underwent great change. This era included the rise of industrial society, the rollback of Reconstruction, and the rise of both populism and Progressivism as responses to the great changes. A search for order implies disorder and a deep unease in the organization of a society.[1]

The Civil War itself may be seen as establishing a new order in the nation's understandings of waste and of race. Although unsanitary conditions killed thousands during the war, progress included the implementation of more than two decades of sanitarians' recommendations in hospitals. This implementation provided an important response to the hazards of waste. On race, the emancipation of American slaves by force had, it seemed, ended the schism on slavery that had shaped the virulent racism of the antebellum period. When General Robert E. Lee's April 1865 surrender at Appomattox ended the Civil War, it seemed the nation was ready to rebuild a healthier, more egalitarian society.

On April 11, President Lincoln announced at the White House: "We meet this evening, not in sorrow, but in gladness of heart. The evacuation of Petersburg and Richmond, and the surrender of the principal insurgent army, give hope of a righteous and speedy peace whose joyous expression can not be restrained." The Union was preserved, the president remarked, and the business of reconstruction could begin (although, he added, that there was considerable debate as to the mode, manner, and means of reconstruction).[2]

Lincoln's Emancipation Proclamation of 1863 shaped the end of slavery throughout the United States. The economic rationale for white supremacy was removed, and 1865 brought hope to freed slaves to perhaps enjoy the full rights of American citizenship. Although the terms of Reconstruction—and how freed slaves might or might not own property, vote, or otherwise enjoy the benefits of citizenship—were not established, the end of bondage was.

America Transformed

Emancipation was just one of the major changes upsetting the established order of the United States. Leaps in industrial development and urbanization continued after the war. In the seventy years between 1850 and 1920, the population of the United States soared by 357 percent while the world population increased by only 55 percent. The most phenomenal growth occurred in the cities, primarily because of immigration and rural-to-urban migration. During this period, nearly thirty-two million people entered the United States, most of them from Southern and Eastern Europe. City growth was especially dramatic; in 1860, the only American cities with populations greater than 250,000 were New York City, Brooklyn (an independent city until 1898), and Philadelphia. By 1890, eleven cities were that large, with New York City, Chicago, and Philadelphia each hosting more than one million residents. Forty-one percent of American city dwellers in 1910 were foreign-born. About 80 percent of the new immigrants settled in the Northeast. Migration from rural areas of the country was also impressive as farmers came to cities; one estimate had fifteen million rural people moved to the cities between 1880 and 1920, with rural whites and blacks alike moving within the country to industrial cities like Detroit and Chicago. During those years, the rural population fell from 71.4 percent to 48.6 percent.[3]

Abolition and sanitary reforms promised to resolve some of the problems on race and waste that had vexed the nation since its founding. Yet the cultural history of the antebellum period informed what would happen at war's end. When President Lincoln admitted little agreement on the terms of Reconstruction on April 11, 1865, he anticipated the political debate of the next decade. Opining that at least some "very intelligent" freed men in Louisiana ought to have the right to vote, the president infuriated at least one member of the crowd witnessing Lincoln's speech. Three days later, John Wilkes Booth shot him.[4]

If Lincoln's evolving views on emancipation were a logical conclusion of Jefferson's struggles over egalitarian values, Booth's murder of Lincoln was a logical continuation of Calhoun's assertions of white supremacy. Assassinating the president who proposed that black men could vote was the first shot in the post-slavery constructions of race in the United States. These constructions were informed by the tensions that resulted in the Civil War and also by new developments in the economies of the North and South alike.

Lincoln's death triggered a decade of political turmoil. His successor Andrew Johnson vetoed several attempts to establish Reconstruction. Subsequently, Congress impeached Johnson but fell short of removing him from office. Reconstruction involved federal imposition on governments in the states that had seceded, inspiring resentment of both the federal government and freed African Americans. Opposition to Reconstruction grew in the South; support to maintain Reconstruction ebbed in the North. The ultimate result was a rollback of the Reconstruction laws that had existed as part of the congressional negotiations to settle the disputed 1876 presidential election.

During Reconstruction and its aftermath, the United States struggled with the question of race in a free society. A nation with slavery written into its Constitution—and that had seen despicable justifications for subjugating peoples from Africa under the guise of benevolent paternalism—would not become an egalitarian utopia once abolition, at the barrel of a gun, had become the law of the land. The form and enforcement of Reconstruction acknowledged these tensions. At the conclusion of the Civil War, the states that had formed the Confederacy were placed under military rule to ensure compliance with federal law.

In the immediate wake of the Civil War, the South attempted to preserve the racial status quo. The provisional state legislatures established by President Johnson adopted a series of Black Codes to establish servile working conditions resembling slavery. Florida, Mississippi, and Texas established laws racially segregating passenger cars on railroads. Yet racial segregation, as the historian C. Vann Woodward argues, was a more complex historical process with different outcomes in different states. North Carolina, for example, saw freedmen serve on juries. African Americans served in Congress and state legislatures in the South.[5]

Reactions, however, were fierce. The abolition of slavery did not eradicate legal structures of racism. States and the federal government established new laws relating to immigration, marriage, and citizenship based on "common sense" definitions of race. What emerged was a more detailed construction of rights and privileges based on white identity, and white identity was based on a variety of often contradictory, complex social and legal constructions. Immigrants who did not meet the criteria of whiteness were denied citizenship. Struggles to define these criteria are evident in the fifty-two racial prerequisite cases reported in American courts between 1878 and 1952, cases that introduced evidence ranging from published academic scholarship to vernacular common sense.[6]

Legal constructions of race culminated the passage of the Johnson-Reed Immigration Act of 1924, which was the nation's first comprehensive restriction of immigrants. It established numerical limits on immigration based upon (in the words of the historian Mae M. Ngai) "a global racial and national hierarchy that favored some immigrants over others," with European migrants favored over those from other nations. East Asians were particularly subject to restrictions between the 1850s and the Johnson-Reed Immigration Act.[7]

Racism based upon physical appearance was not new in 1865. Whiteness emerged as an explanation of power relations in the colonial era between people of European heritage and American heritage and between people of European heritage and African heritage. The language of dominance shifted progressively from religious (Christian/savage) to physical appearance (white/black/red). This obsession with color informed the ways in which power relations in the new nation were understood both in the early nineteenth century and in the late nineteenth century. The understanding, however, was not static. The ways in which white identity was shaped, achieved, and threatened evolved, contingent on specific social anxieties at different times of the century.

Notably, anxieties over environmental and materialist threats to economic and physical health shape constructions of whiteness. Industrialization shaped not only class relations but also race relations through the entire United States as industrial capacity grew. The benefits and damage of industrial capitalism produced new ways of describing race, and new inequalities based upon racial identity. The inequalities manifested in who was allowed to enter the nation. Anti-Chinese sentiment in California emerged with the first wave of Chinese immigration in the 1850s, culminating in Congress passing the Chinese Exclusion Act of 1882.[8]

Europeans were allowed to enter the country but encountered derision and discrimination based upon their religion, language, and "dusky" skin color, limiting employment and residential opportunities. The American military continued to push indigenous peoples west into reservations, fueled by constructions of the original Americans as "red" and "savage." The question of where black Americans who were no longer slaves fit in society was most contentious of all.

Economic transformations informed these social interactions and the relationships Americans had with the materials in their lives between the Civil War and World War I. Industrial production and mass consumption produced new definitions and volumes of unwanted, potentially dangerous materials. Americans classified larger volumes and greater varieties of materials as wastes. The decisions informing these classifications reveal the acute insecurities of the immediate postbellum period.

The Waste Age

The industrial urbanism Jefferson feared accelerated after 1865. Sanitary revolutions produced more sophisticated attempts to manage waste materials. The proper places for discards moved from streets to bins, separate sewers, dumps, and junkyards. Technologies developed to store and transport wastes; new occupations developed to manage wastes. Unprecedented volumes of human wastes were removed from households via sewers into waterways. Waterways also became home to effluent from factories and refineries, such as heavy metals, petroleum, and an ever-growing range of synthetic compounds. The volume of sewage spurred the creation of wastewater treatment technologies, which could ably manage bacterial hazards though not necessarily chemical hazards.[9]

The reorganization of land to serve industry accelerated. If the antebellum period saw transportation advances in the form of canals and railroads, the postbellum United States became networked in ways that allowed the rapid, reliable transport of raw materials and finished commodities.[10]

In the post-war period, waste became a more complex concern. At the same time that the United States grappled with the realities of race after emancipation, the nation also contended with the complex realities of urbanization. Cities were vital cogs in the nation's economy even in Jefferson's time; as industrialization grew in the nineteenth century, the centers of New York, Boston, and Philadelphia remained crucial centers of trade.

The act of transporting people and commodities produced wastes. The horse was a vital part of urban transportation in the late nineteenth century, with over 180,000 horses working in Manhattan in the 1880s. The manure and carcasses of overworked horses were constant nuisances on city streets.[11]

Horses were vital to intra-urban transportation, and steel horses drove inter-urban transportation. The railroads, which networked cities across the continent with faster, more dependable movement of people and goods (thus growing the economic productivity of cities), exacerbated the waste burdens of urban residents. Coal powered railroads; by 1880, soft bituminous coal constituted over 90 percent of American railroad fuel, producing dense smoke that blackened the skies of industrial cities such as Pittsburgh, Chicago, and Saint Louis. Residents complained of damage to buildings, higher costs of cleaning, and chronic health problems associated with the smoke. Stationary sources of air pollution included factories and homes that burned coal for heating in the winter; at the worst times, urban skies were black at noon with the coal soot urban dwellers inhaled regularly.[12]

Industrial activities made city air unpleasant to the eyes and nose. The increased capacity of meat processing made the already unpleasant trade of rendering worse. One Cambridge, Massachusetts, slaughterhouse in 1873 so befouled the air that residents from a five-mile swath of the Boston area were nauseated. Between the smoke from fuel and odors from manufacturing processes, industry dirtied urban air.[13]

Urban land and water also bore greater waste burdens after the Civil War. Cities had wrestled with the problem of sanitation prior to the war, and the explosive growth of postbellum urban society increased the hazards of waste. American cities achieved unprecedented residential density in the late nineteenth century, creating enclaves, some of which earned names (Little Italy, Chinatown, Ukrainian Village) that described the dominant demographic groups moving in. In 1894, New York City's Sanitary District A averaged 986.4 people an acre in thirty-two acres, which translated to 300,000 people in a space of five or six blocks, often living in cramped tenement buildings. Bombay, India, the second-most crowded area in the world, had 759.7 people an acre; Prague, the European city with the worst slums, had 485.4 people an acre. American cities surpassed any in Europe for the ills Thomas Jefferson had railed against one century earlier.[14]

Chicago's explosive growth from a swampy outpost in the 1830s to an industrial metropolis six decades later was perhaps Jefferson's worst nightmare. At the time of the Columbian Exposition in 1893, sociologists predicted this "City of the Century" would soon surpass New York City as the nation's largest. This did not happen (in part because New York City annexed Brooklyn), but the ills Jefferson associated with cities were visited upon the city. Jefferson might have appreciated the polemic *If Christ Came to Chicago!*, written by the British journalist William T. Stead in 1894 as a condemnation of the rampant corruption, "frosty smoke-mist" and the "poisonous drippings of what has become the *cloaca maxima* of the world."[15]

One decade later, the journalist Upton Sinclair found Stead's description of the city accurate. Sinclair described the experience of entering Chicago as witnessing "perplexing changes in the atmosphere" and land, where "the grass seemed to grow less green." The air was filled with thick smoke and "a strange, pungent odor" so strong that "you could literally taste it, as well as smell it—you could take hold of it, almost, and examine it at your leisure."[16]

The victory of industrialized meat production over the environment of Chicago was awe inspiring. Stockyards were filled with cattle as far as the eye could reach. Slaughterhouses transformed between eight and ten million animals into food each year, using most part of the animal as commodity. The parts that could not be sold were dumped into the adjacent South Fork of the South Branch of the Chicago River, called Bubbly Creek. This weak tributary was overwhelmed by the waste. The offal, blood, and feces sealed off one terminus and left the remaining waterway thick with organic wastes and bubbling from released methane.

Sinclair echoed Stead's reference to the *cloaca maxima* and called this waterway "Chicago's Great Open Sewer." Local reform groups identified it as a shameful blight upon the lives of the immigrants unfortunate enough to work and live near it. In 1911, the *Chicago Daily News* published photographs of a chicken and a man standing atop the wastes on Bubbly Creek. Industry had made it possible for man to walk upon the water.[17]

Cities concentrated wastes from their growing population and industrial processes. Local waterways were transformed. Brooklyn's Gowanus Canal became a repository of wastes for the industries at the canal's banks. Petroleum runoff from Cleveland's refineries so polluted the adjacent Cuyahoga River that the waterway periodically caught fire. Bubbly Creek was but the most infamous of the Chicago River's polluted stretches; the river handled so much sewage that the city decided to reverse the river's flow away from Lake Michigan's drinking water and southwest in the direction of Saint Louis.

Mass consumption lead to escalating solid waste disposal. Between 1903 and 1907, Pittsburgh's garbage almost doubled, increasing from 47,000 tons to 82,498 tons. Other metropolitan areas saw their creation of garbage increase to the point that many engineers, chemists, city officials, journalists, and sanitarians voiced concern over excessive waste being a problem. Cities developed programs to rid their streets of refuse and collect garbage. They began using incinerators to reduce the amount of garbage stored in dumps and, in New York City, briefly employed scavengers to sort through dumps for salvageable material.[18]

The problems were far worse than any Jefferson had witnessed in London or Paris. Amid the unsanitary conditions produced by density, epidemic diseases ran rampant. Typhoid spread throughout New Orleans from sewage standing in unpaved streets. In 1873, Memphis lost nearly 10 percent of its population to yellow fever. Mortality figures for "Murder Bay," a black district in Washington, DC, not far from the White House, were twice as high as those for white neighborhoods. The residents of that slum lived in ghastly surroundings, picking their dinners out of garbage cans and dumps. By 1870, conditions in New York City had deteriorated to the point that infant mortality rates were 65 percent higher than those of 1810, and yellow fever epidemics in Memphis killed so many residents that the state of Tennessee moved to revoke the city's charter in 1878. Correlations between living conditions and disease in tenements led to some understanding of the debilitating effects of a bad environment on health, but improvements would not come quickly.[19]

Responses to Wastes

Sanitary occupations to address these issues fell within two distinct classes. One, constituting civil engineers and medical doctors, involved individuals with formal educations who had established themselves as experts. These sanitarians, influenced by antebellum sanitarians such as Edwin Chadwick, Florence Nightingale, and Lemuel Shattuck, belonged to professional organizations such as the American Public Health Association, the American Society of Civil Engineers, and the American Society for Municipal Improvements (founded 1894 as ASMI, later renamed the American Society for Municipal Engineers). They employed scientific approaches to recommend public health measures. These professionals enjoyed great social prestige, using scientific methods to assess environment problems, developing reports, collecting statistics, and advising political leaders on how best to address pollution of the air, land, and water.[20]

These professionals frequently coordinated with civic associations composed of middle- and upper-class women (in many cases, the spouses of political and economic leaders) to define waste problems and offer prescriptive solutions. Women's clubs often asked sanitary experts to conduct reports on urban pollution and then pressured city government to act on the conclusions of the reports. The Women's Health Protective Association of Brooklyn, New York, for example, could boast in 1901 of getting the city to stop dumping garbage into the ocean (where it would wash up on and befoul the beach) and instead to incinerate household wastes. The association also instructed households on keeping ash cans inside their properties rather than on sidewalks and advocated for improvements in the plumbing of Brooklyn's public schools.[21]

Jane Addams, founder of Chicago's Hull-House, framed the urban waste problem in starkly moral terms: "In a crowded city quarter, if the garbage is not properly collected and destroyed, a tenement-house mother may see her children sicken and die." Therefore, keeping the city clean was the duty of local authorities in consultation with sanitary experts.[22]

A second class of sanitary occupations involved a wide set of tasks handling waste materials. Some of the people involved were employees of municipal departments, others worked for private waste management businesses. Several waste-trading businesses were as small as one-person operations. Even those with as many as a dozen employees involved the proprietor handling waste materials along with the employees. Few of the people in these occupations received formal educations, and their work lacked the status of the sanitary professionals in the first class. Their operations were often scorned as nuisances and threats to public health; they were seen as dirty people performing dirty work. At times, these waste workers came into conflict with the sanitary experts and reformers seeking to remove harmful materials from residential areas.[23]

These two classes did not necessarily correlate to economic wealth, although those in the professional set tended to be more likely to grow up in conditions allowing them to experience formal educations. A fortunate few in the informal set established ownership of profitable waste handling businesses and became prosperous. Some became community leaders and philanthropists. The Dutch immigrant Harm Huizenga arrived in Chicago during the 1893 Columbian Exposition. He soon established an incinerator ash hauling operation, growing it into a garbage-hauling business with his sons. This family business successfully expanded to handle garbage collection for municipalities across the United States (and eventually, worldwide). Waste Management, Inc., the largest waste handling corporation on Earth, began as a small immigrant-founded family business. The majority of people employed in the waste trades, however, did not grow wealthy, were not unionized, and were subjected to great risks on the job.[24]

As industrial society grew, so too did wastes and the business of waste management. Trade in old metals, textiles, rubber, and glass was not merely local but international, and a few enterprising waste traders amassed considerable wealth. Work sweeping streets, hauling garbage, and sorting discards became both the basis for successful businesses and a standard division of basic municipal services such as police, fire, and street maintenance. In 1909, the Census Bureau enumerated 22,560 individuals employed as street cleaners in cities with populations above 30,000.[25] The number of rag, junk, and scrap businesses listed in city directories grew steadily between the Civil War and World War I, then experiencing a major increase during the war as trade in scrap iron and steel rose to fuel war production.[26]

These economic developments were informed by new cultural constructions of hygiene. Native-born Americans expected to keep themselves clean and expected others to keep themselves clean as a matter of moral responsibility. Unclean people could spread cholera, typhoid, scarlet fever, or any number of contagious diseases, threatening the safety of all. A responsible individual had to bathe regularly, wear clean clothes, and keep a sanitary household. By the end of the nineteenth century, Progressive reformers and settlement-house workers attempted to teach the urban poor and recent immigrants to adopt the rising American standards of hygiene, conflating cleanliness with American identity.[27]

Many new immigrants in this war against germs lacked the facilities to uphold hygienic standards as easily as people living in middle-class neighborhoods could. Upton Sinclair's novel *The Jungle* shocked American readers with its depiction of the squalid living and working conditions of Lithuanian meatpackers in Chicago's stockyards. (Though what really disturbed the American people was Sinclair's vivid descriptions of contaminants in the meat they purchased and ate rather than the dehumanizing conditions the immigrants worked and lived in.) The dank Packingtown conditions contrasted with rising standards of living as Chicago's middle class began living in newer houses further away from the crime of the city's productive neighborhoods, leaving the housing by the stockyards to be filled by immigrants from Southern and Eastern Europe. As of the 1920 Census, about half of the people living near the stockyards were foreign-born Europeans, and infant mortality in the area was estimated by one study to be double the rate of that in the more affluent Hyde Park neighborhood to the south.[28]

Progressive efforts to aid residents in befouled neighborhoods focused on the link between poor sanitation and death. Mary McDowell and Jane Addams founded settlement houses in Chicago in the 1890s, bringing in educated middle-class women to both acculturate working-class residents and advocate on their behalf with the often apathetic and corrupt city government. Reports on sanitary conditions aided the latter effort; in 1901, Chicago's City Homes Association surveyed forty-four blocks of the city's South Side, finding a high mortality rate owing to "the filthy and unpaved streets and alleys, to the dampness of the many lots the surfaces of which were below the street level, to the dilapidated and unsanitary frame houses, and to a dense and poverty-stricken population."[29]

The cramped, filthy conditions new urban residents faced brought with them scorn by those who saw them as unwelcome contributors to the problem. Observing social conditions in New York City, the journalist Jacob Riis summarized: "The once unwelcome Irishman has been followed in his turn by the Italian, the Russian Jew, and the Chinaman, and has himself taken a hand at opposition, quite as bitter and quite as ineffectual, against these later hordes."[30]

Riis described the living conditions of the urban poor as miserable and unsanitary, as if the worst excesses of Jefferson's European cities were multiplied. The tenements of New York City's Lower East Side were packed with humanity in closer quarters than any London had experienced, and even the alleyways were crowded. "Through dark hallways and filthy cellars, crowded, as is every foot of the street, with dirty children, the settlements in the rear are reached."[31]

The War on Waste: Hazard

In order to address these concerns, cities drew upon the advances made in sanitary reforms in the 1850s and 1860s. One of the most important figures in post-war sanitary reforms was Col. George E. Waring, Jr. Prior to the war, Waring was a successful scientific agriculturalist in New York State, managing farms for Horace Greeley and Frederick Law Olmsted. Olmsted hired him to work as a drainage engineer in the construction of Central Park, after which Waring worked on a variety of drainage and sewerage projects nationwide until the outbreak of the Civil War. He joined the Union Army as a major and was commissioned a colonel in 1862. Waring left the military in 1865 to build drainage and sewerage systems in several communities in Massachusetts and New York.

Waring's response to the yellow fever epidemics in Memphis, Tennessee, brought him to national prominence as a sanitary engineer. In 1878, more than one-sixth of the city's population died of the disease. In 1879, civic leaders repealed the city's charter and established a commission to govern the city and rebuild its sanitary systems from scratch. Local and state officials invited the National Board of Health to investigate and make recommendations; Waring was one of the investigators invited. He proposed that Memphis build a sewer system to discharge household sewage on a regular basis while not handling stormwater (which would instead be handled by surface streets). Despite some opposition from local property owners and some engineers about the city paying for such a system, Waring's plan gained sufficient support from the state legislature that Memphis had completed the new sewer by the end of 1881.

Waring's success eliminating the source of diseases at a low cost meant other municipalities adopted his system in the 1880s and 1890s. In 1881 and 1883, Waring patented aspects of his Memphis System, created a company (the Drainage Construction Company), and marketed his innovation to cities throughout the United States. Not only did attention to the Memphis System produce sewer contracts for Waring, it led to his 1895 appointment as street cleaning commissioner of New York City.

Waring was sent to New York City to both literally and figuratively clean up the town. By 1895, the Tammany Hall political machine had received such widespread scorn for corruption and doling out patronage jobs that, when reform mayor William L. Strong took office, he sought to appoint qualified professionals untainted by the machine to run city services. Thus, Theodore Roosevelt became police commissioner and Waring became street cleaning commissioner. Armed with a mandate to eliminate political cronies from sanitation jobs, Waring sought to instill an efficient military structure based upon the principles of sanitation as he understood them. Under Waring, New York City adopted the best sanitation methods attempted piecemeal throughout the country. Waring directed households to use a "primary separation" system in which garbage, rubbish, and ashes were kept in separate receptacles awaiting collection. The Street Cleaning Department could then easily use different methods of disposal for the separate waste materials.

Waring used a variety of waste disposal methods, including dumping wastes in the ocean, developing a reduction plant to extract value from discards, and initiating the White Wings program to combat the horse manure and litter filling the city's streets. Uniformed street sweepers, working under close watch from supervisors, descended upon the streets with military precision. Dressed entirely in white to emphasize their role sanitizing the city, these workers drew positive attention to the city's efforts, and citizens and newspapers remarked upon the new standards of cleanliness in New York's streets.

George Waring's accomplishments in Memphis and New York were adopted in part or in whole by cities across the United States. The sewage and drainage systems he implemented were intended to remove noxious odors, under the theory that miasmas produced epidemic diseases. Sanitary experts working in the 1880s began to realize the presence of specific pathogenic organisms (bacteria), rather than miasmas, transmitted diseases. By 1900, public health professionals understood the "germ theory" of disease as the operating theory to implement effective measures against contagious diseases. A focus on bacteria rather than odor advanced water treatment and control of solid wastes.[32]

Identification of germs as the cause of disease led to a focus on sewage and garbage management at the expense of controlling industrial wastes. The historian Joel Tarr argues that because industrial wastes were toxic, rather than containing germs, public health authorities reasoned that, "from a purely pathogenic standpoint, their relation to sanitation is remote." As cities worked to curb the dangers of germs, smoke continued to fill the air despite protests from reform groups, and industrial wastes proliferated on the land and in the water.[33]

Exactly how these wastes were controlled and who was charged to control them varied from municipality to municipality. If waste was managed at all in the antebellum period, it was done so on a local level, and not by the federal or state governments. Private means of collecting some waste commodities such as rags and bones had existed as far back as the colonial era; however, the responsibility for collecting and disposing of garbage and sewage was not decided as a public or private matter as late as the 1890s.

Systems varied from town to town. The 1880 U.S. Census (the first census in which comprehensive urban statistics were compiled) reveals no national trend favoring one system over the other. In only 48 of 199 cities surveyed was there a municipal system for collection and disposal

A GROUP OF "WHITE WINGS" AT THE STARTING POINT OF THE ANNUAL PARADE.

A SECTION FOREMAN WITH HIS SWEEPERS READY TO MARCH.

A SWEEPER AT WORK WITH BROOM, SHOVEL, BRUSH, WATERING CAN, AND BAG CARRIER.

"The 'White Wings' of New York at Work and on Parade." Picture Collection, The Branch Libraries, The New York Public Library, Astor, Lenox, and Tilden Foundations.

of garbage and ashes. Only 38 cities employed the contract system, while 59 cities left the responsibility to private parties. Public municipal collection tended to occur in larger cities with larger tax bases. Cities with populations over 30,000 were more likely to have a formal, citywide system of collection than did smaller cities. Furthermore, smaller cities were more likely to favor private collection than were larger cities.[34]

Municipalities could either contract the service by taking bids from private scavenging companies or establish a municipal service. Cities initially embraced the contract system as it required little or no capital outlay by the city, while still allowing for some municipal supervision. This arrangement encouraged the proliferation of private businesses to collect garbage, scavenge for scrap materials, cart incinerator ashes, and manage dumps. Such operations were increasingly profitable and also prone to corruption. Reformers in cities like Chicago and New York City attacked the contract system as corrupt and argued that municipal operation of services would effectively and efficiently reduce the hazards of wastes in cities.[35]

Urban reformers championed sanitary reforms in the 1890s. Because air, land, and water pollution affected many or all urban residents, several community protest movements developed to address pollution concerns. Two reactions to industrial capitalism emerged. One, which manifested in various ways as anarchism or socialism, sought to dismantle the political and economic structures of industrial society. Actions to achieve these goals ranged from labor walkouts to assassination attempts (including several successful ones) on presidents and mayors, including President James Garfield's 1881 killing by Charles Guiteau, President William McKinley's 1901 killing by Leon Czolgosz, and Chicago Mayor Anton Cermak's 1933 killing by Guiseppe Zangara (who intended to kill President-Elect Franklin D. Roosevelt). These killings, as well as labor uprisings by people with Southern and Eastern European names, stoked fears of immigrants and the disorder they might bring to America.[36]

A second reaction sought to temper the worst ills of industrial capitalism while preserving the modern society it shaped. This Progressive approach sought to reform social and environmental ills under the assumption that transparent, efficient systems would benefit the public and reduce the acute problems facing modern society. Business leaders championed efficiency on the shop floor under the influence of Frederick Winslow Taylor, who stated in 1911 that "we can see and feel the waste of material things," and "the need for greater efficiency is widely felt."[37]

This ethos informed a political movement. Wisconsin Governor Robert LaFollette pioneered income tax collection and workers' compensation schemes. President Theodore Roosevelt battled trusts and advocated active regulation of businesses ranging from oil to foods and drugs. Sanitary engineers adopted the gospel of efficiency from Progressivism, and social reformers and civil groups embraced its moralistic rhetoric.

Allowing waste materials to collect endangered the public, especially vulnerable children. As the historian Martin Melosi puts it, "Primitive collection and disposal practices were signs of backwardness and barbarity; civilized societies were well kept and sanitary. One could hardly expect citizens to seek moral and material progress in a despoiled habitat polluted by litter and disease-breeding refuse. In the broadest sense, filth bred chaos, while cleanliness promoted order." As Americans tried to produce order from their rapidly changing lives and communities, effective waste collection was a crucial part of that effort.[38]

Fears of waste matter as a hazard continued, and many of the sanitary reforms recommended in the antebellum period that were implemented during the Civil War were crucial in making urban society safer in the postbellum era. Sanitarians such as Waring developed methods of removing human waste, refuse, rubbish, and garbage from homes and neighborhoods. Sewers, water treatment facilities, garbage collection, and (after 1916) zoning were organizational and technological advancements providing order to communities across the United States. These efforts won results. Between the Civil War and World War I, American cities reduced outbreaks of cholera, typhoid, malaria, yellow fever, whooping cough, and scarlet fever. (Other diseases, such as influenza and polio, were not so easily eradicated, remaining threats after 1920.) The American city in 1920 was demonstrably cleaner than it had been half a century earlier.

Hygienic reform did not stop at the private doorstep. As Suellen Hoy demonstrates in her book *Chasing Dirt*, American households and individuals also changed sanitary habits after the Civil War. Mass production of soaps, as well as of clothing and household goods, made keeping one-self and one's house clean easier and more affordable in the early twen-tieth century. Magazines such as *Good Housekeeping* instructed women on proper hygienic practices; often the sanitary engineers who devel-oped public works systems also doled out advice to women on keeping a sanitary home.[39]

The War on Waste: Inefficiency

At the same time, the expansion of industrial capitalism and its quest for profit brought new scrutiny to waste as inefficiency. Fears that west-ward expansion and voracious industrial production might deplete the natural resources of the nation led to efforts in business and govern-ment to wisely manage resources through conservation. Such efforts were not meant to attack industrial capitalism but improve it. President Theodore Roosevelt saw the fundamental problem facing the United States as the "problem of national efficiency, the patriotic duty of insur-ing the safety and continuance of the Nation."[40]

Scientific expertise informed the quest for efficient resource use. Frederick Winslow Taylor and Henry Ford revolutionized industrial production in part because they optimized time, labor, and materials used. Innovations included the assembly line and a vast increase in reclaiming wasted materials as well. Materials discarded because they were old, obsolete, or perhaps dirty had potential value as scrap or shoddy material in industrial production. Trades in cotton and linen rags emerged in the nineteenth century as paper manufacturers sought the materials for the pliable and durable paper into which they could be fashioned. The transatlantic rag trade flourished for most of the cen-tury, slowly declining after the advent of cheap wood pulp allowed for more affordable paper manufacture after the 1880s.[41]

Metals, which could be remelted and refashioned, had been used in production for centuries; the biblical reference to fashioning swords from plowshares and plowshares from swords evidence of how mal-leable and sturdy scrap metals could be. In the late nineteenth century, the United States became what historian Thomas J. Misa calls a nation of steel. Steel was the building block upon which skyscrapers were con-structed, ships were built, railroads criss-crossed the continent, and any manner of tools and machines were fashioned. Andrew Carnegie's ascent from Scottish orphan to railroad inventory clerk to steel tycoon is but the most famous example of the amount of iron and steel circulating in the United States—and the amount of money used to buy and sell that metal. Railroads, steel mills, and later, automobile manufacturers sought old metal, which was cheaper to acquire than mining virgin ore.[42]

The quest to salvage wasted materials brought a tension between waste as inefficiency and waste as hazard. Old rags could make paper; they could also harbor infectious diseases. Old metal could make new trains; it could also give handlers tetanus and puncture wounds. The dual identities of waste emerged as industrial capitalism transformed American society.

Industrial capitalism also reshaped the demography of American cities. Demand from factories for labor attracted millions of migrants from Europe, Mexico, and Asia as economic and political instability led many to leave their home countries.

The outbreak of World War I effectively sealed the borders to new immigrants, yet industry continued to require new pools of labor. They turned to migrants within the United States, especially people leaving rural areas for cities. Some came from the Midwest, but the South especially saw millions of migrants leave sharecropping for the prospect of work in the cities. Southern whites came to Detroit to work in the automobile industry, to Gary to work in steel, and to Chicago to work in meat. African Americans left the South in such large numbers that the exodus became known as the Great Migration. Between 1914 and 1920, the wave of migrants transformed black communities from New York City to San Francisco, utterly reshaping most of the new industrial cities of the Midwest (including Detroit, Pittsburgh, Cleveland, Chicago, and Saint Louis).[43]

The economy of the South evolved in a different way. Gone were the giant plantations, but cotton reigned supreme. Despite debate over economic redistribution to freedmen, the economic order of the South saw vast inequities of wealth persist. The landed gentry retained their lands and loaned space upon them to small sharecropping farmers. In practice, this arrangement effectively tied labor to the land, burying farmers in unsupportable debt. Sharecroppers' situations worsened when monocultural cultivation of cotton invited plagues of boll weevils that feasted on and destroyed the crops. Faced with ever-declining economic prospects in the fields, sharecroppers found themselves the subjects of appeals to move north as factory labor. Factories that had depended on immigrant labor for decades now saw the spigot of new foreign workers shut off owing to the war. Millions of sharecroppers, black and white, had new prospects.

These changes transformed the nation. In the 1920 Census of Population, more Americans were enumerated as urban residents than rural residents. Progress in sanitation had combined with vast increases in employment capacity to make urban life compelling for a majority of the nation. A century after Thomas Jefferson's death, his country had transformed from the yeoman farmer ideal to embrace urban industry.[44]

His fears of such an embrace were warranted. While a few individuals like Andrew Carnegie grew immensely wealthy, class inequalities became more dramatic than ever. While sanitary reforms made urban living possible, residents in working-class and poorer areas were more likely to be exposed to human and industrial wastes. Increases in production capacity and population density concentrated wastes further.

Purity and Danger: "Redeemers" of White Supremacy

No understanding of the search for order between the Civil War and World War I is complete without discussing the Ku Klux Klan (KKK). This secret society's purpose was to establish social order on the basis of white supremacy. Opportunities—be they new political rights for freedmen in the South or economic opportunities for millions of new immigrants in Northern cities—brought great insecurity and fear to those who had once enjoyed privileges and comfort and who were threatened by emancipation, by immigration, by industrialization, or by urbanization.

Approaches to alleviating this anxiety built upon appeals to tradition, but not a tradition of Jeffersonian Enlightenment ideals. The traditions that gave comfort in postbellum America were the scientific appeals to white supremacy that had evolved between 1820 and the Civil War. With slavery gone and pastoral society threatened by industrial growth's appeals to immigrant free labor, this noxious residue of

American racial history endured to shape a new chapter of American racial constructions.

The ways in which existing ideas of white supremacy endured were not merely a restoration of the antebellum era but a reaction against new and heightened fears. Fears of emancipated African Americans, fears of waves of new migrants, and fears of contagion produced new and qualitatively different stereotypes. These stereotypes in turn shaped new forms of racial inequalities.

Reconstruction, enforced by the Union Army, upended the political order of the South. Freedmen had access to the vote, and in a region dominated by Democratic politics, Republicans gained a foothold. Reconstruction brought the promise of social and economic change. The institution of slavery was no more. The large plantations remained, but whether they would be divided up among the freedmen, retained by the existing landowners, or otherwise redistributed was an open question in the early days of Reconstruction. The racial order was in flux; lower-class whites lay vulnerable to being considered equal to the freedmen.[45]

Southern white politicians castigated black suffrage as a fundamental threat. Reconstruction, declared South Carolina Governor Benjamin Franklin Perry, would throw control of the South into the hands of "ignorant, stupid, demi-savage paupers." North Carolina Whig leader William A. Graham believed enfranchising blacks would "roll back the tide of civilization two centuries at least."[46]

Free, enfranchised blacks, politically, constituted the greatest threat to white Southerners. The success of plantation slavery had produced not only dependence on slaves for the economic order but a realization that slaves were a large (if disparaged) segment of society in the region. In South Carolina, Mississippi, and Louisiana, the majority in each state of the population was black; Alabama, Florida, and Georgia had populations almost 50 percent black, North Carolina and Virginia were about 40 percent black, and Arkansas, Tennessee, and Texas were approximately 25 percent black. In a democracy, these numbers boded ill for maintaining the racist order. Beyond the worries about black voting power, establishment whites feared the possibility that some whites might support blacks politically, leading to formidable political blocs. Because of this fear, "carpetbaggers" (migrants from the

North) and "scalawags" (native Southerners who cast their lot politically with the freedmen) found themselves subjected to a torrent of abuse by their Democratic opponents, an odium that persisted in the morality play of traditional Reconstruction historiography. The promise of a black-white Republican coalition was deeply upsetting to whites in the defeated Confederacy, and it was among the resentments that festered during Reconstruction.[47]

Black enfranchisement proved unpopular with Northern white voters as well. In the fall of 1867, the Democratic party made large gains in Union states in large part because of the question of what political power blacks would have. From Maine to California, Democrats gained ground dramatically, winning in New York by more than 50,000 votes, coming within 3,000 of electing Ohio's governor and gaining control of the legislature, sweeping California, and reducing Republicans' massive majorities of 1866 by three quarters.[48]

Race, then, was a highly divisive issue in the North as well as South, West as well as East, in the early years of Reconstruction. Emancipation had provided the potential for equality, but that potential met furious resistance in all corners of the newly unified nation. Issues of the vote, of access to education, property rights, rights in courts, and all of the rights of citizenship were hotly contested.

Fears ran rampant about the prospect of blacks and whites marrying and what that meant to constructions of race. A factor in the Southern conception of racial purity was fear of sexual pollution, or miscegenation, characterizing the progeny of such unions as tainted. In 1869, the Georgia Supreme Court used scientific racism as a rationale for upholding the miscegenation law, proclaiming: "The amalgamation of the races is not only unnatural, but is always productive of deplorable results. Our daily observation shows us, that the offspring of these unnatural connections are generally sickly and effeminate, and that they are inferior in physical development and strength, to the full-blood of either race."[49]

The phrase, "of either race," is crucial because it shows how badly judges wanted to reconcile the scientific goal of racial purity with the constitutional veneration of equality. The abstract ideal of racial purity, judges and legislators implied, might apply to people with black or white skin, or, for that matter, to indigenous Americans or people from Asia (though it was primarily concerned with notions of distinct *black* and *white* races).[50]

The invention of the term "miscegenation" marked a new and highly significant turn in the longer history of the regulation of interracial marriage. Between 1864 and 1967, lawmakers and their supporters routinely called laws that banned interracial sex and marriage "anti-miscegenation" laws; they did so in order to signal their belief that sex and marriage between people of different races was a distinctly different phenomenon than sex and marriage between people of the same race. The progeny of interracial unions were labeled various kinds of mongrels, mulattoes, quadroons, and octaroons, and crucially, their legal perception was on a par with their black ancestors rather than their white ancestors. The language of pollution had irrevocably tainted these Americans as too impure to be white.[51]

When judges who were charged with enforcing miscegenation laws had questions about racial categories, there were two obvious places to look for answers: the precise wording of the race definition laws passed by state legislatures and the authoritative expertise of race science. Anti-miscegenation laws and the assumptions behind the word "miscegenation" itself all pointed to the idea of blacks as pollutants potentially staining white purity, which appeared to be self-evident.[52]

The obsessions with white supremacy in the South meant that the region's Democratic party rapidly became devoted to one issue—opposing Reconstruction and its threat to white supremacy. In a widely publicized letter written on the eve of the 1868 Democratic convention, vice presidential candidate Frank Blair argued that voting for the Democratic ticket was a vote to restore the established order of the South. A Democratic president could achieve this by declaring Reconstruction state governments "null and void" and using the army to disperse them. This statement had immediate setbacks for the Democratic ticket in 1868, but the sentiments informed Democratic rhetoric over the next decade.

Blair subsequently stumped for this idea, proudly articulating white supremacy and assailing Republicans as damaging the established order of society. To Blair, Republicans had placed the South under the rule of "a semi-barbarous race of blacks who are worshippers of fetishes and polygamists" and longed to "subject the white women to their unbridled lust." Like Calhoun before him, Blair's racist thinking was informed by reading contemporary scientific literature. In Blair's case, his interpretation of Charles Darwin's *Origin of Species* had only amplified his long-standing fear of racial intermixing. Blair—in a reading that in no way expressed Darwin's ideas on race—argued that miscegenation would reverse evolution, produce a less-advanced species incapable of reproducing itself, and destroy "the accumulated improvement of the centuries." These were the convictions of the Democratic candidate for vice president of the United States in 1868.[53]

The Democratic party's redefinition of itself as the political mechanism for asserting white supremacy came at the same time that a secret society developed to assert white supremacy by force. Founded in 1866 as a Tennessee social club, the Ku Klux Klan had spread into nearly every Southern state within two years, launching a "reign of terror" against Republican leaders black and white. Although largely confined in 1868 to Piedmont counties where whites outnumbered blacks, violence in Georgia and Louisiana spread into the heart of the Black Belt (that portion of the South dominated by plantation agriculture where millions of African Americans lived and worked).[54]

The Klan, dressed in white hoods and robes, terrorized African Americans from exercising their rights as citizens and intimidated sympathetic whites. In some areas, armed whites prevented blacks from voting in the 1868 presidential election, although systemic disenfranchisement of Southern blacks would not be complete until the turn of the century as Jim Crow laws and terror campaigns gradually denied the ballot to blacks across the region.

The Klan attempted to intimidate blacks from voting, holding office, becoming economically prosperous, or even getting educated. Institutions like churches and schools, embodiments of black autonomy, frequently became targets. "Nearly every colored church and schoolhouse" in the Tuskegee area was burned during the fall of 1870. Female teachers were attacked as well as male, and white as well as black educators were victimized.[55]

This terrorist activity was in the mainstream of Southern society. Over the years, the Ku Klux Klan flourished in rural and urban areas, with community leaders frequently being members. This arrangement was without shame for decades; only in the late twentieth century would the U.S. senator from West Virginia Robert Byrd be compelled to apologize for his membership in the organization. The Klan was mainstream in many pockets of American life, a purifying force bent on restoring the racist order of slave society.[56]

The Klan had varying waves of popularity, with a resurgence after the turn of the century. Writers and entertainers romanticized the Klan as redeemers of an older, white social order. Thomas Dixon, Jr., popularized this image in his plays and films. The North Carolinian, born in 1864 and raised during Reconstruction, was furious at a performance of the abolitionist play *Uncle Tom's Cabin*. It inspired his book *The Leopard's Spots: A Romance of the White Man's Burden, 1865–1900*, an unapologetic championing of the antebellum racial order enduring under the imposition of reconstruction after the war. This book became an instant best-seller upon its 1902 publication, and Dixon followed it with 1905's *The Clansman: An Historical Romance of the Ku Klux Klan* and 1907's *The Traitor: A Story of the Rise and Fall of the Invisible Empire*.

These books demonized abolitionists and compared black men to animals. If in the 1840s John Calhoun's rationale for slavery was a benevolent paternalism, Dixon's interpretation of emancipation was, as Eric Foner puts it, the story of "the southern black man's innate bestiality and bloodlust." Once free of that paternal guidance of their white masters, as Foner characterizes Dixon's narrative, African American men reverted to "their primitive evolutionary state, subjecting southern whites to an incessant reign of terror." The greatest fear in this reign of terror was the sexual subjugation of white women by black men, who, unable to control primitive urges, became rapists. Sexual pollution remained an acute anxiety of white supremacists.[57]

The only defenders against this threat in Dixon's narrative were the white-robed crusaders of the Ku Klux Klan, redeeming the white race and purifying the South from Northern tyranny and black sexual violence. The Klan's reputation among self-identified whites was, far from being agents of terror, as a collection of noble knights representing an old and beloved social order. In this characterization, all the KKK's actions were not only justified but heroic, as the organization defended whiteness against, initially, freed African Americans in the South and whites sympathetic to their cause, then expanding to threats from the new immigrants (Anglo-Saxon Protestants excepted).

Dixon's romantic view of the Klan gained an even wider audience when the filmmaker D. W. Griffith released *The Birth of a Nation* in 1915. A breakthrough in long-form cinema that held the box-office record in the United States for decades, *The Birth of a Nation* reproduced this heroic image of the Klan as redeemers of a lost and noble South against the threat of animalistic black terror. President Woodrow Wilson championed this view. The former president of Princeton University had already moved to resegregate the federal workforce after the Progressive hiring practices by Presidents Roosevelt and Taft. An unapologetic white supremacist, Wilson was quoted in Griffith's film, adding legitimacy to the racist imagery Griffith presented. *The Birth of a Nation* was not simply a regional phenomenon in the South; it was a film that drew audiences in the urban and rural areas of the North as well. The KKK in the early twentieth century, as the historian Kenneth Jackson notes, developed followings in cities and became especially widespread in the state of Indiana. According to estimates from within the Klan, the 1924 distribution of chapters throughout the nation was about 40 percent in the region of Indiana, Illinois, and Ohio (with about an equal number below the Mason-Dixon line). The redeemers of white supremacy were not only popular in the former slave states but also throughout the country.[58]

The images of a mass of angry whites "heroically" menacing a cowering African American victim were reproduced not only in books and films but also in the mass-market newspapers expanding their reach into American households. Representations of African Americans in newspaper cartoons became more dehumanized, strengthening visual stereotyping. The cartoonist William Marriner's popular *Sambo and His Funny Noises* ran in newspapers between 1905 and 1914, exposing readers to the character's crude dialect, wide eyes, and supposed insensitivity to the rain of violent acts white characters inflicted upon him. Advertisements of smiling, servile African Americans for products, such as the smiling Rastus for Cream of Wheat and Aunt Jemima, introduced during the 1893 World's Fair, became popular during this time.[59]

These popular images contributed to the dehumanization of African Americans amid an increasingly hostile cultural, political, economic, and social climate. Racial lynchings became more common in the 1890s and increased further after the turn of the century. The terrorist violence of the Klan was important in maintaining white supremacy in the century after the Civil War, with the Klan gaining popularity at times when white supremacy was challenged. The Klan's focus on whiteness as purity, and the organization's image as redeemers of the appropriate social order, gave it a powerful rationale as being socially sanitary, ensuring people were in their appropriate places. Klan publications boasted that the KKK was "an American organization" in which immigrants were not welcome, a "Gentile organization" in which Jews (or even non-Protestant Christians) were not welcome, and "a white man's organization" asserting the supremacy of "the White Race."[60] At a time when fears of disorder upended American society, the Ku Klux Klan sought to restore order. While the concept of a pure white race was illusory, the organization's tactics were effective at subjugating people deemed impure.

The Klan's goals were consistent with a series of racist laws enacted in Southern states after the compromise of 1877 effectively ended Reconstruction. Over the next two decades, states developed patterns of racially restrictive laws. Crucially, the U.S. Supreme Court upheld several of these key laws, most famously the decision in *Plessy v. Ferguson* (1896) that established the "separate but equal" justification for segregation. This legal basis of racial discrimination shaped the approaches Southern states took to restrict access to train cars, hospitals, schools, restaurants by race and to otherwise racially reshape the spaces of life in the South. Black people were deemed out of place in a variety of public accommodations in the former Confederacy.[61]

Purity and the Search for Order

At the end of *The Search for Order*, Robert Wiebe concludes that, after a long period of turmoil in the late nineteenth century, the United States had "in a general sense . . . found its direction early in the twentieth century."[62] Indeed, the methods of addressing fear and insecurities concerning the vast political and economic upheavals after the Civil War led to a clear direction by 1920. Some aspects of this direction, including the construction of the most effective sanitary systems the nation had seen, had started to overcome the acute hazards of waste in cities. Other aspects were more troubling, including a renewed valuation of white

supremacy across the country. If upholding the notion of white supremacy had roots in the antebellum period, postbellum whiteness would be
constructed, described, and maintained in new, disturbing ways reflecting the dominant concerns of an industrializing society. The Klan's tactics and iconography were extreme, but the ideas informing them were
in the mainstream of a newly toxic attitude about race in the United
States. That attitude, conflating sanitation and white identity, informed
every sector of society and proved difficult to undermine or remove.

"How Do You Make Them So Clean and White?"

The Ku Klux Klan (KKK) was the most visible and extreme representation of white supremacy in the years after the Civil War. The KKK cast white identity as purity, mingling with Christian iconography to ensure white supremacy in elected office, in economic relations, and in sexuality. The KKK was only the most extreme version of this racial construction. State legislatures wrote miscegenation laws that based public health on white purity at risk of pollution, and assumptions that whiteness and purity were intertwined dominated white culture.

The politicization of biology extended beyond sexuality to produce newly corrosive explanations of skin color in the late nineteenth and early twentieth centuries. In high and low culture alike, Americans identifying as white found new ways to justify subjugating non-white people in keeping with the explanations of racism in John C. Calhoun's time. These justifications shared the Klan's obsession with purity to conflate white identity with sanitation at a time when the language and science of sanitation were lauded as saving American civilization.

Reconstructing Whiteness

Whiteness suffered two blows in the wake of the Civil War. Abolition of slavery appeared to dismantle the rationale for white identity that had developed in the South. Mass immigration from Europe, Latin America, and Asia challenged nativist white identity throughout the United States. Reconstruction offered the potential of a more egalitarian society in keeping with some of the ideals Thomas Jefferson espoused. Freed slaves might own property, vote, and hold office. The influx of new immigrants threatened to further reshape the nation as a multi-hued, multi-cultural society.[1]

This idea terrified many Americans who had come of age in a society that asserted white privilege. If the initial period of Reconstruction offered greater political and economic opportunity to African Americans, it also produced a reaction championing white supremacy. In all walks of life, from Harvard and University of Wisconsin professors espousing eugenics to Klansmen intent on "redeeming" the racial order of the antebellum South through terror, Americans redefined whiteness by linking skin color to cleanliness in the years after Lee's surrender at Appomattox.

Even as racial purity was challenged by the new political order; concerns over purity continued to shape the way Americans perceived their cities. In these dense settlements, the notion of purity had public safety concerns. By 1900, American cities were crowded like never before. New York City, Philadelphia, and Boston were far more densely populated than they had been just fifty years earlier. Chicago had been a small backwater on the edge of Lake Michigan when incorporated in 1833; in 1893 its progress as an industrial and transportation center had vaulted it to the status of "City of the Century," with a workforce of millions manning its modern mills, railroads, grain elevators, and slaughterhouses. Chicago's growth was so rapid in those sixty years that it was chosen to host the Columbian Exhibition, where observers predicted that the city's population would exceed fifty million by 1930. Such a number was unimaginable before the Civil War; the rapid urbanization of American society in the wake of heavy industrial development had led Americans to live in quarters more cramped than their grandparents could imagine. In such an environment, a cough by one person could quickly be shared by thousands.[2]

Pollution and Purity

The racialization of hygiene produced tensions within racial categories. Although this process was meant to secure white supremacy, within whiteness lay deep insecurities. "White trash," an insult used to marginalize poor Americans of Western European heritage, emerged in the 1820s but became especially widespread after the Civil War. This construction allowed the wealthy plantation class to maintain contrasts with poor farmers during Reconstruction. Adding the word "trash" to an individual's racial identity threatened to remove the power and privileges of whiteness. It was used to demean individuals convicted of drunkenness or theft in newspapers from Georgia to Oregon.[3]

A Michigan newspaper used the slur to increase poor whites' racial insecurity. The *Jackson Citizen Patriot* in 1886 declared: "The laboring men of the North have no desire to be reduced to the condition of the 'poor white trash' of the South, who were despised and ridiculed by the colored slaves."[4] The threat of marginalization at or below the level of blacks compelled poor whites to engage in the rhetoric of white supremacy even in areas that did not have large African American populations. Such insecurity may explain why Robert Byrd's participation in West Virginia's Ku Klux Klan and opposition to desegregating the military in the 1940s advanced his political career.[5]

Within African American society, the politics of skin color could become inverted. A new insult against lighter-skinned African Americans emerged in the late nineteenth century that appropriated the most dangerously dirty material in racial terms in order to demean people of lighter-colored skin: "shit-colored nigger." A vicious insult, equating a human's skin with excrement. The legendary jazz musician Charles Mingus heard it often from other children on the streets of Watts, California, during the Depression. Years later, he remembered (writing in the third person) that "they loved to crowd around and torment him, kicking at his cello, feigning punches, calling him sissy, Mama's boy and schitt-colored nigger till they finally made him cry."[6]

Born to parents of African, Chinese, English, and Swedish descent in 1922, Mingus internalized the scorn of his skin color. His memoir *Beneath the Underdog* is littered with the phrase "schitt-colored nigger," sometimes accompanied by the modifier "half-ass yella phony." Even after a career composing and performing some of the most elegant, sophisticated music of the twentieth century, the man was tormented by the taunts of his youth.[7]

If Mingus's spelling of the word "schitt" was unique, his experience unfortunately was not. By the time he tried to avoid the Watts gang, the insult "shit-colored" had become a way for dark-skinned African Americans to belittle light-skinned African Americans who may have had Irish or Mexican or Italian or Jewish heritage. The historian Henry Louis Gates recalled in his memoir that members of his own family (who, he noted, qualified as octoroons, an attempt at precisely measuring the percentage of black blood versus white blood in a Louisianan) heard the term from other people. The insult became an informal measure of racial purity among African Americans.[8]

The journey that led these Americans to hear their skin compared to the most foul material commonly produced by humans involved the central assumptions behind racial purity between the Civil War and World War II. On Watts street corners, in Klan meetings, in some of the most acclaimed literature of the age, and in the halls of Ivy League universities, associating "impure" skin with pollution became the norm. If the insults Mingus heard promoted a form of blackness, they came from a process that reaffirmed white identity. This process, though rooted in the existing inequities of antebellum America, was a product of new concerns and insecurities that developed after the Civil War.

In this context, the insult "shit-colored" had deadly ramifications; having one's skin compared to potentially infectious waste was on a par with being called a leper. Your own biology betrayed you, marking you as a contaminant to the surrounding community. Young Charles Mingus did not literally believe his skin was infectious as excrement, but the insult stained his soul, leaving scars evident even when he was one of the most accomplished musicians in the world.

The hygienic connotations of that insult was not limited to urban areas. Urbanization was more intense in the North than South; though the slaves had been emancipated, the economic focus of the region remained agricultural production of cotton, now by sharecroppers working planter's lands. Still, the conflation between dark skin and filth was ever present. The conflation was fiction. No matter that African Americans regularly used soap and washcloths. No matter that African Americans established educational institutions that instructed students on hygienic practices that were more advanced that what many middle-class white people undertook in advocating the use of "Bible, bath, and broom." The conflation of dark skin color with dirt had become racist common sense.[9]

The assumption transcended geographic and political divides in America, a statement that could be made about precious few things in the 1880s and 1890s. When we tell American history of this period, we often do so with a bifurcated model. The historian James Grossman argues that Wiebe's model of a search for order is one of two frameworks—the other presented by Grace Elizabeth Hale in 1998—that historians have developed to understand how the North and South modernized between the Civil War and Warren G. Harding's "return to normalcy" in 1920. Progressivism, argues Wiebe, was the ideological and political expression of a middle class engaged in a "search for order" amid heavy industrialization and urbanization. Grossman notes that Hale, in her book *Making Whiteness*, identifies a Southern version of that quest. "Making whiteness" through the construction of a "culture of segregation" enabled white Southerners simultaneously to identify their place in a modernizing nation and to fix the place of increasingly disorderly African Americans within the region."[10]

Grossman's framework equating Wiebe's search for order in Northern society, economics, and institutions with the Southern construction of white supremacy neatly placed two of the defining characteristics of postbellum American society on parallel tracks divided by the Mason-Dixon line. If this dichotomy appears to provide a useful shorthand for the dynamics of American history, it threatens an artificial cleavage of the nation. In both the North and South, substantial attempts to reshape American society between 1865 and 1920 included attempts to rationalize the space and race of the nation across regions using race as the basis for creating order. The actual processes of reordering the American labor force and residential patterns are the subjects of the following two chapters; the rest of this chapter is concerned with how the idea of a white race became conflated with the ultimate standard in hygiene.

The racialized search for order was not simply one that produced a Southern "culture of segregation" (as Hale puts it), but one in which those considered white throughout the nation were granted particular privileges, including economic opportunity, legal rights, and consideration among eugenic advocates as the most advanced, intelligent, cultured, and generally superior race. Above all, in both the North and South, the search for racial order after emancipation took place in a context in which the urbanizing nation grappled with a search for hygienic order freeing the nation's communities from the specter of epidemic disease.[11]

The New Sanitary Order

Attempts to rid the cities of miasmas and plagues produced a new class of sanitary engineers. The accomplishments of the sanitary engineers were substantial in both the immediate and long term after the Civil War. Col. George E. Waring's sanitary reforms in Memphis and New York City led to a period of civic improvements across the nation. Engineers reversed the flow of the Chicago River, allowing the rapidly expanding city of the century to continue to use Lake Michigan for drinking water as excrement made its way southwest away from the population. Between the Civil War and World War II, sanitary engineers purified drinking water, devised ways to control smoke in the air, regulate solid wastes, and, above all, make the cities safer, cleaner places to live. Their efforts were dramatically successful; urban infant mortality rates declined despite urban growth. The United States becoming a majority urban nation by 1920, which would not have been possible without reducing the hazards of late nineteenth-century urban life.

Sanitary engineers developed institutions, including trade associations and publications, to proliferate their technological and managerial systems. A few, such as Waring and Raymond Tucker, achieved measures of fame after performing miracles that cleaned the land, air, and water of entire cities. Tucker's perceived effectiveness managing the city of St. Louis's smoke control measures led to his election as that city's mayor.[12]

Aside from the engineers trained to develop sanitary systems, magazines and books instructed middle-class homemakers on how to keep a clean home. If immigrants were dirty, assimilation involved cleaning them up. Progressives, including the women who worked in urban settlement houses, attempted to civilize new immigrants by teaching them English, American cultural customs, and modern hygienic practices. The project was urgent and immediate, for a filthy home was the home of diseased, inferior people. Mothers had to be taught cleanliness, else they be blamed for corrupting their families with dirt.

Jane Addams had been instructed in the value of hygiene as a young student at the Rockford Female Seminary in the late 1870s, where she learned that "the consciousness of clean linen" was "close to the consciousness of a clean conscience."[13] Taking that wisdom from Rockford to Halsted Street on the West Side of Chicago, Addams established a curriculum at Hull-House to teach Eastern and Southern European women to do away with heavy drapes and rugs in favor of more austere décor. Hardwood floors were easier to sweep than thick carpets. Light white curtains collected less dust than thick drapes did. Addams instructed the neighborhood's women not only to sweep their own doorways and keep their own houses clean but also to help keep the city clean. In a working-class neighborhood where garbage collection was not consistent, Addams advocated residents taking sanitary reform into their own hands.[14]

These lessons were taken to heart by her students. When new immigrant women hung white curtains in industrial communities, they were claiming respectability and hope. Visiting Braddock and Homestead, Pennsylvania (two industrial towns on the edges of the Smoky City itself, Pittsburgh), the labor journalist Mary Heaton Vorse noted that working-class immigrant women made time out of their busy days to stop working and "attempt this decency" of hanging white curtains.[15]

Race and Dirt

Addams supposed that the new immigrants could be reformed and assimilated into American standards of hygiene. Not every observer felt that the newcomers could be reformed. Several experts, some self-appointed, others legitimized by academia and the marketplace, referred to skin darker than pale yet lighter than brown as "dusky," indicating the inhabitants of this skin were less than white and innately, biologically, less than clean. Racial terms like "greaser" and "sheenie" became common insults by the 1920s. These terms presupposed that Italians, Mexicans, and Jews had greasier, oilier skin and hair and that this condition was somehow a biological fact.[16]

Such a classification put these people perilously close to the status of African Americans by 1890, leaving them vulnerable to violence and marginalization. Some of these justifications came from the most learned corners of society. Academics created new pseudoscientific disciplines to confirm racist assumptions that blacks were intellectually and morally inferior to whites.[17] Above all, the rationale for these classifications was based in a deep sexual anxiety. If blacks were biologically, morally, and intellectually inferior to whites, any attempts by blacks and whites to interbreed would, in effect, be polluting to the white race. Particularly in the South, this worry led to bans on interracial marriage and the establishment of separate "but equal" accommodations that ran the spectrum from drinking fountains to hospitals. Fear of racial contamination shaped laws, behaviors, and space.

If black people were pollutants, dusky people were as well. The new immigrants from Southern and Eastern Europe may not have been black, with the stigma blackness had in a society that equated it first with bondage and then with filth, but neither were they white. With these biological markers of grime and grease, it was unclear at the turn of the century how they might achieve whiteness, rather than (as the historian David Roediger puts it) their "inbetween" racial identity.[18]

The implicit assumption of these lessons was that sanitation was a necessary requirement of American identity. Assimilated immigrants internalized this virtue, evident in the transformational rhetoric attached to the Statue of Liberty. The inscription is "The New Colossus," written by the poet Emma Lazarus, herself the descendant of Jewish immigrants, writing in celebration of the statue arriving in New York in 1883 as a beacon to newcomers: "Give me your tired, your poor, / Your huddled masses yearning to be free, / The wretched refuse of your teeming shore." Lazarus implied that America would transform this refuse into vigorous, prosperous, and clean Americans. The sentiment resonated with the symbolism of the statue enough that in 1903 the poem was engraved on the statue, welcoming the millions who entered the United States through New York City.

Academic Racism

Less optimistic perspectives on the place of new immigrants filled the halls of the United States's most prestigious universities. New immigrants were characterized as pollutants threatening American purity, rather than as raw materials just waiting for the transformative power of Americanization, in both sociological and biological disciplines by the turn of the century. The sociologists John R. Commons and Edward Alsworth Ross—among the elites of their discipline—saw the new immigrants as racial inferiors to native-born whites. Ross, in his book *The*

Old World in the New (published on the eve of World War I), laid out a complex and occasionally contradictory classification scheme for the newcomers to American shores. On the differences between Jews from different parts of Europe, Ross claimed that the type of Jew depended upon the region, with Roumanian Jews being of "a high type" and Jews from Galicia (a Eastern European region currently in Poland and Ukraine) being the lowest: "Besides the Russian Jews we are receiving large numbers from Galicia, Hungary, and Roumania. The last are said to be of a high type, whereas the Galician Jews are the lowest," people whose town "is but a hideous nightmare of dirt, disease, and poverty."[19]

At times Ross argued that such misery was based in innate biology; elsewhere he allowed for the potential of the immigrant's condition to improve with a better environment. Intimating that hygiene is learned and not innate, when discussing Italian copper miners in the Southwest, he wrote that "at first the Italians live on bread and beer, never wash, wear the same filthy clothes night and day, and are despised. After two or three years they want to live better, wear decent clothes, and be respected."[20] In contrast, he observed that Slavs seemed to be "immune" to the dirt that "would kill a white man," so Slavic men and women did the dirty jobs Americans were unable or unwilling to do. Dirty people, in this construction, were simultaneously degenerate and physically robust, allowing whites to justify passing unpleasant yet necessary work off to new immigrants who were "biologically" suited for it.

In industrial society, such people were necessary. "If it wasn't for the Slavs," Ross quoted the superintendents of the Mesabi Mines, "we couldn't get out this ore at all, and Pittsburgh would be smokeless. You can't get an American to work here unless he runs a locomotive or a steam-shovel. We've tried it; brought 'em in, carloads at a time, and they left." When Ross asked about raising their pay, the superintendents replied, "No, it's not a matter of pay. Somehow Americans nowadays are n't any good for hard or dirty work."[21] Ross's distinction of Slavs from whites was by no means unique, nor was his assumption that Slavs could handle dirt far better than whites could. Such distinctions would have important consequences for labor markets during the Progressive Era.[22]

Whether the differences were biological or environmental, Ross was consistent in one conclusion: Whites from Northern Europe were clearly superior in intellect, culture, and physical form to any other people on earth: "That the Mediterranean peoples are morally below the races of northern Europe is as certain as any social fact." Here Ross implies that a certain evolution took place for the white people, noting that at one point in history they were "dirty, ferocious barbarians." However, even in this primitive state, the proto-whites were still superior to the Mediterranean immigrants Ross witnessed in the early twentieth century. For Ross these forerunners of white Americans, "these blondes," were truthful, and whether it was pride, superior ethics, or inability to creatively invent falsehoods, "something has held them back from the nimble lying of the southern races."[23]

By the turn of the twentieth century, a racial hierarchy in which white skin denoted the most advanced evolution of mankind was in place. In 1903, the same year "The New Colossus" was engraved on the Statute of Liberty, the director of the Baugh Institute of Anatomy, Dr. Edward Anthony Spitzka, published a long treatise on brain size and form in "men of eminence," commenting that "the jump from a Cuvier or a Thackeray to a Zulu or a Bushman is not greater than from the latter to the gorilla or the orang." A racial hierarchy had emerged in which darker skin meant lower levels on the evolutionary scale, and comparing non-white peoples to dirty animals and dirt itself was common.[24]

Popular Constructions of Race and Hygiene

The corrosive effects of the assumptions about waste and race were already evident in the early twentieth century. Definitions of race and cleanliness used by working-class residents became charged, as new immigrants attempted to distance themselves from African Americans. Living in 1930s Connecticut, a Slovak woman in a neighborhood where black and white children often played together confessed to a researcher her worries about how associating with African Americans might make her children vulnerable to charges of being as filthy:

> I always tell my children not to play with the nigger people's children, but they always play with them just the same. I tell them that the nigger children are dirty and that they will get sick if they play. I tell them they could find some other friends that are Slovaks just the same. This place now is all spoiled, and all the people live like pigs because the niggers

they come and live her with the decent white people and they want to raise up their children with our children. All people are alike—that's what God says—but just the same it's no good to make our children play with the nigger children, because they are too dirty.[25]

The Slovak woman's religious upbringing could not overcome the explicit racial definitions of hygiene she had learned in the United States. God was now subservient to fear of contamination in her life as an American attempting to figure out her family's place in society.

Marketing Racism

Whether in the ivory tower or the working-class street, the rhetoric and imagery of hygiene became conflated with a racial order that made white people pure and anyone who was not white, dirty. A crucial concept in this reasoning was the idea that white skin was pure. The notion of purity was central in advertising during this period—purity in soaps and purity in food. Purity was synonymous with health and with reliability, and advertisers could convince the public that their products were safe and reliable with declarations of purity.

The idea of purity was an obsession as manufacturing and distributing processes divorced consumers from seeing how the goods they purchased originated. For food, concerns about swill milk (from cows fed spent liquor mash, which was often adulterated and contaminated) and adulterated meat in the early part of the era lead to local, state, and federal regulation. These concerns were exacerbated in the first decade of the twentieth century, not least because of public revulsion to the meatpacking process described by Upton Sinclair in *The Jungle*. These concerns led to the Pure Food and Drug Act in 1906—no question what the first word in the name of that populist legislation would be—and creation of the Food and Drug Administration. *Pure* foods and drugs were *safe* foods and drugs, allaying the concerns of worried consumers in an increasingly complex and bewildering society.[26]

Purity extended to the tools Americans could use against filth, including the toothbrush, household cleanser, and, above all, soap. Soap emerged as a potent weapon against dirt. Industrial development brought the masses many products at affordable prices, and soap was no exception. In the years after the Civil War, several manufacturers in the United States marketed soaps on a national basis. Among these were companies still recognizable in the early twenty-first century, including Proctor & Gamble, the makers of Ivory Soap. Less recognizable manufacturers to our eyes included the nationally distributed products of Kirkman & Sons, Soapine, and Lautz Brothers.

All of these firms engaged in print advertising in the late nineteenth and early twentieth centuries. The marketing of soap, like that of many products, grew increasingly visual between 1865 and the end of the century. As magazines and newspapers proliferated, growing larger and longer in circulation, the number of black and white and (more often in magazines) color illustrations in their pages increased.[27]

Manufacturers also used the U.S. mail to send advertisements out, often in the form of small cards and pamphlets. The archivist Fath Davis Ruffins, who oversaw the organization of hundreds of these advertisements for the National Museum of American History, observed that advertisers felt greater license to use humor in these targeted advertisements (as opposed to placement in magazines, which might be read by a broader audience), and the humor displayed in the soap cards reflects tropes in both regional and national humor.[28]

Many of the cards display comic scenes unrelated to the function of the product. Some poke fun at children, others use caricatures based on people's appearance. Of the latter, caricatures of Jews, Indians, Irishmen, Asians, African Americans, bald men, fat women, and Southern Europeans are common. Many products, such as the Gold Dust line of cleansers, employed African American caricatures as logos. The Gold Dust Twins were two young African American boys, naked from the waist up, pitch black in appearance, who "did the work for you" in cleaning floors, kitchenware, and other household goods. Other racial stereotypes used as logos included Indians and Chinese for laundry.

Grace Elizabeth Hale does not ignore the soap advertisements in her history of the South. She notes that these ads were early innovations using black skin to boast of their products' effectiveness; the advertisements, however, were well within mainstream claims about race and hygiene at the end of the nineteenth century, as closer inspection reveals.[29]

"Me Wash-ee all Clean-ee, Me use-ee Soapine-ee." Warshaw Collection of Business Americana—Soap, Archives Center, National Museum of American History, Smithsonian Institution, Washington, DC.

Much of the racial illustrations in the advertisements are not remarkable in and of themselves; they were present in much humor and advertising of the age, and the unpleasant caricatures (large-lipped African Americans, slant-eyed Asian Americans, hook-nosed Jewish Americans) are as predictable as they are offensive to twenty-first-century eyes. An important subset of the advertisements, however, went beyond these stereotypes to explicitly racialize dirt. Several soap companies in the 1890s conflated the words "clean" and "white." Proctor & Gamble's marketing of Ivory Soap boasted of it being 99 44/100 percent pure white soap, and long into the twentieth century, its advertisements consistently emphasized the white color and its almost absolute purity: The sallowness of "smoky city" complexions (a problem long after Trollope left Pittsburgh, after which he presumably was able to wash the soot off of his skin), the advertisements maintained, "usually results not from ill health, or bad blood, but from dirt and can only be dispelled by the regular application of a pure soap," and Ivory "has no equal, on account of its absolute purity." It was so pure that it claimed to remove tan and freckles.[30]

Often its advertisements featured a young woman's face with smooth, milky white skin. Frequently, Ivory ads employed blonde, blue-eyed children, as did other soap companies' ads, including a Lautz Brothers campaign featuring the fair-skinned "Snow Boy." In a 1900 ad titled "Envy," a dozen black cats sat around staring at a white cat sitting next to a washtub with a floating bar of Ivory. The lucky white cat was fortunate enough the wash the black away.[31]

Similar to the Ivory Girl was the Fairy Girl, an icon for Fairbanks's Fairy Soap. An 1898 booklet promoting the soap featured a poem:

THE FAIRY GIRL
Here's a dainty Fairy girl,
Neat and clean from foot to curl,
Whitest frills of snowy lace,
Soft white hands and winsome face.

In her muslin dress so white,
She's a picture of delight!
No more lovely sight than this
Dainty happy little miss.

She will tell you if you call,
FAIRY SOAP has done it all,
Washed her dress and cleaned her lace,
Made white hands and beaming face.[32]

Lest this connection seem obscure, other advertisements used whiteness to connote cleanliness. An 1882 card advertising David's Prize Soap features an illustration of two African American women doing laundry. One asks the other, "How do you make them so clean and white and get them out so early?" The other replies, "Clean and White? Well I uses DAVID'S PRIZE SOAP." African American laundresses were often used in soap advertisements, in no small part due to the widespread perception that such work was fit for African American women.[33]

The leap from these claims to explicit descriptions of dark skin as dirty was small. Several manufacturers boasted of cleansers so effective

"How Do You Make Them So Clean and White?" Warshaw Collection of Business Americana—Soap, Archives Center, National Museum of American History, Smithsonian Institution, Washington, DC.

that they made black features appear white. Several advertisements featuring the Gold Dust Twins showed them scrubbing the bottom of kettles and pots clean. The confirmation that the job was done was when one twin saw his reflection clearly in the pot. Staring back at the pitch black face was a white face with light brown hair. Sapolio used similar imagery with a black woman looking at her white reflection as the white family she served looked on approvingly.[34]

The ultimate proof of a cleaner was to claim to actually remove black skin, leaving the clean white skin beneath it. Some advertisements implied this ability, as in N. K. Fairbank & Company's card for Fairy Soap. In this ad, a young blonde, blue-eyed white boy is looking at a young black boy in wonder, asking the question, "Why doesn't your mamma wash you with Fairy Soap?"[35]

If this message was too subtle, other advertisements rammed the point home. Lautz Brothers sent out at least two separate cards with white men washing young African American boys with their soap.

Top, left and right, "Why Doesn't Your Mamma Wash You with Fairy Soap?"; *bottom, left,* "Beat That, If You Can"; *bottom, right,* "Golly! I B'leve PEARLINE Make Dat Chile White." Warshaw Collection of Business Americana—Soap, Archives Center, National Museum of American History, Smithsonian Institution, Washington, DC.

In both of these images, the blackness was literally washed away by the white soap. The caption of each was "Beat that!" Several other companies advertised soap that literally washed dark pigment off of skin; Pearline, for example, featured an illustration of an African American woman scrubbing a young child and exclaiming "Golly! I B'leve PEARLINE Make Dat Chile White."[36]

If pictures and their racist captions did not convey the message, poems and stories would. On the back of the Pearline card described above, the James Pyle Company walked back its claim, admitting that "we are not sure that it will make black skin white." Other manufacturers were bolder in their claims. In "Soap Bubbles," a booklet similar to Fairbanks's mailer with the Fairy Girl, John Kirkman & Son printed a poem claiming that Kirkman's Wonder Soap, and only Kirkman's Wonder Soap, could clean skin white:

> There were two little nigger boys,
> Two little nigger boys,
> Whenever they were sent to bathe
> They made a dreadful noise,
> Because their mother did believe
> That white they could be made,
> So on them with a scrubbing brush
> Unmerciful she laid.
> She tried a combination of
> Many kinds of soap;
> But the result of all her labor
> Gave her but scanty hope.
> Although the lather that she got
> Was very soft and white,
> It did not make her offspring so,
> Though she scrubbed with all her might.
> So she got KIRKMAN's WONDER SOAP,
> Composed of rare ingredients,
> She used it once, and then she knew
> How vain her past expedients.
> Sweet and clean her sons became—
> It's true, as I'm a workman—

> And both are now completely white,
> Washed by this soap of Kirkman.[37]

Washing pigment white was not limited to African American skin. Proctor & Gamble, in advertisements distributed at the time of the Columbian Exposition in 1893, boasted that Ivory Soap could civilize Indians. Using two images of Indians given Ivory by Uncle Sam, the newly cleaned and civilized Indians happily exclaim, "We once were factious, fierce, and wild, / To peaceful arts unreconciled," but fortunately "IVORY SOAP came like a ray / Of light across our darkened way" making them "civil, kind, and good" as well as "clean and fair to see."[38]

By 1893, such portraits of indigenous Americans could be used quite comfortably in humor without raising fear or discomfort among whites. The American military had largely subdued Indians almost two decades earlier, using treaties and force to sequester tribes on reservations. This caricature, showing savagery defeated by the civilizing forces of soap, claims to document a taming white Americans assumed was their history. (Neither blood nor bullets existed in this telling of the story.)

Other people who were not considered white were subject to racial cleansing. Kirkman & Sons released an advertisement sometime after 1906 (it references that year's Pure Food and Drug Act) showing three white women washing three wealthy Turkish men's skin from brown to white. The accompanying poem tells the story of how the women were the Turkish men's maids. They convinced the men to let them wash them with the soap, transforming their features to milky white. The story ended happily, with the now-white men marrying each of the maids. Cross-racial and cross-class lines were transcended, all through the miracle of a pure, cleansing soap.[39]

Such a message may not have resonated with eugenicists and Klansmen fearful of the polluting dangers of miscegenation to their innate, static ideals of white purity. It was, however, consistent with the trope that skin darker than white was somehow impure and dirty. Products boasting of absolute purity were so powerful that they could literally wash away the stain of race. In an era in which advertising played with the national imagination in so many ways, these pokes of humor instilled the idea that nothing could be more powerful than soap with the capability of washing away race.

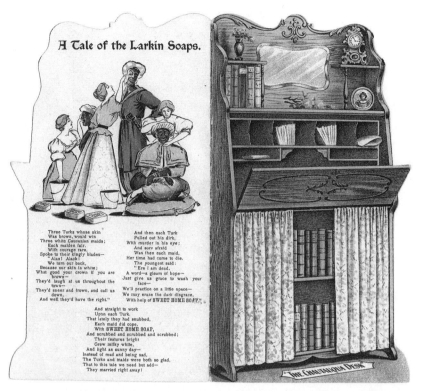

"A Tale of the Larkin Soaps." Warshaw Collection of Business Americana—Soap, Archives Center, National Museum of American History, Smithsonian Institution, Washington, DC.

Implicit in the joke was the understanding that what remained as pure was milky white skin. In ad after ad in national magazines, young, white skin was employed to hit that message home. Although the explicit racial jokes of the advertising cards faded away in the early twentieth century, the norm of whiteness in soap advertising endured for the rest of the century.

Invading Germs

Discussing white skin as clean skin fit into a lexicon of scientific racism; at the same time that advertisements boasted that their soaps could make you clean and white, eugenicists measured skulls and argued that those noses, jaws, and craniums possessed by humans from Northwestern Europe held demonstrably superior brains to the skulls possessed by humans from Southern Europe, Africa, and the Americas.

The scientific justification for racial superiority came at a time when science and engineering promised to rid society of several pressing problems. Given the high priority placed on ridding cities of dirt and disease, if white skin was clean skin, then white skin was also healthy skin.

If, however, black skin was dirty skin, what was the connection between black-skinned people and disease? In a world where dirt could kill (and in densely packed cities, it could kill thousands quickly), an influx of black-skinned people were thus defined as pollutants that could threaten the health and well-being of otherwise healthy men, women, and children.

Nor was the classification of hygiene simply about black and white; demarcations between white and less-than-white skin would subject the latter to a dirtier stigma. The idea of Eastern and Southern Europeans as filthy, backward people was observed—or at the very least, satirized— by some of the most accomplished authors of the era. Henry B. Wohlman's work on ethnic caricature reveals this in the work of Mark Twain, and Henry James. In his story "Three Thousand Years among the Microbes," Twain imagined himself as a cholera germ—one of the most feared contagions in American society in the late nineteenth century— coursing through the veins of an "incredibly dirty" tramp "shipped to America by Hungary because Hungary was tired of him." James, in *The Golden Bowl* (1904), provided a contrast of American and Italian racial types that Wohlman identifies as divergent: "Amerigo's ethnic origin 'sticks out' of his exquisitely typical profile, whereas Mr. Verver's American face is 'colourless,' *clear*, and in this manner somewhat resembled a small decent room, clean-swept and unencumbered with furniture."[40]

These ideas were not unique to writers of fiction; sanitary engineers and others who employed workers to handle wastes believed them as well. New York City's Department of Streets and Sanitation employed Italians to sort waste because, as I discuss in the next chapter, Col. Waring believed Italians were racially suited to do so. But not everything Waring's department said about immigrants racialized waste. One of his supervisors, David Willard, lamented the "ignorant foreign population crowded into the East Side districts," disrespecting the city's sanitary code. Willard's description of the East Side residents inferred an opposition to the biological definitions of race and waste; these people, for him, were *ignorant*. Ignorant people could be taught to know better; as with poverty, it was a condition correctable through social control. Willard argued that getting to their children was the way to educate them, thus elevating them from the low status of filth: "To use for this end the influence of the children, who are recognized by their parents as superior to them in education and intelligence, is not a new idea, but one practically untried to any extent." Willard created street-cleaning teams of children that uplifted the area, "removing litter from the streets, inducing others not to throw out refuse, or noting certain blocks or houses where the people were careless in their habits or had a disregard for the sanitary laws."[41]

Although Willard's methods assumed an environmental rather than biological model of hygiene, they were consistent with an assumption that the new immigrants were dirtier than native-born whites. When discussing the ideal of native-born whites as the pinnacle of cleanliness, we should remember that belief and practice often did not resemble each other. If production of garbage was a measure of filth, immigrants were cleaner than native-born white Americans. In 1912, the sanitarians Rudolph Hering and Samuel A. Greeley conducted a survey of waste management practices in Chicago. Their survey concluded that native-born whites produced 751.4 pounds of garbage, rubbish, and ashes per capita per year. The new immigrants, which in Chicago included substantial numbers of people born in Italy, Poland, and Russia, produced only 672.8 pounds per capita per year of the same refuse.

An alternate explanation is not charitable to native-born Americans yet makes logical sense. By removing more garbage, rubbish, and ashes from their homes and bodies, these people were enforcing stricter standards of hygiene on their immediate environs. A clean home was a home that actively removed as much old and dirty material as possible as quickly as possible. That this disposal led to more waste that had to be managed by other people in other places was of no concern as long as that waste was out of sight and out of mind.[42]

By the beginning of World War I, the United States had already established the idea that white Americans were above living with waste. If white Americans were to be clean and waste had to be placed elsewhere, it was left to non-white people to move that waste, and perhaps to a place where non-white people lived. The beginnings of environmental inequalities had begun in an idea espoused by sanitary engineers, Progressive reformers, and advertisers.

Resistance and Reaction

Non-white people did not experience this marginalization unaware. Nor did non-white Americans ignore the sanitary revolution going on in the country. Americans with dark skin had the same concerns about dirt and disease as Progressive whites like Jane Addams and George Waring. These articulated standards belied the academic racism espoused by Edward Alsworth Ross, Edward Anthony Spitzka, and their colleagues; if African Americans were concerned with hygiene and uplift, what did that mean for classification schemes presuming innate, uncivilized status for non-whites?

The conflation of race and waste was part of the increasingly hostile racial climate of the period. The increasingly hostile racial climate at the turn of the century led to varied responses from African American thinkers. Historians see these responses as falling into two camps. One, represented by W. E. B. du Bois, fiercely resisted the injustices of white supremacy. Among the actions du Bois took was helping convene the 1905 meeting on the Canadian side of Niagara Falls (where hotels were not segregated, as they were on the American side) to discuss options. Out of this meeting (the members of which became known as the Niagara Movement) came several meetings before it disbanded amid uncertainty of direction in 1910. One year before its demise, however, du Bois had organized the National Association for the Advancement of Colored People (NAACP), with the purpose to "eradicate caste or race prejudice" in the United States and fight for equal opportunities in education, the legal system, employment, and throughout American society. That organization endured, with its activities in its first decade focused on drawing attention and outrage to lynchings, including advocating for passage of Congressman Leonidas Dyer's Anti-Lynching Bill. By the end of the decade, the NAACP had organized protests against screenings of *The Birth of a Nation* in cities like Chicago. This institutionalized response to white supremacy would prove durable and important to challenging racism in the twentieth century, and the NAACP's legal branch developed the strategy that ultimately produced the landmark 1954 Supreme Court decision in *Brown v. Board of Education*, which refuted the rationale of "separate but equal" accommodations based upon race. The massive legal framework of white supremacy, however, meant that blacks were denied the full legal status of citizens in much of the United States a century after the Civil War.[43]

A second approach, associated with Booker T. Washington, was to accommodate white society's norms and prejudices in an attempt to assimilate and uplift African Americans into the benefits of the modern industrial white society. Washington was frequently assailed in his lifetime for meeting (privately) with President Theodore Roosevelt and developing vocational training to make African Americans students into suitable employees in industrial society.

It is worth remembering that among Washington's accomplishments was being the most famous African American proponent of the sanitary revolution. In this context, his actions may be understandable as resistance against the encroaching injustice of racialized waste. He was a vocal proponent of the hygienic advances that Progressive reformers advocated, equating sanitation with civilization and modernity, a path to uplift his fellow freedmen into respectable society.

Washington's autobiography *Up from Slavery* revealed a man at war with dirt. Of his youth, he recounted dreading of work in the filthy coal mine, for any one who mined "was always unclean, at least while at work, and it was a very hard job to get one's skin clean after the day's work was over."[44] Instead of mining, the young Washington found a place at the Hampton Institute, where the founder, former Union Army general Samuel C. Armstrong shaped his views on hygiene and morality. When Washington came to the Tuskegee Institute in 1881 to train young African Americans in vocational pursuits, a large part of the school's mission was training in the gospel of the toothbrush: "In addition to the usual routine of teaching, I taught the pupils to comb their hair, and to keep their hands and faces clean, as well as their clothing. I gave special attention to teaching them the proper use of the toothbrush and the bath." For Washington, these hygienic practices were vital to his students' education. "In all my teaching, I have watched carefully the influence of the tooth-brush, and I am convinced that there are few single agencies of civilization that are more far-reaching."[45]

Civilization was a crucial term, the antonym of savagery. Scientific justifications of white supremacy depended upon assumptions that whites were more civilized, smarter, and more advanced than other races. Equating hygiene and civilization made sense, as a people orderly enough to banish dirt would advance further than people unable to address problems of disease and disorder. That Washington, an African American, made this equation was a challenge to the notion that civilization and hygiene were uniquely the provenance of whites. "I do not believe that any person is educated so long as he lives in a dirty, miserable shanty. I do not believe that any person is educated until he has learned to want to live in a clean room made attractive with pictures and books, and with such surroundings as are elevating."[46]

Washington's efforts were part of a larger movement of championing hygiene among African Americans. Similar efforts were under way in both the North and South, some well before Tuskegee was established. New York City's Colored Home and Hospital, found on the corner of Sixty-Fifth Street and First Avenue in 1840, noted in its annual report in 1888 that "applicants for admission must be bathed, and, if necessary, have their clothing changed, before passing to the wards," and once inside, "each inmate must take a bath once a week, unless excused by the Physician."[47] New York City's Colored Orphan Asylum (founded in 1836) boasted similar hygienic care of its charges in 1889, noting that "strict observance of hygienic rules" restored the children to a sound state of health.[48]

In the South, Tuskegee's influence spread to other institutions. The Nashville Institute for Negro Christian Workers trained young African American men and women as reformers in the mode of the settlement houses movement, with the hopes that in a segregated society these reformers would uplift African Americans living in filthy, poor conditions. The Nashville Institute explicitly used the terminology of professional sanitarians. It described the social worker as sanitary engineer, training its students "to clean up the Negro slums and to teach his people how to apply modern methods of sanitation and hygiene." In a

brief pamphlet describing the school's curriculum, its leaders sardonically noted the dangers to public safety posed by segregation: "Disease
has no regard for the color line." In 1913, service work in the South was
primarily done by blacks for whites, a form of inequality that exacted
a price from all. "Thousands of colored nurses, cooks, and laundry
women in the South go every morning" from homes where "there are
contagious and infectious diseases." The pamphlet claimed that "at least
seventy per cent of all the white homes in the South are entered daily
by these colored women," indicating that neglect of the homes and
neighborhoods of black women could spread epidemic disease even
in the ostensibly pristine homes of white people. (Raising the possibility of such an epidemic would send chills down the spines of contemporary observers knowledgeable of recent European history. Twenty
years earlier, the German city of Hamburg blamed a cholera epidemic
that killed ten thousand people in six weeks on the supposedly poor
hygienic standards of servant girls contaminating affluent households.)
The conclusion of the institute was that social justice would produce a
cleaner, safer society: "In order for America to build a civilization that
is physically and morally sound, it is imperative that white and negro
people should co-operate in developing and maintaining a healthy and
righteous community life."[49]

African American newspapers employed columnists to instruct readers on how they and they children could lead healthy, clean lives. An
article in the *Pittsburgh Courier* proclaimed that using soap was beneficial to the teeth and keeping a bit of curd soap to use on a person's
toothbrush was a simple way to practice good dental hygiene.[50]

The *Chicago Defender* between 1911 and 1929 employed the South
Side surgeon Dr. Albert Wilberforce Williams as a regular columnist
instructing readers on proper household sanitation, avoidance of tuber-
culosis, and preventative measures to take to ensure healthy lives. A
prominent surgeon whose specialties included treatment of tuberculo-
sis, Dr. Williams repeatedly urged his readers to attend to sanitation as
a preventative measure. In 1913, he warned against "dirty surroundings,
vacant lots in filthy condition; alleys unpaved and strewn with garbage
and decaying refuse of every kind; stables unscreened and neglected
manure piles; privy vaults. . . . the presence of trades or industries that

are offensive in residence communities and which are a menace to both your healthy and comfort." He urged readers exposed to these hazards to, if at all possible, select their next house or apartment in neighborhoods and buildings that meet modern sanitary requirements.[51]

Dr. Williams equated dirt and morality, proclaiming that housing "is a mighty factor in the moulding of the character of a people" and that people should seek "the best sanitary condition that their means can afford."[52] In 1917, he reported on the "Health Improvement" campaign at the annual Tuskegee Negro Conference as a timely movement consistent with the concerns he had reported on in Chicago for years.[53] One year later, he argued that cleanliness bore a close relation to health, personal cleanliness was best achieved with "plenty of soap and water with elbow grease," and also that clean surroundings were crucial to maintain a healthy environment. He instructed readers to ensure that their front and back yards were free of food scraps, old papers, rags, and other debris that "will cause decomposition, gas, fumes, foul odors, etc., that will prove very deleterious to your health."[54]

In 1921, Dr. Williams argued that teaching proper hygiene to children was vital to the betterment of the race. "If the future generation is to be improved, the present one must be properly educated" to take care of them, and "to make a race strong and hardy, there must be developed within them powers of resistance against their natural enemies."[55]

Dr. Williams's columns appeared in a nationally distributed African American newspaper, so his ideas were disseminated far and wide. These ideas reflected Washington's gospel of the toothbrush. Contemporaries and historians attribute Washington's methods to attempts to placate the white power structure in the South and that schools like the Tuskegee Institute prepared young African Americans for menial occupations like maids and janitors. That interpretation reflects frustration with the rollback of Reconstruction and its consequences to black America.

An alternate interpretation understands Washington's ideas in the context of how hygiene was discussed during his life. His insistence on the gospel of the toothbrush refuted the corrosive new racial order and sought to place African Americans at the forefront of modern, hygienic society in hopes that attention to hygiene would improve the community, rather than making it servile to the needs and wants of whites.

Washington, like the leaders of the Nashville Institute, chafed against the hardening color line near the end of his life. In a speech he gave to the Negro Organization Society of Virginia in Norfolk in November 1914, he argued that both white and black races should work to uplift the conditions of rural blacks in the South and that racial segregation would be detrimental to these efforts. "The two races in Virginia can cooperate in encouraging the Negro wherever he lives to have a clean, sanitary, healthy community." Washington drew upon his observances to argue that segregation would make such efforts impossible. "Wherever the Negro is segregated, it usually means that he will have poor streets, poor lighting, poor sidewalks, poor sewerage, and poor sanitary conditions generally. These conditions are reflected in many ways in the life of the race to its disadvantage and to the disadvantage of the white race."[56]

Washington's criticisms of white Southerners were tempered by his claim that "[the Negro] is not likely to thrust himself on any community where conditions are not congenial, where he is not happy, and where he is not wanted," but his conclusion that segregation was not only unnecessary but, in most cases, unjust was among his strongest statements in opposition to the color line.[57]

One of Washington's efforts on hygiene near the end of his life became an annual event for more than thirty years. Beginning in 1915, a variety of organizations—including the annual Tuskegee Negro Conference, the National Negro Business League, the National Medical Association, and the National Negro Insurance Association—organized an annual National Negro Health Week. This annual event, with campaigns to clean yards and instruct children on proper hygiene, was organized annually until it ceased in 1951 because its goals of elevating hygiene had largely been accomplished.[58]

Hygiene Racialized

Washington did not live to see National Negro Health Week become an institution as he died of hypertension half a year after the first event. He did not live to see the age of sixty. (Conversely, du Bois lived a long life, long enough to see the NAACP's legal team win the 1954 *Brown v. Board of Education* decision before dying in Ghana in 1963.) Washington did not live to see the color line harden further in the years ahead or to see African Americans internalize the measure of skin with hygiene. Even inverted in a model that assumed African heritage was the pure apex, that blacker skin was pure and that yellow skin was "shit colored," this model condemned people who had been called "colored," "mulatto," or "octaroon" to an untouchable status. Calling the skin of mixed-race people filthy boded ill for the prospects of an integrated society. Sadly, white Americans in both North and South did not heed the Nashville Institute's advice that whites and blacks should work together in ensuring a clean, safe environment for all. Instead, Americans who identified as white chose to escape waste whenever and wherever possible, leaving the consequences of their escape to others. Soap and cleanser advertisements, though less overtly racial after the 1920s, continued to champion whiteness as a form of purity. Immigrants trying to assimilate used soap on their own skin and dirt-related insults to separate themselves from others. Wastes collected from communities inhabited by whites was handled and dumped in communities inhabited by non-whites. All were justified by racist ideas of cleanliness.

In an era when slavery had been abolished and the promise of equality for African Americans and new immigrants emerged, a biological justification for white supremacy pouncing on the fears of contagion developed. Dirt and disease permeated the language of racial purity, and racial constructions permeated discussion of public health. A new biopolitical understanding of the body and society had been constructed and was understood by both those attempting to assert domination and those who would be dominated.[59] Versions might be subverted (such as a racial hierarchy prizing darker skin over lighter skin in African American communities), and assumptions of this understanding might be challenged by affected peoples, but the new, powerful stereotype was established and would have consequences. By the time Charles Mingus heard the caustic insults to his skin in the streets of Depression-era Watts, both employment practices and residential patterns across the United States revealed the increasing significance of color throughout the nation. Waste, and the racial hierarchies now associated with waste, shaped material realities in American life. The racial constructions of waste informed what work particular Americans performed, where particular Americans lived, and the proximity of waste materials to those work and residential patterns.

PART III

Material Consequences

5

Dirty Work, Dirty Workers

If dirt was the enemy of modern society, modern society organized workers to fight dirt and disorder. On streets, in homes, in clothes, on faces, Americans—to paraphrase the historian Suellen Hoy—chased dirt with more vigor, more soap, and more labor in the years after the Civil War. By 1930, the public and private systems Americans used to get cleaner had grown larger and more complex in half a century than they had in the century before. When attitudes toward waste changed, they brought demands. Clothes needed to be washed more often. Who would clean them? Streets needed to be swept. By whom? Mass production opened up a new world of goods to possess. All sort of old materials were considered dirty and unwanted. Who would take them away, and where would they go? These questions created and reshaped sanitary services between 1870 and 1930, with many of the public and private systems we recognize in twenty-first-century American society taking form.[1]

The war on dirt created new opportunities and new burdens. Entire industries developed, niches that allowed entrepreneurs chances for upward mobility. Work handling wastes intensified, exposing laborers to filthy, unpleasant, and dangerous conditions in greater concentrations and longer hours than was known before the Civil War.

Sanitary occupations have existed throughout civilized history. A series of developments saw an expansion of both sanitation-related occupations in the United States and the number of people employed in those occupations.

Industrialization both created wastes and demand for waste materials. Factories processed raw materials and generated pollution. Some also could process post-consumer or post-industrial wastes, diverting materials from disposal.

Sanitary standards and practices became more rigorous. In part owing to the experiences of the Civil War, nursing, sanitary engineering, and public health became more widely recognized as important in the maintenance of modern society. As American society became more able to handle wastes, the rise of a larger, more affluent middle class meant more people had the capital to have their clothes, bodies, and homes cleaned.[2] They also could purchase more goods at a time when industrial capacity created a larger world of mass-marketed goods.[3]

Industrial cities expanded city services, including modern streets and sanitation departments. The cities welcomed millions of newcomers to the United States who were either unaware or unconcerned with the developing aversion to waste among the American people. Cities also grew owing to the migration of African Americans from the rural South.

These factors led to more materials classified as waste for disposal, an increase in both private businesses and public services devoted to sanitation throughout the United States, and an increase in the European immigrants, Asian immigrants, and African Americans who performed these services. Between 1860 and 1930, the variety of sanitary occupations performed in the United States led the Bureau of the Census to develop new classifications to enumerate the people working to collect garbage, trade junk, wash clothing, sweep streets, and clean homes and businesses. One imprecise occupational category gives an idea of the expansion. In 1860, 1,080,000 people worked in domestic service in the United States. In 1930, 2,550,000 people worked in domestic services in the United States, more than doubling the workforce in seventy years.[4]

More precise occupational data are available for the twentieth century. In 1900, 91,000 workers above the age of fourteen were identified as laundry and dry-cleaning operators; in 1930, 265,000 workers were identified as such.[5] In 1900, the number of private household workers (including housekeepers and laundresses who took in laundry or worked in others' homes) was 1,579,000; forty years later the number was 2,412,000.[6] The number of charwomen and cleaners grew from 29,000 in 1900 to 52,000 in 1930.[7] The number of janitors and sextons grew from 57,000 in 1900 to 310,000 in 1930.[8] The growth of these sanitary occupations outpaced the increase in both the overall population and the population of working individuals over fourteen in the United States.

Population not only grew but shifted. By 1920, the United States was primarily urban, with cities gaining population from rural areas (including a mass migration of African Americans and whites from the rural South to the urban North) and foreign countries. Newcomers shaped the labor force of numerous industries in the cities—for example, the steel mills of Pittsburgh and Chicago were quickly staffed by thousands of Slavic laborers. Italian-born individuals helped shape the construction industry in several cities. Mass migration resulted from a combination of economic and social pressures in Europe and the rural United States and opportunities emerging in American cities due to industrial expansion. The archetypal stories of immigrant life and work in the United States during this period revolve around factories. The Slavs in the steel mills of Thomas Bell's *Out of This Furnace*, the Lithuanian meatpackers of Upton Sinclair's *The Jungle*, and the young Jewish and Italian girls killed in the Triangle Shirtwaist fire in Manhattan portray the immigrant as industrial employee, usually in a menial position defined as unskilled. As David Roediger notes, many of the most unpleasant factory positions were the domain of Eastern and Southern European immigrants who were ridiculed on the shop floor for being filthy.[9] Native-born white Americans had access to a wider choice of employment options than immigrants and African Americans did, a pattern that replicated itself regardless of region.[10]

Migrants to American cities who did not—or owing to discrimination, could not—seek work in the large mills could find sanitation work either in the employment of cities, in a private individual's firm, or by starting a new small business. The emerging sanitary trades in the late nineteenth and early twentieth centuries had what the sociologist Roger Waldinger calls an opportunity structure conducive to high levels of immigrant business ownership. In his study of the garment trades in New York City, Waldinger identified several characteristics within industries that featured large proportions of entrepreneurship from foreign-born individuals. Two important characteristics were little competition from established natives and low required investment costs.[11]

The emerging sanitary occupations were not likely to have many native-born whites engaging in them for two reasons. First, the work was unpleasant compared to other occupations open to native-born whites. Second, the economic opportunities in these trades was nascent at the end of the Civil War, providing little guarantee that toiling in scrap or laundry might be a path to upward economic mobility. The work required uncomfortable physical labor in city dumps, cramped laundries, and other settings considered unhealthful and unsanitary. The materials handled posed risks to the workers; rags were flammable and could harbor diseases. Junk heaps could contain jagged objects, poisonous materials, and any number of hazards to the people working in them. The work may have been vital to maintain new standards of hygiene, but it was also low status and high risk, the kind of work identified by the sociologist Stewart E. Perry as "dirty work."[12] Since waste materials were considered unsanitary and contact with them exposed the handler to disease, scorn, and injury, those who scavenged were poor, usually immigrants with few business contacts. Journalists observed that immigrant women and children scavenged for scraps in mid-nineteenth-century cities for subsistence, and immigrant men scavenged and peddled scrap materials.[13]

Consigning "dirty work" in mills and factories to immigrants and African Americans was common throughout American industry (the essayist Alois B. Koukol observed in 1914 that the status of Slavic workers in Pittsburgh mills was "little better than hunks or clods of dirt"), and demographic trends in these occupations were evident to the sociologists St. Clair Drake and Horace Roscoe Cayton. In the study *Black Metropolis*, Drake and Cayton observed that Chicago's expanding white-collar middle class was composed of native-born whites and that the people employed to serve them were not. Drake and Cayton estimated that, by 1930, "the native-born, the 'successful' foreign-born, and the children of the immigrants left the city's heavy work and dirty work to the rapidly dwindling 'new' foreign-born population and to the constantly growing Negro population."[14]

Analysis of national census data between 1850 and 1930 indicates that Drake and Cayton's observations of Chicago are consistent with employment trends in the rest of the United States. Workers and, in some occupations, business owners were overrepresented with first- and second-generation immigrant groups. In some sanitary services, native-born African Americans were overrepresented. The demographic structure of sanitation work between 1870 and 1920 has historical contexts in specific occupations, but an overarching trend is the underrepresentation of native-born people who identified as white handling wastes.[15]

As concern about keeping clean increased, the number and volume of occupations involved with managing and removing wastes increased. By 1930, more individuals removed rubbish from city streets than had done so in 1870. More individuals collected and sold scrap materials. More worked in sewers and municipal sanitation departments. More worked in laundries or as janitors.

The occupations in sanitary services ranged widely from easily replaceable "unskilled" laborers to owner-operators of waste-hauling businesses. The paths to work in these occupations were varied, dependent on historical timing, geographic factors, gender roles, and a host of other variables.

While the history of these trades after the Civil War is far from monolithic, the occupations share two common threads. The trades expanded, and a disproportionately large share of the people working in them did not identify as native-born whites. Whether Italian-born garbage haulers, Eastern European Jewish scrap-metal dealers, African American laundry women, or Chinese American laundry men, stereotypes of waste handlers of the time are divorced from native-born white identity.

These types are rooted in both contemporary narrative accounts and occupational data. Two broad themes emerge for the period between 1870 and 1930. First, the period saw sustained growth in variety of occupations and number of workers addressing sanitary concerns, ranging from janitorial work to laundry to waste disposal. Second, the people doing this work by and large were not people who were considered white by the standards of the day.

Between 1850 and 1900, relevant occupations enumerated in the U.S. Census of Population included janitors, launderers and laundresses, traders and dealers in junk, and ragpickers. In 1910 and 1920, the Census expanded its occupational codes, and relevant occupations included traders in junk, garbage men and scavengers, charwomen and cleaners, janitors and sextons, launderers and laundresses—not in laundry, laundry operatives—foremen and overseers, laundry operatives—laborers, and cleaners and renovators—clothing, etc.

Much of the sanitation workforce was foreign born or the children of foreign-born individuals. For all sanitary occupations between 1870 and 1930, excluding laundry, the participation of native-born individuals from native-born parents was significantly smaller than their representation in the general population. In most occupations, the broadest overrepresentation was from foreign-born individuals.

The broad trend of native-born whites being less likely to work in the sanitary occupations and foreign-born and African American individuals being more likely to work in the sanitary occupations is borne out by particular histories of particular occupations. Each grew in size and importance, and each developed particular occupational patterns.

Collecting Garbage and Sweeping Streets

Per capita garbage generation from households increased by the turn of the century, as consumers could shop for new, affordable goods rather than mending older items around the house. Household wastes, including rubbish and biological wastes, had historically been thrown into dirt roads. As horses gave way to trolleys and automobiles, the composition of city streets evolved from dirt to wood to cobblestone to asphalt. The uses of streets evolved from dump and playground to traffic artery, making roads less suited as sinks for garbage.

Indoor plumbing solved the question of what to do with the contents of chamber pots. Waterways became effective sinks to take fecal matter and urine out of sight and out of mind. Sewers addressed worries over the malodorous effects of sewage at a time when the miasma theory of disease transmission still had cachet in public health.

Sewers proved suitable sinks for human waste, but households generated other rubbish that could not be easily flushed. Food wastes had also gone into the street to await consumption by livestock; with automobiles supplanting horses and pigs, these wastes presented nuisances.

Mass production allowed Americans to purchase more clothing, more utensils, more books, more toys, and more goods of all kinds. With mass consumption came mass disposal of old clothes, shoes, cookery, and the wide variety of goods Americans could replace by purchasing new goods from catalogs and stores.

One option for disposing of garbage was incineration. Cities built large incinerators, and tall buildings (including residential apartments and office buildings) constructed incinerators for on-site use. Such disposal was convenient, offered the use of waste as fuel for heat, and reduced solid matter. Solid waste was not eliminated, as incineration generated ash that had an acrid smell (and could contain dioxins, heavy metals, and other toxins).

Businesses developed to collect incinerator ash and household wastes. The most famous of these was the business of Dutch immigrant Harm Huizenga. Huizenga and his son took his truck through the streets of Chicago and Cicero in the 1920s collecting wastes and transporting them to Lake Michigan to use as landfill for Lake Shore Drive. After his 1936 death, his descendants transformed the business into Waste Management, Inc., which grew to handle garbage and recycling services for municipalities and private businesses around the world.[16]

Much solid waste was not burned but instead collected to be disposed of in dumps. How this was done depended upon the local authority. New York City established a Department of Street Cleaning in 1881 to address the growing amounts of garbage, fecal matter, and horse urine in the streets, but effective removal of wastes in New York's streets would wait more than a decade. George Waring transformed the city's Department of Streets and Sanitation into a giant workforce by 1895 as part of a drive to uplift local sanitary standards that included juvenile street-cleaning groups and White Wings marching down clean streets. Waring's department was popular, as regular collection removed noxious odors from neighborhoods; even as germ theory became the accepted model of disease transmission, public concerns about smells endured. Public employees swept the streets clean and collected garbage from residences, sorting it for materials that might have economic value and dumping the rest into the East River, the Atlantic Ocean, or landfills. To perform these tasks, Waring specifically hired Italians. Similar hiring occurred in Philadelphia's Division of Housing and Sanitation and other public sanitation departments.[17]

In San Francisco—a large-city exception to municipal collection and disposal—competition was ferocious among independent scavengers until 1920. In that year, the first scavenger cooperative, the Sunset

Scavenger Company, was formed. Emilio Rattaro, who started his own scavenger company in 1916, was instrumental in bringing competitors together to form Sunset, a group dominated by members of northern Italian heritage. The bond of ethnic and family ties likely aided the cooperative association's success.[18]

This private cooperative grew throughout the twentieth century, and the Italian immigrants who founded it remained in the trade. Stewart Perry quotes a descendent of the founders in 1978, who said that "it was good work for immigrants—even if you couldn't read or write, you could scavenge; if you had a horse, a wagon, and a gun you could get what you needed and protect yourself enough to do business."[19]

Entry into the trade might be gradual. "Scores of immigrants moved into [the garbage business], perhaps working with relatives at first until they could save enough to buy a wagon and a horse for their own. Then they would strike out independently. Ties with friends and relatives and from the same or nearby villages in the old country probably restrained a man in his choice of potential customers to canvass and concomitantly increased the ferocity of his competition with those with whom he had fewer ties."[20]

If private garbage collection offered the opportunity to start a business from nothing, public services allowed a measure of job security. As municipal departments of streets and sanitation grew, employment within them became opportunities for political machines to offer patronage jobs. Many recent immigrants found work this way. Antanas Kaztauskis, a Lithuanian living and working in the Chicago stockyards, reported that work in the streets and sanitation department was a reliable fallback for those who were active in the machine:

> Summer was over and Election Day was coming. The Republican boss in our district, Jonidas, was a saloon keeper. A friend took me there. Jonidas shook hands and treated me fine. He taught me to sign my name, and the next week I went with him to an office and signed some paper, and then I could vote. I voted as I was told, and then they got me back into the yards to work, because one big politician owns stock in one of those houses. Then I felt that I was getting in beside the game. I was in a combine like other sharp men. Even when work was slack I was all right, because they got me a job in the street cleaning department.[21]

Italian immigrants participated in New York City's garbage sorting in large numbers. In 1881, the *New York Times* reported that the people who "separate from valueless material the atoms that can be put to use again are almost entirely Italians . . . as industrious as ants, and, apparently, have eyes for nothing but the bits and particles that go to fill their bags."[22]

The *New York Times* report was perhaps biased because the reporter filed his story from the heavily Italian Five Points neighborhood of the city, but New York City Street-Cleaning Commissioner Waring employed Italian immigrants in the 1890s as scow trimmers. Waring reasoned that Italians were "a race with a genius for rag-and-bone picking and for subsisting on rejected trifles of food."[23]

Waring's stereotyping reflected the tendency of immigrants to handle garbage. In 1910, the proportion of garbage men and scavengers who were foreign born was 47 percent, more than two standard deviations larger than expected in proportion to the general population. The proportion of garbage men and scavengers who were native born to native-born parents was also 47 percent, but this represents two standard deviations less than what would be expected in the general population. In 1920, the foreign-born made up 41 percent of garbage men and scavengers (again more than two standard deviations larger than expected), and native-born individuals made up 45 percent. The population of garbage men and scavengers in 1920 was less white than the general population. African Americans made up 27 percent of garbage men and scavengers, again more than two standard deviations larger than expected, as African Americans were 9.9 percent of the general population in 1920. Whites, including the foreign-born, made up 73 percent of garbage men and scavengers, more than two standard deviations smaller than expected.

The occupation codes in the 1930 Census changed, with some new sanitary occupations arriving and others leaving. In one such occupation, garbage men and scavengers, both foreign-born individuals and African Americans were represented in numbers more than two standard deviations above what would be expected in the occupation of garbage men and scavengers. Native born to native parents constituted 52 percent of garbage men and scavengers in 1930. Half of these workers were African American (25 percent of the total workforce).

Foreign-born individuals constituted 29 percent of the workforce, and native-born individuals to at least one immigrant parent constituted 19 percent of the workforce.

Another new occupation enumerated was street cleaner. A plurality of the individuals enumerated as street cleaners in 1930 were foreign born (43 percent). An additional 20 percent of street cleaners were native born to at least one foreign-born parent. Native-born street cleaners to native-born parents constituted 37 percent of the occupation. Native-born African Americans constituted 18 percent of street cleaners in 1930, more than two standard deviations greater than one would expect given their representation in the general population.

The work these people performed was hazardous; a 1917 survey of New York City White Wings by the Department of Sanitation's chief physician Dr. S. I. Rainforth revealed that 5,484 workers (constituting 80 percent of the department) were disabled doing their work. Keeping in mind that New York City's Department of Sanitation was unusual in even having a chief physician who provided the workers medical care at cost to the department, the workers had endemic issues with injuries and exposure to the elements. Other municipal departments and private waste handling businesses did not have physicians assessing the workers' health.[24]

Garbage collection and street sweeping were among the most visible sanitary occupations of the early twentieth century, and thanks to public efforts such as Waring parading White Wings down city streets, urban residents grew to expect raised hygienic standards owing to their work. This provided workers with leverage—when New York City's garbage collectors went on strike for higher wages in 1907, the clutter and odor filling streets quickly drew notice of residents, increasing pressure on the city to negotiate with the strikers. Not for the last time, garbage collectors drew attention to their work with a successful labor action.[25]

Charwomen, Cleaners, and Janitors

Work removing wastes from streets, demolition sites, and public places grew. Work removing dirt from homes, businesses, and clothing also expanded, with racial and nativity dimensions to these occupational patterns similar to those found in garbage hauling.

Domestic work in 1900, as it had been throughout the nineteenth century, was a major occupation for women. One-third of all employed women in the United States worked in some sort of service capacity (about two million workers in homes, restaurants, and hotels), with more charwomen and maids employed as middle-class families employed someone else to do the cooking and more rigorous cleaning. Domestic service had been an entry point for women from Northern and Western Europe, including Irish women in large numbers starting with the mass migration at mid-century. By the end of the century, women from Germany and the Slavic nations could find work cleaning houses in Northern homes without a lack of English-language fluency hindering them. In the South, domestic cleaning work was almost monolithically the responsibility of African American women from the end of the Civil War onward.[26]

The occupations of charwoman and domestic cleaner grew after the Civil War, though status and pay remained low. Though several attempts to organize domestic workers occurred during this period (for example, 300 Chicago-area domestic working women successfully negotiated union procedures to settle grievances with employers in 1901), workers found it difficult to maintain labor organization, and job security was perilous.[27]

In 1910, foreign-born individuals made up 44 percent of charwomen and cleaners, children of at least one foreign-born parent made up 22 percent, and native-born Americans born to native-born parents made up 36 percent. Ten years later, the percentage of native-born Americans born to native-born parents rose to 40 percent, still more than two standard deviations smaller than their proportion in the general population. Charwomen and cleaners were 45 percent foreign born and 15 percent born to at least one foreign-born parent.

Similar patterns emerged for janitors. In 1910, Americans born to native-born parents constituted less than half the occupation, and while that number grew to 52 percent in 1920, the majority of native-born individuals in this occupation category were African American men. The number of foreign-born individuals in each year was more than two standard deviations above their numbers in the general population.

Janitorial work was dirty and low status, but just as junk and scrap trading provided opportunities to Jews, it offered an economic strategy for the African American men who performed it. The racial barriers that existed to many occupations were absent in janitorial work. For example, in 1889, Brittain Oxendine, a Reconstruction-era member of the North Carolina state legislature, fled the racial violence of the South for Seattle, Washington, where the only work he could find was as a janitor at the city's largest newspaper, the *Seattle Post-Intelligencer*.[28]

In the 1920s, a group of African American janitors in Chicago organized the Service Employees International Union (SEIU) and had success unionizing janitors in New York City and Chicago, winning relatively good wages for the work. A majority of the janitors in Kansas City in 1920 were African American men, and as the historian Charles Edward Coulten observes, not only did the janitors receive regular wages, but the job might also come with living quarters for the janitor and his family. As residential segregation practices became more stringent in Kansas City during the 1920s, the possibility of adequate living space was a significant benefit of the job. Janitorial work among African Americans was so widespread in Kansas City that the local Urban League office instituted a Janitorial Training School in the 1930s to best place community members in the wake of massive unemployment and few opportunities in other occupations.[29]

Perspective on the status of janitors during this period may be gleaned from a survey that took place some years later. Between the fall of 1949 and winter of 1950, the sociologist Ray Gold interviewed thirty-seven Chicago-area janitors for his doctoral dissertation. Their responses helped him characterize how janitorial work could, even if the janitors were making good money, be stigmatized as "dirty work." Although Chicago-area janitors received good wages in the years after the SEIU formed in 1921, the position itself was low status, owing, according to Gold, to the following factors: "(1) many janitors are foreign-born and therefore strange and suspicious; (2) the janitor is always seen to be wearing dirty clothes, so the tenants seem to feel that he habitually disregards cleanliness; (3) the janitor lives in the basement, which symbolizes his low status; and (4) the janitor removes the tenants' garbage, which subserves him to them."[30]

Gold also noted class and racial jealousy among tenants. One African American janitor expressed the resentment he received after purchasing a new car: "They say 'How is the nigger with the big car?' meaning I am a 'nigger' because I got a Buick and my car is bigger than theirs." Even in the period after janitors were able to organize for better wages and working conditions, their work remained dirty and demeaning.[31]

The Junk and Scrap Trade

Trade in junk and scrap was related to garbage hauling but involved different opportunities for economic mobility. Garbage removal was performed by a combination of public and private entities; few public entities engaged in the scrap trade until the era of recycling as an environmental act came in the late twentieth century. For more than a century before, such dealing was the provenance of thousands of businesses of varying size, loosely organized into a trading network collecting scrap from homes, worksites, dumps, and demolished buildings, processing them, and returning the materials to manufacturing industries. (A related trade, taking in secondhand goods for either resale or charity, grew as households sought to remove old, unwanted goods that might still have utility in someone else's home.)[32]

A common thread in the histories of American Jewish families is having a father or uncle in the junk trade. Jewish involvement in the scrap trade transcends settlement patterns by region or urbanization. Lee Shai Weissbach, the pre-eminent historian of small-town American Jewry, observed that "a remarkable number of Jewish men in small-town America" got their start as junk dealers. Jews moved to towns like Roswell, New Mexico, to establish a scrap trade; rare was the small-town junk dealer at the turn of the twentieth century who was not a Jew who was either an immigrant or the son of immigrants from Eastern Europe.[33] Furthermore, junk was the vehicle that propelled many Eastern European Jews into the heartland—often the initial Jews to settle in small towns worked in junk. Weissbach notes that of the thirty-five Eastern European-born heads of Jewish households listed in the census of Appleton, Wisconsin, in 1920, 40 percent were in the junk business.[34]

Most sanitary occupations grew owing to a growing concern over the definition of waste as filth. The trades in junk, scrap, rags, and other secondary materials grew in part because more people were disposing of old materials under that working definition but also owing to increased attention to the definition of waste as squandered value.

Industries extracted value from nature as primary sources, transforming forests into lumber, ore beneath the planet's crust into metals, and plants into fibers. Railroads, mills, shipyards, publishers, construction companies, and, by the early twentieth century, automobile manufacturers had hearty demands for the raw materials that would become mass-produced goods.[35]

American waste trading emerged as an industry over the course of the nineteenth century. The first period of growth concerned linen and cotton rags, in part because more clothing was available to Americans in the early nineteenth century, but primarily because there was new demand for these rags. Machinery that mechanized paper making proliferated across New England by 1820, making mass production of books and documents possible. Bleached and dried rags were fodder for paper production, and the largest scrap trade through the Civil War was in salvaged textiles.[36]

During and after the Civil War, demand for ferrous scrap metal expanded. In part this was due to the expanding importance of iron and steel in structuring industrial society, including building construction, transportation, tools, and agriculture. Steel fabrication, particularly after the proliferation of the open-hearth process of production, allowed for the use of scrap iron to forge new, stronger steel. Similar techniques allowed for the recycling of copper. The abundance of scrap metal in demolition sites, from homes, and from industry made it more affordable to harvest than digging into the earth for iron ore.[37]

The growing cities provided many sources for scavengers. City dumps replaced streets as centers for refuse, allowing scavengers to sort post-consumer waste at centralized locations.[38] Enterprising peddlers traded new consumer products for obsolete household items. The urban poor had opportunities to generate income from scavenging and selling their collections to junk shops or mills.[39]

Rural hinterlands beyond city centers provided opportunities to reclaim old materials. I. H. Schlezinger was a Jewish immigrant from Austria-Hungary who came to Columbus at the turn of the twentieth century. His son Edward recalled that I. H. worked as a peddler, going out in the country with his horse and wagon to visit the area farmers. "The women would give him orders to bring out to them things—to pick up for them—and then he would trade—trading—it was called—then if they accumulated—like the husbands had a pile of old iron on the farm—scrap iron—he would take that in return."[40] Thus households and farms produced commodities for industry as well as consuming them.

My family history reflects Schlezinger's experience. Austrian Jew Abraham Zimring left Vienna in 1904. Landing at Ellis Island, he immediately set out for Waterloo, a small town in northeastern Iowa, where a "cousin"—in actuality an acquaintance from Austria who was not a blood relative—had prospects for Abraham traveling from farm to farm collecting scrapped equipment and kitchenware. He continued this work as he sent for his wife and children, never making much money and eventually abandoning the trade to work in tobacco and liquor sales.[41]

Over 90 percent of the American labor force trading in junk, however, was urban, reflecting the more concentrated wastes and access to customers in cities. Historical accounts of American cities in the nineteenth century suggest heavy participation by immigrants in scavenging, junk collecting, and scrap dealing in the late nineteenth and early twentieth centuries, and demographic data indicate that this suggestion is accurate. A correlation between place of birth and occupation in the 1880 Integrated Public Use Microdata Series (IPUMS) sample indicates that over 70 percent of the workers in the waste trades in 1880 were born in Europe. The typical waste trade worker in 1880 was a male, married, head-of-household born in Europe, with the largest groups coming from Germany, Ireland, and Poland. While narrative accounts suggest women continued to scavenge, they did not enumerate "waste trade" as their occupation, indicating a limit in enumerators' questions that may have accentuated the gendered nature of the work. (It is possible that individuals who scavenged to augment household incomes did not identify themselves as scavengers to the Census.)[42]

The census data identifying work with waste materials as an almost uniformly male activity conflicts with anecdotal accounts of female scavengers yet also reflects a growing formalization and gendering of the industry. While men and women alike had scavenged dumps, streets, demolition sites, and the waterfront, the Census did not enumerate women as being employed in the waste trades, possibly owing to bias by enumerators to identify individuals working in scrap yards as workers and not enumerate scavengers. Furthermore, if a wife helped her husband keep the books for the business, as was common, she would not be enumerated as a junk worker. It is possible that Census data collection methods reduce documenting women's roles in the trade.

The Census's methods also revealed a very white workforce—if we consider whiteness as defined by the Census with caveats over how "white" native-born Americans viewed Jews, Italians, and Slavs between 1870 and 1930. Most of the men enumerated were classified as white (93 percent) as opposed to African American or Chinese. As with the data indicating that waste trade workers were mostly male, the conclusions defining a white workforce may have been a function of the method used to enumerate workers. Stories of African Americans working as scavengers in Northern cities abound: African Americans worked as yard labor in urban scrap yards and ran secondhand goods and junk businesses in the South. These individuals, however, may have been missed by the Census. Transient scavengers (regardless of race or sex) likely were not listed as waste trade workers if they were even recorded for the Census. And while African American junk shop owners may have had stable businesses, they may not have tapped into the industrial network feeding large mills, perhaps causing census takers to not consider them with the larger workforce. Finally, even individuals working in yards that were in that industrial network were often people who worked multiple jobs or were employed seasonally and may not have described themselves primarily as waste trade workers to the census takers. The Southern and Eastern European male image of the waste trades as developed by Census information is overwhelming, but it may be obscuring a more varied portrait of the business of reclamation and waste management in the late nineteenth century.

Keeping reservations about biases involving race and gender in mind, the Census provides a portrait in keeping with the idea that the waste trades offered opportunities for European immigrant men who wished to start their own businesses. A large proportion of the individuals born in Germany and Poland were likely Jewish, though the 1880 Census does not feature a positive indicator of Jewish status, such as native tongue. By 1920, so many Jews—many fleeing repression in Russia and the Ukraine—had started businesses trading in scrap iron, rags, and other secondary materials that the public face of the scrap dealer was the face of a Jew.

The 1920 Census allows for a more precise measure of Jewish identity than does the 1880 Census. As Susan Cotts Watkins observed in her work on the 1910 Census, the presence of native tongue of both the enumerated individual and the individual's parents as a category allows for the most precise measure of Jewish identity in census records. As Jews were the only group likely to identify Yiddish or Hebrew as a native tongue, identifying Yiddish-speaking individuals (and the children of Yiddish-speaking individuals) as Jews is a reasonable inference.[43]

Sixty-eight percent of the junk workers in the 1920 IPUMS were from countries in Eastern and Central Europe, where Jews had emigrated from in large numbers over the previous four decades. A majority of the junk workers from Eastern Europe spoke a native tongue of Yiddish, Hebrew, or "Jewish." Even leaving aside the caveat that this technique may omit Jewish individuals whose mother tongue may have been recorded as Russian, German, or another language, defining workers' ethnicity by native tongue indicates that first-generation Jewish immigrants were by far the most represented group in America's junk trade in 1920. Contemporary observations agree with the statistics. By the mid-1930s, the editors of *Fortune* estimated that the scrap metal industry was 90 percent Jewish owned.[44]

The rag trade that dominated secondary material trading for most of the nineteenth century included a large proportion of Italian-born workers in the late nineteenth century. An 1874 *Chicago Daily Tribune* report on their living conditions decried the squalor in racial terms:

> From the underground burrow, called the basement, to the topmost garret, the houses are filled with Italians—men, women, and children—of the lowest order. Their chief vocation is THE NOBLE ART OF RAG-PICKING, and the entire charnel-house smells of tainted raiment, steeped in swill beer and stale alcohol. The men who hang around the place are the lowest types of human society—almost black—a cross between Polish Jews and the very worst class of plantation darkies. It is impossible to suppose that these beings have in their veins the blood of

the conquerors of the ancient world. They must have descended from
the camp-followers of Hannibal who sojourned many years in the sunny
plains of Italy.[45]

The large Jewish and Italian representation in the scrap metal and
rag trades was in part due to the mass waves of immigration from Eastern Europe coinciding with the growth of demand for scrap materials
by American industry; certainly the timing provided easy entry into a
trade where demand was high, initial investment costs were low, and
an individual who could assess good material from worthless material
and offer the goods to an industrial customer could enjoy rapid upward
economic mobility.[46]

Timing was an important reason for the presence of Jewish immigrants in the scrap trade, but the goals and needs of the immigrants
were also crucial. Jews in both Europe and the United States had a long
tradition of entrepreneurial activities from peddling to shop keeping.
For Jews, the impulse to start a business was due in part to the advan-
tages of not having a supervisor who could discriminate against their
religious practices, fire them at will, or refuse to hire them. The historian Alan Kraut argued that, even if a shopkeeper or peddler's income
was lower than a factory worker's, business ownership provided more
freedoms, including the ability to close early on Fridays.[47]

One dimension to the expansion of the waste trades is that they provided opportunities at a time when other occupations were declining.
Jewish immigrants in the United States had peddled produce and other
goods and operated a variety of shops since the first era of mass migration from Germany in the middle of the nineteenth century. The skills
and logistics in the scrap trade were similar to those of the produce
trade. Both required little initial capital investment yet required evalu-
ation of inventories suitable for sale, as well as the ability to network
with other buyers and sellers. Census data support the historian Oliver Pollak's contention that the retail peddler trade was on the wane by
the turn of the century as competition from established shops led to a
loss of customers. Junk peddlers benefited from mass consumerism and
planned obsolescence, and junk peddling became a growth occupation
for newcomers who had little capital or established clientele.[48]

Jewish participation in New York City's secondhand goods trade was widespread by 1880, including scrap yards, junk shops, and pawnbrokers. A *New York Times* report in 1866 on the trade in stolen goods observed that Jews had "a monopoly of the pawnbroking business in this City, and many of them have acquired great wealth nearby. They are sharp and shrewd, always driving a hard bargain." A combination of natural talents and constant practice, the *Times* argued, "made them as good judges of human nature as they are of the value of an article. They can tell at a glance whether or not their customer is a constant visitor at the pawnbroker's counter, and woe be to the individual whose manner shows him or her to be a novice in such transactions."[49] Dealers in secondhand goods were not respectable citizens but "low, degraded people, of Irish origin generally, although many who speak the German language are engaged in the business." The "degraded people" reflected both xenophobia and middle-class disgust of the trade.[50]

As the *New York Times* report made clear, Jews were one of several immigrant groups who traded junk and scrap after 1880. Traders in junk deviated from the occupational patterns in garbage collection in that the vast majority enumerated throughout the period were individuals born in the United States to two foreign-born parents, with that category containing all of the individuals in the occupation in the 1910 sample and most of the individuals in the 1920 sample. When this occupation is analyzed by native tongue of the individual and of the individual's parents, the 1920 sample reveals that individuals speaking Yiddish, Hebrew, "Jewish," or Russian—who collectively constituted approximately 1 percent of the American population—constituted 58 percent of all individuals trading in junk in the United States. Individuals whose native tongue was either English or not available constituted 21 percent of the traders in junk. Other language groups represented in traders in junk well above their numbers in the general population included Italian (11 percent), German (4 percent), and Roumanian (4 percent).[51] In the 1920 sample, 100 percent of traders in junk were individuals born in the United States to two foreign-born parents.

As opportunities to sell scrap to mills increased, more small businesses founded by immigrants clustered in cities. Without established businesses filling demand, newcomers starting out with little more than a sack of bottles, a pushcart full of scrap metal, and a small list of local customers found a way into entrepreneurship.[52]

Some scrap and junk businesses operated out of the yard or house of the proprietor, producing sounds, odors, and sights that neighbors might find objectionable. A junkyard might be founded by a peddler who had raised enough money from door-to-door inquiries or scavenging to buy land. The yard would then purchase collections from other peddlers and sell them to mills. The demand for ferrous scrap during World War I saw a new type of dealer emerge. With enough capital, a junk dealer might purchase warehouses and become a broker, combining purchases from several yards and shipping them to, say, the Ford Motor Company. Within thirty years (and two generations), the Luria Brothers business of Reading, Pennsylvania, grew from one junkyard founded by Jewish immigrant patriarch Hirsch Luria to a brokerage in sixteen cities operated by his sons.[53]

Labor in these new, small businesses often involved relatives. Luria Brothers drafted several members of the Luria family into service in the yards in the early years, and many firms employed their children once they became old enough to handle tools in the yard. As an adult, Louis Galamba recalled that "Father opened a waste material business [in Webb City, Missouri, in 1903] and in 1905 I assisted him after school hours and worked during vacation periods." The business thrived, and Galamba grew up to be president of the international trading firm Sonken-Galamba half a century after his after-school labors.[54]

Decisions concerning firm growth depended upon both market forces and family structure. Though hard decisions concerning the direction of the business were common, an individual attempting to start a firm could do so without worrying too much about financing. Immigrants could enter the scrap industry with minimal investments in technology. Scavengers and peddlers could function with little more than a sack. Peddlers often invested in pushcarts or rented horses and buggies in order to increase the amount of materials they could collect. The low level of capital needed to start in the industry was one condition that allowed immigrants opportunities to start scrap businesses. The rigors of the work constituted another condition. Most of the labor involved manual sorting. When and where the trade was mechanized, the technology employed in scrap yards increased the hazards of an already-dangerous industry. Cranes tipped over. Alligator shears and sledge hammers could speed processing of metal, but they also resulted in the loss of fingers, hands, and arms in mishaps.[55] Gas torches elevated the possibility of burns and explosions in yards. Scrap yard workers risked death and dismemberment as they turned junk into usable commodities.[56]

At the end of World War I, the United States had experienced half a century of heavy industrialization and mass immigration. Both factors transformed the waste trades to the extent that by 1920 dealers in rags, old metals, and other secondary materials had established a multi-million dollar industry operated in large part by men whose families had not lived in the United States forty years previously. Demand for scrap iron during World War I made ferrous metal—already becoming a standard material for industrial production—even more valuable, expanding the market and making some dealers wealthy men.

If the trade in junk and scrap differed from garbage collection in that demand from manufacturers could generate significant income to junk traders, these two waste trades shared similar problems. The emergence of garbage and scrap as trades dominated by foreign-born entrepreneurs led to stereotypes of crime and fraud. Complaints by dissatisfied customers and Progressive reformers were couched in rhetoric that conflated the scrap dealer's unethical business practices with his status as a mysterious, unscrupulous foreigner, related to the Shylock characters perpetuated in European and American folklore since European Jews were accused of usury in the Middle Ages. By the late nineteenth century, the crooked Fagin in Charles Dickens's *Oliver Twist* represented popular perceptions of the child-corrupting, thieving Jew. Official correspondence and trade journals were more reserved in their criticism but warned customers that scrap dealing was done largely by foreigners and "classes of collectors who are constantly going beyond the limit of the law"[57] and that one must be cautious in dealing with "a firm composed entirely of Jews."[58]

The demographics of the scrap trade did not change much between 1920 and 1930. Despite the era of mass immigration coming to a close, a full 58 percent of individuals identified as retail dealers of junk and rags in 1930 were foreign born. An additional 15 percent were native born to at least one immigrant parent. Only 27 percent were native born to native-born parents. African Americans were represented in the population of junk and rag dealers more than two standard deviations less than their representation in the general population. African Americans either could not or did not enter in this occupation that could serve as an opportunity for business owning. In the first third of the twentieth century, the junk and scrap trade was highly masculine and almost monolithically immigrant oriented, and the Census statistics reinforce contemporary attitudes that Jewish men dominated the trade.

Laundry

The growing laundry business in some respects paralleled the scrap trade. Both emerging trades offered foreign-born individuals the opportunity to start new businesses, and both trades have stereotypical associations with particular immigrant groups. The history of laundry during this period is notably distinct in its labor structure. The half century after the Civil War saw transformation of laundry from work done largely by hand in homes to mechanized systems in facilities that could be run by one person or staffed by dozens under complex managerial structures. By 1920, affluent and middle-class Americans could contract out the cleaning of their clothes on a regular basis.

The 1860 Census lists a majority of laundry workers in the United States as Chinese. Asian American men were limited in available occupations, restricted from professional occupations such as medicine and teaching. Laundry work, however, was open to them, both as employees and as business owners. Like scrap for Jews, laundry for Chinese in many communities in the Northern and Western states became a niche occupation. Not only could marginalized immigrants find work in these fields, but enterprising men could start businesses of their own. The initial niche became self-perpetuating, so that at the end of the twentieth century, laundries owned and operated by Chinese men remained common in much of the United States.[59]

The "Chinese laundryman" was an American phenomenon. "The Chinese laundryman does not learn his trade in China; there are no laundries in China," stated Lee Chew, who arrived in America in the early 1860s. "The women there do the washing in tubs and have no washboards or flat irons. All the Chinese laundrymen here were taught in the first place by American women just as I was taught." In China, observed Chin Foo Wong of New York, laundry work was a "woman's occupation," and men did not "step into it for fear of losing their social standing."[60]

Why did Chinese men in America enter this line of work? Unlike the retail or restaurant business, a laundry could be opened with a small capital outlay of from seventy-five to two hundred dollars. The entrepreneurial rationale is similar to why European-born Jews became scrap dealers in the United States. In laundry, as with scrap and junk, the opportunity structure for recent immigrants to open these businesses during this period was very high—strong demand for their services, yet with few established firms from native-born entrepreneurs as competition. Further, each business could be started with minimal capital costs. Much of the dirty work in which the workers were also the firm owners were in such businesses, rather than in large factories. The requirements were minimal: a stove, a trough, a dry room, a sleeping apartment, a sign, and the willingness to spend almost every waking hour of one's day washing other people's clothes. A Chinese laundryman did not need to speak much English to operate his business. "In this sort of menial labor," said one, "I can get along speaking only 'yes' and 'no.'" He could also manage without knowing numbers. "Being illiterate, he could not write the numbers," another laundryman said, describing a fellow operator. "He had a way and what a way! See, he would draw a circle as big as a half dollar coin to represent a half dollar, and a circle as big as a dime for a dime, and so on. When the customers came in to call for their laundry, they would catch on to the meaning of the circles and pay accordingly."[61]

But if "Chinese laundrymen" had reasons to be drawn to this work, they were also pushed into it by racial barriers. Laundry work was one of the few opportunities that were open to Chinese. "Men of other nationalities who are jealous of the Chinese have raised such a great outcry about Chinese cheap labor that they have shut him out of working on farms or in factories or building railroads or making streets or digging sewers," explained Lee Chew. "So he opens a laundry."

Chew's experience took him from rural to urban settings. Initially opening up a laundry in the West to service railroad workers and miners, he left when drunken miners destroyed the business. He then went east to Chicago, operating a laundry for three years, then moved on to four years in Detroit. After returning to China in 1897, one year later he began a laundry business in Buffalo.[62]

The "Chinese laundry" represented a retreat into self-employment from a narrowly restricted labor market. "You couldn't work in the cigar factories or the jute or woolen mills any more—all the Chinese had been driven out," elderly Chinese men later sadly recalled. "About all they could be was laundrymen or vegetable peddlers then." In the 1900 Census of Population, about one quarter of all employed men of Chinese ancestry living in the United States worked in a laundry.[63]

The laundry trade by this time had started to evolve so that Chinese representation as a fraction of the workforce in laundry was shrinking. This was less due to alternative labor options for Chinese men as it was to demand for more laundry work throughout the United States. Between 1850 and 1920, the representation of native-born whites and blacks rose and individuals of Chinese origin shrank until the vast majority of people employed in laundry services were native born to native-born parents. Most of the people working in laundry services enumerated by the 1920 Census were white; however, all laundry work was not equal. By 1920, when the Census broke laundry work into different occupations, management and ownership was significantly more represented by whites, and laborers by African Americans.

Drake and Cayton observed in Chicago in 1930 that about 3,000 women earned their living by washing clothes in the homes of their employers or by taking laundry to their own homes, and of these, over half were African American women. They observed the toils of one such woman: "She is expected to do all the washing, including the linen and towels as well as all the clothes for the five members of the family. She is supposed to finish the work—that is iron the entire wash—and then clean the house thoroughly—all for $2 a day."[64]

The burdens of laundry work observed in Chicago extended to the South. Successful laundries could make their owners wealthy. For example, Henry Loeb, Sr., a man of German Jewish ancestry, founded Loeb's Laundries in Memphis in 1887. Employing hundreds of African American women to wash the clothes, Loeb generated enough revenue to purchase competing laundries, consolidating them into the largest laundry business in the city. As a result, he became one of the wealthiest individuals in Memphis. The historian Tera Hunter observed that, as discretionary income among nineteenth-century women increased, they contracted out laundry to other people so they might avoid the onerous chore of washing clothes all day. Even poor urban women might send out at least some of their wash. Options by the end of the nineteenth century in Northern cities included sending dirty clothes to large commercial laundries. The South did not adopt mechanized laundry technology as quickly, and instead laundry continued to be largely manual labor, with both affluent and poor whites sending out laundry to African American women.[65]

This work might be completed in the homes of upper- or middle-class employers, but most laundresses worked in their own homes and neighborhoods, where segregation in housing and segregation in work endured, with whites concerned about contagion caused by sending dirty work to black neighborhoods where "stinkin' nigger wimmin" (in the words of one customer) performed the necessary work to rid the clothes of filth.[66]

Hunter observed that Atlanta's trade in laundry grew significantly after the Civil War. By the end of the 1870s, demand for laundry services in the city had not led to higher wages, and laundry workers organized to strike for better pay. In 1879 and 1880 Atlanta's washerwomen had already engaged in one major strike and had formed a short-lived protective association. In the summer of 1881, concerned over inadequate pay, they formed a new organization, the Washing Society, and called a strike. The resulting protest was the largest among African Americans in Atlanta during the late nineteenth century.[67]

Although laundry was not considered high-status work, the importance of clean clothes allowed the striking workers to demonstrate resistance. The Washing Society recruited non-affiliated washerwomen to the strike, some of whom had already taken in wash loads. Convinced to join immediately, they returned the clothes unwashed or wet. Pressure from employers led the police to arrest organizers of the strike (among them Matilda Crawford, Sallie Bell, Carrie Jones, Dora Jones, Orphelia Turner, and Sarah A. Collier), charging them with disorderly conduct and quarreling and fining them $5.00 each, except for Collier, who received a $20.00 assessment that she refused to pay. Collier was then sentenced to a chain gang for forty days. This did not end the strike, which extended to some white laundresses (likely poor, single, widowed, and Irish) in Atlanta. Within three weeks, the strike grew from twenty workers to three thousand, facilitated by communal laundry work allowing mobilization and coordination to spread rapidly. Despite the success in organizing, laundresses continued to earn low wages, resulting in another strike ten years later.[68]

Which is not to say that washerwomen lacked agency. Some women took laundry into their homes, allowing them to set their own daily routines as they soaked, wrung, and dried other people's clothing. Such work augmented the family budgets of married women.

Laundry wages remained low in Northern cities, where mechanization reduced menial work yet did not elevate the remaining work to skilled status. Most of Chicago's laundry in 1930 was done in large commercial enterprises employing about 15,000 workers. Drake and Cayton calculated that, in 1930, 55.4 percent of all the women working in Chicago's laundries were African American, as were 26.3 percent of the men working as semi-skilled operatives in the industry. The scale of Chicago laundries was amenable to labor organizing, with local workers affiliating with the American Federation of Labor by the end of the 1930s (including about 2,000 white members and 8,000 African American members).[69]

By 1930, technological changes shaped the service sector, with industrial machinery replacing human energy for many tasks. The mechanization of household sanitation—which, the historian Ruth Schwartz Cowan observed ironically, led to both higher sanitary standards and more hours spent by women using the new technologies to keep a clean home—was not complete; however, laundry had been transformed from what it had been half a century earlier. The technological advances did not lead to a more egalitarian society. The work of turning dirty clothes clean fell disproportionately upon black women.[70]

In the 1930 IPUMS sample, 355,154 individuals were enumerated in the occupation "launderers and laundresses—not in laundry, other domestic and personal service," with the vast majority native-born African Americans. This was an acutely distinctive pattern compared to other sanitary work in 1930.

While native-born whites made up a slight majority of laundry deliverymen, they were represented at a rate more than two standard deviations less than their representation in the general population. Foreign-born individuals and the children of foreign-born individuals were represented at more than two standard deviations greater than would be expected. African Americans, Chinese, Japanese, and Pacific Islanders were represented at more that two standard deviations smaller than would be expected. Overall, however, the participation of African Americans in laundry services of some sort remained far higher than their representation in the general population.

The Sanitary Labor Force in 1930

Sanitary services developed to fill new societal demands concerning hygiene after the Civil War. Context and opportunity shaped specific sanitary occupation structures, but the people employed to perform these services between 1870 and 1930 were, well beyond their representation in the general population, foreign born or African American. White Americans born to native-born parents were far less likely to engage in the sanitary occupations.

If the rhetoric of "clean and white" marginalized non-white people into dirty work, it also unwittingly provided economic opportunities. In some cases, the white revulsion to handling waste allowed marginalized people to become entrepreneurs. In the face of overwhelming discrimination, often the only path to business ownership for Chinese men was owning laundries. This was true not only in Western states but also in large cities of the North, such as New York and Chicago. Thousands of first- and second-generation Jewish immigrants started businesses collecting and trading scrap metal. Hundreds of Italian scavengers in and around San Francisco formed collectives that created the modern garbage-hauling systems for the Bay Area.

Opportunities for advancement existed but were limited. Competition among waste-related businesses was fierce. In rare cases, a scrap or garbage-hauling firm could become the source of wealth, and the histories of scrap recycling and garbage have a few famous cases, such as the development of Waste Management, Inc., from Harm Huizenga's family operation. For the most part, however, these waste handling firms competed against each other. They eked out livings when times were good and struggled to survive when depressions and recessions hit.

Although the work involved was dirty, identifying the people who performed it as unskilled labor does a disservice to their efforts. The skills required to ably perform this work were many. Not everyone could succeed as a scrap peddler or as a laundry operator. A laundry worker lacking the fortitude to work long, hard hours would deliver shabby clothing that would cause customers to turn to another of the many options they had for the service. A scrap dealer who could see commodities in the junk-heap yet was unable to identify appropriate market prices for them would soon lack customers. Failure came too easily to those who could not perform these jobs that so many industries and consumers needed to have done.

Yet the skills for dirty work—skills necessary for consumers and producing industries and vital to the health of communities—were not valued as skills by most Americans. Popular stereotypes of these workers presented them as dirty people of low morals and intelligence and unworthy of public respect. These were not jobs that the American Federation of Labor, the Knights of Labor, or the various craft guilds that developed in the nineteenth century found worthy of organizing. The Congress of Industrial Organizations (CIO), founded much later in the period, had a different philosophy, attempting to organize workers in trades ignored by many of the other unions. Several CIO attempts to organize scrap yard workers took place in the 1930s. But the CIO was an exception. Whether it be due to racial attitudes or a lack of respect for the work itself, few considered work in the waste trades skilled.[71]

The evolving structure of laundry services as dominated by native-born African Americans by 1930 anticipated trends that would develop in other sanitary occupations after World War II. Definitions of whiteness evolved after the war. Burdens of waste and waste work continued to fall heavily on those who were not considered white, and changing criteria shaping white identity resulted in removing many Americans from the perils of not being white.

6

Waste and Space Reordered

The conflation of non-white skin with dirt formalized spatial relationships in American society during the twentieth century. Central cities' association with dirt, codified in Jefferson's time, grew complicated. Cities became cleaner in many important respects. Waste was a far less acute urban public health hazard in 1920 than it was in 1870. Modern sewer and water treatment systems greatly reduced the spread of epidemic diseases in cities, and the population of the United States was majority urban for the first time in the 1920 Census. Cities improved their abilities to keep their residents alive.

Urban association with dirt and grime continued, however. The urban response to industrial wastes was far less aggressive than the urban response to biological wastes. Lacking an immediate public health threat, smoke and water pollution associated with industrial productivity continued to make urban life aesthetically dirty.

In keeping with Jefferson's pastoral ideal, those urbanites with the means to do so longed to live on the cleaner periphery of urban areas. Transportation advances in the form of commuter rail, and then mass-marketed automobiles, allowed for residential developments several miles away from central cities, their factories, and their wastes. By the time the United States became majority urban in 1920, suburban developments had emerged as refuges from the dirty cities. Developers actively marketed their new communities as innately cleaner than urban dwellings. The new suburban residential developments represented an escape from urban dirt. They also represented an escape for self-identified white people from the racial impurity of diverse urban populations. Racially restrictive covenants prevented owners of houses within subdivisions from selling to African Americans or Jews. Mass suburbanization, which began with transportation advances at the end of the nineteenth century and accelerated after World War II thanks to a combination of federal regulations and a growing economy, represented an escape from undesirable space with undesirable neighbors.[1]

Within cities, spatial reorganization that conflated the locations of waste materials and non-white people became concentrated between 1915 and 1960. University of Chicago Settlement House founder Mary McDowell addressed the City Club of Chicago in 1913, castigating a local lawyer whom she quoted as saying: "Gentlemen, in every great city there must be a part of that city segregated for unpleasant things, and of course, you know that people in that part of town are generally not sensitive." McDowell found the sentiment "outrageous" and urged Chicago's leaders to ensure sanitary conditions for all in the city.[2]

At the time McDowell quoted the insensitive lawyer, unsanitary conditions were common for the immigrants who had recently arrived in the city from Europe and Mexico, as well as Chicago's African American community. In the decade after her appearance at the City Club, however, spatial dynamics within Chicago and in cities across the United States altered the exposure of particular peoples to unsanitary conditions. The changing dynamic was anticipated by the Chicago poet Carl Sandburg. One day, not long after World War I had ended, Sandburg observed the action on a streetcorner on the South Side of Chicago. He recounted how an African American woman and three of her children were walking on the block of Michigan Avenue and East 31st Street. Just a couple months removed from life in Alabama, this family was part of the Great Migration that swelled the population of Chicago. Suddenly, Sandburg saw a big limousine swing to the curb. "A colored man steps out, touches his hat to the mother and children and gives them the surprise of their lives." Sandburg recalled the man from the limousine lecturing the family:

> We don't do this up here. It isn't good for us colored folks to send our children out on the streets like this. We're all working together to do the best we can. One thing we're particular about is the way we take the little ones out on the streets.
>
> They ought to look as if they're washed clean all over. And they ought to have shoes and stockings and hats and clean shirts on. Now you go home and see to that. If you haven't got the money to do it, come and see me. Here's my card.[3]

Sandburg saw the man give the mother the card of a banker and real estate man at an office where they collected rent monthly from over 1,000 African American tenants, thus introducing her to the existing network of African American businesses and communities in Chicago. Sandburg noted that such stories were common, as between 1914 and 1918 Chicago had become home to more than 70,000 African Americans arriving from the South.

The newcomers had an adjustment period from life in the rural South, one, Sandburg argued, that included different standards of sanitation in their new home. In Chicago, he observed, now they have learned what garbage cans are for. "From all sides the organized and intelligent forces of the colored people have hammered home the suggestion that every mistake of one colored man or woman may result in casting a reflection on the whole group. The theory is, 'Be clean for your own sake, but remember that every good thing you do goes to the credit of all of us.'"[4]

The experience of Chicago between World War I and 1960 is important for understanding the spatial reorganization of waste management processes in the United States during this period. While Chicago is especially well documented by journalists and sociologists, the social, economic, and political forces that altered the city's demography were at work throughout the nation, as were the cultural attitudes concerning waste and hygiene. The appeals to cleanliness that Sandburg observed in Chicago were being made in African American communities across the nation. The insistence upon "hammering home" the lesson was being made because hygiene just might be an effective weapon in resisting the racist discrimination facing African American communities experiencing a new upheaval. The American people in 1919 had just experienced two waves of mass migrations to and within the country and were about to embark on an unprecedented racial segregation of residential space, a change that continues to affect the spatial organization of people, resources, and wastes in the United States.

An Urban Nation

The first step of this change was intensive urbanization. If Chicago's ascent to metropolitan giant was the most dramatic, it was not in isolation. In 1920, for the first time, the U.S. Census of Population recorded more Americans living in urban areas than in rural areas. From New York City to San Francisco, Minneapolis to New Orleans, the size of cities grew in terms of both population and physical structures. New York City annexed Brooklyn at the same time skyscrapers with steel infrastructure reshaped its skyline.[5]

The systems required to keep these cities functioning were largely in place by 1920. No perfect system to manage garbage existed, and reliance upon incinerators and dumps varied from municipality to municipality. Yet a consensus in urban waste disposal had emerged: waste should be removed not only from the home but also from the neighborhood as completely and as quickly as possible. Cities allocated their budgets to develop departments of streets and sanitation to ensure clean neighborhoods.

The task was formidable. Cities with millions of inhabitants produced far more sewage, garbage, and rubbish in 1920 than had been generated a mere half century earlier. Further, per capita disposal had increased as personal hygiene standards were raised. Cities were more crowded than Americans ever remembered.[6]

Were cities dirtier? That is arguable. By 1920, the automobile had largely (if not completely) displaced the horse from the urban road, greatly reducing the solid waste problem of horse manure from the streets. Municipal sanitation workers could concentrate more on removing the influx of garbage from neighborhoods rather than dealing with horses.[7]

The achievements of municipalities to address the biological waste hazards of contaminated water in the late nineteenth century allowed cities to continue to house unprecedented densities of humanity. Water treatment and sewage had made considerable strides by 1920. Indoor plumbing was not universal, not in the most crowded tenements, yet it was widespread—a key factor in the elimination of typhoid epidemics. By 1920, 87 percent of Americans living in urban communities had access to sewer systems that effectively reduced instances of epidemic disease. Engineers' claims that urban water was cleaner and safer in 1920 than it was in 1880 had a basis in fact.[8]

The air, however, had not cleared. Both industrial production and the requirements of home heating relied heavily upon fossil fuels. Coal— abundant in fields throughout Appalachia and the Midwest—remained the most affordable fuel factories, trains, and home furnaces could use. Yet coal, particularly the soft bituminous coal found in the Midwest, produced thick, black smoke dense with particulate matter. On cold days when home use of coal was heavy, Pittsburgh's skies appeared black at noon. Boosters and local newspapers in St. Louis, Chicago, Cincinnati, and Pittsburgh bickered as they claimed any city other than the claimant's home was far smokier.[9]

Smoke control was perhaps the great challenge in municipal housekeeping between the wars. Civic clubs had pressured municipal governments to remove or reduce the black clouds over cities since the late nineteenth century. As air quality worsened in the 1920s and 1930s, these demands grew louder. The civil engineer Raymond Tucker proposed a plan for the city of Saint Louis to regulate the coal fuel being sold so that the dirtiest coal would not get into furnaces. St. Louis passed an ordinance on Tucker's model in 1938, and dozens of cities followed suit over the next ten years. Significantly, transitions from coal to cleaner forms of domestic heat (natural and manufactured gas, electricity) were largely complete by 1955, causing the skies to clear. (Tailpipe emissions from automobiles produced less opaque pollution.) In the years prior to this transition, real estate agents selling suburban subdivisions placed advertisements in newspapers imploring urban residents to "escape the smoky city" and come live in the clean air of the suburbs.[10]

If the water was perhaps cleaner, and the air dirtier, the land in the cities of the newly urbanized United States in 1920 was a battleground of hygiene. Progressive educational and advocacy efforts on hygiene continued. Systems devoted to rubbish removal were now in place but not comprehensive. Where incinerators were employed, they largely shifted pollution from land to air. Ash remained as a toxic residue of incineration burdening the land.

The urban dump was specialized space that removed the burden of waste disposal from all the city's streets, concentrating it. Yet if the dump was still situated in the city, would it be adjacent to neighborhoods where the odors and vermin would affect local hygiene standards?[11]

Finally, by 1920, the informal private systems of scrap collecting, processing, and selling took waste materials and fed them back into production. To what extent was this system one that could—or should—coexist with the residential functions of the growing cities?

The answers that governments, businesses, and private citizens settled on for these questions led to the next great shift in the newly urbanized nation. After World War I, metropolitan space—comprising both cities and adjacent suburbs—underwent a variety of changes that reordered where people lived and where waste was put.

Demographic and sanitary pressures had informed the American urban experience since the colonial era. The intensity of industrialization and population density after the Civil War had exacerbated these pressures, and opportunities in monetizing waste handling services also informed urban difficulties. The number of people working to haul, eliminate, or trade waste materials had increased. Opportunities to profit from scrap derived from a set of economic and cultural changes in the United States that made the nation a more intensive industrial producer with a population of more conspicuous consumers. More materials—including textiles, old metals, paper, and rubber, industrial chemicals, as well as existing biological wastes—were deemed waste by industry and consumers alike. Industrial scrap included retired train engines and railroad tracks, scrapped steamships and worn machinery. Railroads, shipping businesses, and factories wanted to remove the old and seemingly worthless material from their premises and were eager to find takers for the old metal.[12]

The increase in industrial scrap was joined by an even greater increase in the amount of materials American consumers disposed of beginning in the late nineteenth century. Industrialization had two important social effects: greater wages and salaries led many Americans to change their attitudes concerning consumption and waste, and industrialization produced new economic opportunities for immigrants. Growing firms after the Civil War created a substantial middle class of managers, bureaucrats, and clerical workers. As the middle class grew, it developed a growing consumer culture in the late nineteenth and early twentieth centuries, with the rise of department stores and catalogs catering to an expanding mass market. New patterns of consumption and waste disposal reshaped the way Americans valued objects, and changing attitudes provided the context for a national scrap trade dominated by immigrants.[13]

Americans had more objects; middle-class consumers consumed consciously. Clothing and accessories had been traditional markers of social status in the antebellum period, so much so that escaped slaves in the North frequently passed as freedman by wearing more refined clothing. By the end of the century, however, the mass production of clothing, watches, and other accoutrements allowed the working classes to afford to look similar to their middle-class counterparts.[14]

Ever mindful of their upward social ambitions and wary of being confused with the working classes, many native-born middle-class consumers developed accentuated attitudes toward appearance and behavior to better identify themselves as early as 1830. Concern over dress sense, proper eating etiquette, housekeeping, and public behavior all led to a proliferation of prescriptive literature and consumer items at the turn of the century designed to set members of the middle class apart from those in the working classes, resulting in what the economist Thorstein Veblen sardonically termed "conspicuous consumption," as he viewed the quest for social standing through the purchase of goods and education.[15]

An important facet of the evolving middle-class sensibility was a focus on hygiene, a focus that helped reshape the systems of American cities. City streets once combined the functions of playground and dump, where children played and household waste was dumped. Even before the automobile began to dominate use of the street, concern for public health developed systems in which public or private entities washed the streets and took refuse to dispose of in dumps or incinerators. Indoor toilets connected to sewers were common in cities of the 1930s. Workers collected garbage from residential neighborhoods on a weekly basis. Americans threw progressively more amounts of a wide variety of materials out of their homes between 1850 and 1930, in part owing to concerns over germs and hygiene, in part because rising standards of living and mass production allowed for easy replacement of consumer goods such as razors and clothing. The American house in 1930 had more things in it that it did a century before, and for its middle-class inhabitants, the desire to have those things be clean and orderly was a driving force in the classification of old materials as wastes to be eliminated from the household.[16]

And there were many, many more old materials on hand to be eliminated by 1920 then there had been in 1860. The United States increased its production capacity, transforming itself into a society of mass production and mass consumption. New production techniques produced items of mass consumption ranging from canned goods and razor blades to automobiles with the advent of Ford's Model T. Chicagoans' ability to purchase products was aided in the early twentieth century by the presence of giant department stores like Marshall Field's and, later, supermarkets like Dominick's.[17]

Running water, gas, and electricity became mainstream features of the new suburbs before World War II, but tenements and aging housing stock in the cities frequently left residents with few means to stay clean. Europeans who had come from areas that saw improvements in water filtration and sewage in the late nineteenth century did not share Americans' unique aversion to waste materials. The differences between native-born Americans and immigrants regarding waste and hygiene manifested in many ways, as settlement house workers and public health officials attempted to reform urban immigrants' practices from using soap, to discouraging the keeping of livestock, to practicing accepted methods of kitchen hygiene. Many efforts were successful; after all, immigrants had their own taboos and practices regarding wastes (including, for example, kosher dietary laws among Jews), and several were adaptable to their new homes. Yet the cultural differences produced different attitudes regarding handling wastes as commodities— and though wastes were taboo, some were also coveted.[18]

Urban Ecology and Modern Environmental Inequalities

Tensions in Chicago concerning wastes fell upon immigrants and African Americans. Immigrants living near the stockyards were subject to noxious odors and polluted water. Jewish and Italian immigrants who worked in the waste trades were blamed by local reformers such as Jane Addams and the Chicago Juvenile Protection Association for being "moral menaces" to urban children. Whether European immigrants and their children were blamed for unsanitary conditions or identified as victims of unsanitary conditions, the local Progressive community actively fought for more sanitary communities for them.[19]

Racial tensions in Chicago evolved during and after World War I, with the 1919 race riots revealing the acute problems of segregation and density facing the community. Settlement houses in the 1920s were less amenable to African American neighborhoods than they were to the European immigrant wards; over the next forty years, sanitary burdens became especially pronounced in majority African American neighborhoods. Diligent though Chicago's African American community may have been about personal hygiene at the dawn of the 1920s, forces converged to dump increasing amounts of waste near their homes and schools.

If Chicago was a large (and well-documented) example of this unhappy development, it was by no means unique in the African American experience. As American communities rationalized the urban landscape into residential and industrial areas, they also intensified spatial segregation based upon skin color. Between 1915 and 1960, the consequences of these developments meant creation (or expansion) of ghettoes seen by public officials as dirty and increasingly seen by public and private waste management systems as repositories for waste. This reshaping of the urban landscape was influenced by the continued idea that blacks somehow polluted white neighborhoods, poisoning the community and devaluing the property. Instead of diminishing over time, this attitude proliferated, ultimately becoming federal policy that reshaped cities and suburbs over several decades.[20]

The seeds for that reshaping were already apparent in 1919, when Sandburg described the interaction between the banker and the newly arrived mother from Alabama. Sandburg did not simply happen upon the corner of Michigan Avenue and East 31st by chance. He was in the middle of writing a series of articles for the *Chicago Daily News* on the undercurrents of the July 1919 race riots that killed dozens and injured hundreds. Later published as a book, Sandburg's articles underlined the growing tensions in the city. Self-identified whites' fear of blacks polluting their otherwise pristine neighborhoods unleashed two extreme responses. One was terrorism. The other was reordering urban space.[21]

Terror in the form of mob violence greeted African Americans in Chicago. A dispute over access to a beach on a hot day escalated into a week of rioting that killed thirty-eight people. The riots of 1919 were years in the making, as appeals to grow the African American labor force in Chicago conflicted with white resistance to living near black people. The rise of urban industry served to pull migrants to cities, including millions coming to the United States for work. Factory work making steel, railways, automobiles, and buildings; refining petroleum; and turning animals into meat, trees into lumber, and plants into processed foods required unprecedented numbers of workers to continually produce commodities. First- and second-generation immigrants often enticed relatives and acquaintances in their home countries with promises of a better life.

African American newspapers such as the *Pittsburgh Courier* and *Chicago Defender* openly recruited readers in the Deep South to relocate to the papers' home cities for better jobs, more money, and perhaps a less hostile society. Immigration restrictions after the outbreak of war in Europe in 1914 meant, potentially, better opportunities for African Americans in urban factories once the flow of cheap labor from abroad had ceased. The combination of push and pull factors to cities meant that the period between the Civil War and the end of World War I marked a dramatic shift toward urbanism; by the end of the war, with the heightened industrial production needed to fight the war, the United States was for the first time a majority urban society.[22]

The rise of urban society brought with it confirmation of Jefferson's fears of inequality, depravation, and disease. Vast economic gulfs between the owners of the means of production and their employees emerged. Some oligarchs, such as George Pullman, attempted to reshape the lives of their workers with planned communities. Others, such as Andrew Carnegie, attempted to enrich the lives of their workers with cultural institutions such as libraries. But most—those two men included—used violence to quell labor unrest, as workers faced dangerous conditions on the job, crowded and polluted conditions in their homes, and often more precarious conditions on the streets of their neighborhoods. Decades of immigration were joined during World War I by a large influx of rural Southern African Americans into urban areas, exacerbating crowded conditions in industrial cities, including New York City, Philadelphia, Boston, Cleveland, Oakland, Detroit, Gary, St. Louis, Kansas City, Washington, DC, and Los Angeles.[23]

With mass migration came tensions over employment opportunities, housing, and other amenities. The Great Migration immediately provoked tensions. In 1914, a *Chicago Defender* columnist lamented that "Afro-American people in increasing numbers are refused the accommodations of public places," violating Illinois state laws. Even

when racist acts made it to the court system, Chicago's courts themselves discriminated, and the police especially degraded black Chicagoans and treated them as inferiors. Thus, black Chicagoans new and old
alike were "more and more being reduced to a fixed status of social and
political inferiority."[24]

The most visible evidence of this hardening racist status was an
increase in residential segregation. Chicago's black community prior to
World War I was largely segregated by both cultural de facto forces and
de jure practices such as the enforcement of restrictive covenants pro-
hibiting sale of homes to African Americans. Such practices were also
used against other groups, including Jews. As the African American
population of Chicago grew, white impulses to restrict neighborhoods
from including black residents intensified. The Black Belt of Chicago
grew on the city's South and West Sides, away from the central business district. Many of the city's wealthier white residents moved to the
North Shore in the early twentieth century, leaving behind older but
nicer housing; Chicago's Bronzeville, Douglas, and Kenwood neighborhoods became central to African American life and business. Smaller
and more decrepit housing abandoned by European immigrants who
had improved their economic prospects was available west of the Loop
(the downtown area of Chicago) in Austin, Lawndale, and adjoining
neighborhoods of the West Side. In smaller numbers than the Great
Migration of African Americans, people from Mexico and Puerto Rico
emigrated to Chicago's Near West Side between 1940 and 1960s. Urban
neighborhoods that had been majority European immigrants before
1915 underwent a transition to majority African American and Hispanic
between 1915 and 1960.[25]

These neighborhoods were crowded and often lacked access to
the services that had become priorities for urban sanitarians after the
Civil War. A 1922 study on race relations in Chicago reported acute
waste management problems in black neighborhoods. In a South Side
neighborhood, the report concluded that "rooms were poorly lighted
and ventilated, the sanitation bad, and the alley and grounds about
the houses covered with rubbish and refuse."[26] Houses in the Black
Belt were observably in poorer repair than houses in majority Polish,
Bohemian, and Jewish neighborhoods. In many cases, the City Commission on Race Relations found houses on the South and West Sides

unfit for human habitation and recommended that the city condemn and raze properties. The report concluded that one of the many necessary actions to improve Chicago's race relations was better enforcement of health and sanitary laws, particular regular collection of rubbish and garbage "in areas of Negro residence, where the Commission has found these matters to be shamefully neglected."[27]

Moving beyond those neighborhoods was difficult and dangerous. The color line made housing a constant struggle for African Americans. James "Jack" Isbell remembered that his family, living on the South Side of Chicago, moved thirteen times between 1929 and 1932, each time in cramped apartments: "Even if you could afford a big apartment, you couldn't find one to rent. The landlords cut up all the larger apartments and converted them into smaller units so they could make a lot more money."

Residential segregation produced longer commutes for workers employed as domestic cleaners. Isbell remembered that his mother "worked out from home for a private family. She would go across [the half-mile-wide] Washington Park and work for the white folks in Hyde Park." After the time spent commuting and working, "She would come home in the evening and she used to do laundry for the people around our neighborhood."[28]

A few enterprising real estate agents such as Jesse Binga developed a technique of "block busting," surreptitiously employing a white buyer to purchase a home in a white neighborhood and then moving African American residents in, causing white neighbors to flee and open up more housing opportunities to Binga's clients. Fears of such activity among white homeowners associations produced warnings and worse. The *Chicago Defender* reported on terroristic threats left on the doors of black newcomers that their homes would be burned down or blown up, the rationale being, as given in a 1919 statement by a homeowner's association in Hyde Park, that every homeowner had the right to defend his property with "every means at his disposal" and that this must happen as Hyde Park's residents were being "menaced by a possible Negro invasion" that would be disastrous.[29]

By 1920, a unique and troubling pattern defined Chicago's African American community. While particular neighborhoods had been defined by a dominant ethnic or racial group—Ukrainian Village,

Chinatown, and Greektown are three Chicago neighborhoods that retain their names in the twenty-first century—all were a good deal more heterogeneous in the Census of Population than the increasingly segregated black belts were becoming. Race determined one's ability to live in particular neighborhoods above and beyond factors such as income, occupation, or longevity in the city.[30]

The most influential explanation for the replacement of one neighborhood population by another was labeled "ecological succession" by the Chicago School of Sociology, especially in the work of Robert E. Park, Ernest W. Burgess, and Roderick D. McKenzie in the 1920s and 1930s, which dealt with the residential succession process. The "invasion and succession" model suggests that suburbanization of the middle class leaves the inner city to new minority groups who create ghettos. It theorizes that newly arrived (and often poor) immigrants/ethnic groups will occupy inner-city neighborhoods first; later, some economically well off people from this group will enter the American mainstream and move to the suburbs to find better living conditions. When immigrants stay in the inner city, most live in segregated neighborhoods. When they move out to the suburbs, their experiences vary from being totally dispersed, to being relatively concentrated, to being highly segregated, depending upon the ethnic group and the time and place in question. With its concern for residential neighborhood change and succession, the model of ecological succession reflected the experiences of many white ethnic groups.[31]

What did the Chicago School mean by "ecological succession"? The city, modelled as an organism, is a biological entity with specialized organs and functions interacting together in a system. When that system undergoes change, or crisis—for example, when it is affected by new factors such as mass migration from Europe and the South—the population of city neighborhoods succeeds in predictable ways. This concept of the city shaped urban ecology (and the planning that would reshape metropolitan areas) and public policy.[32]

This focus on demographics places the urban ecology model squarely in the existing tradition of social Darwinism. The model tests an assumption that assumes that assimilation is the norm and ultimate goal of all in the city, and any problems of crime or other disorder is due to the fact that "the foreign element in our population has not succeeded in assimilating American culture and does not conform to the American mores."[33]

Park and his colleagues, writing in the solo first person, display an evolutionary model of race that assumes eventual progress. Unsurprisingly, given the assumptions social scientists were making at the time, African Americans remained at the bottom of this model, though Park and his co-authors saw hope for all in the future:

> The peoples who are making, or have made in recent years, the most progress in America today are, I suspect, the Jews, the Negroes, and the Japanese. There is, of course, no comparison to be made between the Jew, the Japanese, and the Negro as to their racial competence. Of all the immigrant peoples in the United States, the Jews are the most able and the most progressive; the Negro, on the other hand, is just emerging and is still a little afraid of the consequences of his newly acquired race-consciousness.
>
> What is alike in the case of the Jew, the Negro, and the Japanese is that their conflict with America has been grave enough to create in each a new sense of racial identity, and to give the sort of solidarity that grows out of a common cause. It is the existence in a people of the sense of a cause which finally determines their group efficiency.[34]

Sanitary Conditions in Black Metropolis

Students of Robert Park differed with him on racial categorization and extended the model of urban ecology to assess racial disparities in urban living conditions. The sociologists St. Clair Drake and Horace Roscoe Cayton most famously provided a thorough study of African American life in the same city that Park, Burgess, and McKenzie studied. Published in 1945 as *Black Metropolis*, Drake and Cayton's study provides a portrait of African American living conditions right before the exodus of middle-class whites to the suburbs exacerbated urban racial segregation.

In the wake of the 1919 riot, the governor of Illinois set up a commission to investigate the conditions of African American life in Chicago. Among its findings were recommendations to improve housing and sanitary services. "In such matters as rubbish and garbage disposal, as well, as street repair," Drake and Cayton observed, "Negro communities were said to be shamefully neglected."[35]

Booker T. Washington's turn-of-the-century concerns over hygiene and African American status resonated in 1945. Drake and Cayton reported that community leaders in Chicago were concerned over whether members of the community would enjoy any of the economic gains secured during World War II and that newspapers like the *Defender* carried articles "urging Negroes to be quiet, clean, orderly, and reliable, so that The Race will not acquire an unfavorable reputation."[36]

If racial tensions increased after World War I, so, too, did African American political power. As Chicago's Black Belt grew, Republican African American politician—and ally of Mayor "Big Bill" Thompson—Oscar DePriest rose to power. In 1923, he slated two of his candidates against the Republican "regular" candidates for aldermen of the Second and Third Wards. He charged the incumbents with responsibility for "dirty streets and alleys, the growth of vice, the misery brought upon the families of the discharged officeholders, the lack of adequate police protection, the lack of bathing beaches and recreational facilities." DePriest's People's Movement polled about 6,000 votes in each ward, but its candidates lost. Despite the electoral defeat, DePriest's rhetoric on the stump revealed concerns about crime and sanitation shared by residents in the growing Black Belt. He would continue his campaigning and serve three terms in the U.S. House of Representatives before losing his seat in a Democratic wave election in 1934.[37]

In 1945, Drake and Cayton observed the concentration of waste trading and industrial activities in the Black Belt. During the Depression years, thousands of homeless men and women floated from room to room in the cheap lodging houses and hotels sandwiched in among the junkyards, factories, and warehouses of the rundown Black Belt areas near the Loop.[38]

Industrial cites boomed in the 1940s with wartime demand, and industry grew after the war. Industrial cities' good times were short-lived as suburbanization and the decline of domestic manufacturing in the United States after the late 1950s took their toll. African American concentration in Rust Belt cities coincided with the departure of industrial work and much of the overall population. The historian Thomas Sugrue notes that, in the second half of the twentieth century, Detroit lost nearly a million people and hundreds of thousands of jobs. This process isolated African Americans in persistent, concentrated, and racially segregated poverty.[39]

The historian Kenneth T. Jackson observes that a combination of racist real estate practices in the private sector combined with racially informed federal mortgage insurance regulations to exacerbate residential segregation after World War II, with the urban periphery being whiter and wealthier, with greater access to college educations, professional employment, and the amenities of middle-class life. "Because low-income areas, public-housing projects, and minority groups live so close to city centers, economist Richard F. Muth calculated that the median income in American cites tends to rise at about 8 percent per mile as one moves away from the business district, and that it doubles in ten miles."[40]

In contrast, metropolitan areas in other parts of the world had the inverse, with working-class council estates in Great Britain emerging on the periphery of affluent urban centers and similar socioeconomic spatial distributions found in the metropolitan areas of Egypt, India, Bulgaria, Italy, Spain, Brazil, Argentina, Chile, Venezuela, and Mexico. The American impoverishment of urban areas in the twentieth century was distinctive, representing a cultural distrust of cities rooted in the colonial era. The Jeffersonian distrust of cities endured as cities grew more crowded and polluted in the years between the Civil War and World War II. Streetcars and later the automobile offered urban workers the opportunity to live away from the crowds and grime. Jackson observed that suburbia offered the exciting prospect that disorder, prostitution, and mayhem could be kept at a distance, far away in the festering metropolis.[41]

By that time, suburban developers had found great success luring urban residents out of the smoky cities and into the woods and meadows beyond city lines. The mass exodus from the city to the suburb did not occur until after World War II, when federally insured mortgages allowed millions to purchase new homes for the first time. However, the lure of the suburbs had roots before 1945. Jackson's history of American suburbs argues that a pastoral ideal vital to our understanding of suburban life was in place before the Civil War. Thomas Jefferson's laments about urban industry did not die with the eighteenth century;

Andrew Jackson Downing and Frederick Law Olmsted sought refuge from the city in their park designs. The notion of the urban park was a natural refuge from urban life, even if that natural space (such as New York City's Central Park, designed by Olmsted and Calvert Vaux) was constructed and manipulated by humans.[42]

The pastoral ideal—an environment filled with trees and green grass, without smoke, sewage, and filth—was central to the marketing of suburban subdivisions even before World War I. The historian Adam Rome's account of the rise of the Country Club District (a pioneering suburban development outside of Kansas City) places the desire for clean living at the center of the development's pitch to prospective residents—as well as the desire to live with self-identified white people.[43]

Legal and cultural practices to keep new suburbs white were commonplace at the turn of the twentieth century. The Country Club District sold its spacious homes and yards only to buyers who accepted racially restrictive covenants and who joined the Homeowners Association, the purpose of which was to supervise the quality of private lawn care, the cleaning of streets, and the collection of garbage. These provisions allowed the Country Club District to become one of the most exclusive and desirable areas to live in the Kansas City metropolitan area.[44]

Patterns within the real estate market increased residential racial segregation in the first third of the twentieth century. Obsessions with whiteness dominated real estate appraisals; real estate expert Frederick Morrison Babcock wrote in 1924 that appraisers must pay attention to who were moving into a neighborhood as one should always settle "near persons of the same social standing [and] same races" and that appraisers should factor the rise in the population of less desirable people into predicting price declines throughout the area.[45]

During the Great Depression, concern over the proper value of real estate in a moribund market grew, as did the obsession with desirable and undesirable areas. The Chicago School of Sociology, already concerned with models of urban ecology, contributed to this concern with the publication of Homer Hoyt's dissertation on real estate, *One Hundred Years of Land Values in Chicago* (1933) and book *The Structure and Growth of Residential Neighborhoods in American Cities* (1939). In his work, Hoyt demonstrated that the influx of low-status residents would damage the value of areas in the long term. Observing the "block busting" in Chicago, Hoyt wrote that the introduction of African Americans into a neighborhood would first raise prices (as the pioneers had to pay a premium to break the color barrier) and then precipitate a drastic decline.[46]

Noxious urban industry, Hoyt argued, triggered residential mobility for those who had the economic and cultural capital to move away from the central city. One factor in suburbanization and residential movement toward the urban periphery was unpleasant conditions in industrial areas of the city. "In the case of the Stock Yards," Hoyt observed, "the higher class of employees sought to get away from the noise and odors of the industrial district as well as from the old neighborhoods occupied by unskilled laborers of the new immigration or of the colored race."[47] Hoyt elaborated that "there can be little doubt, however, that the presence of the colored population in the areas east of State Street is the specific cause of lower land values there" and that "the undesirable racial factor is so merged with other unattractive features, such as proximity to factories, poor transportation, old and obsolete buildings, poor street improvements, and the presence of criminal or vice elements, that the separate effect of race cannot be disentangled."[48]

By 1933, then, urban areas with black residents were already identified as sufficiently undesirable that whites with the means to do so would move away. Provisions within the New Deal exacerbated and catalyzed unprecedented segregation between the end of World War II and 1980. Faced with a stagnant housing market, the federal government moved to insure home mortgages in 1935, relieving banks of the worry of loaning money to people over periods of twenty to thirty years. A new government entity, the Home Owners Loan Corporation (HOLC), evaluated the wisdom of loans to particular people in particular places. How the HOLC did this was by adapting existing appraisal methods from various markets and systematizing appraisal across the nation. In doing so, the HOLC made assumptions regarding the useful or productive life of housing it financed. The method it used was to divide cities into neighborhoods and send appraisers into them with elaborate questionnaires asking about the occupation, income, and ethnicity of the inhabitants and the age, type of construction, price range, sales demand, and general condition of the housing stock. The answers to these questions allowed for investors all over the country to evaluate whether an area was on the rise or on the decline.[49]

The data generated by the HOLC's questionnaires could be generated visually, creating maps of metropolitan areas showing patterns of desirable and undesirable neighborhoods. In doing so, the HOLC created a new form of systematic racism, "redlining." The rating system that emerged from the HOLC's questionnaires undervalued neighborhoods that were dense, mixed, or aging. Four grades of quality—imaginatively entitled First, Second, Third, and Fourth, with corresponding code letters of A, B, C, and D and colors of green, blue, yellow, and red—were established. First grade/A/green areas had every desirable trait—new buildings and prosperous and ethnically appropriate residents, and they would be in demand regardless of the overall state of the American economy. Such neighborhoods had to be "white"—at the time of the maps' creation, that did not include Jews. Jewish neighborhoods, or even those with an "infiltration of Jews," could not be considered "best" any more than they could be considered "American."

Jews might be able to live in the Second grade/B/blue areas, ones that were "still desirable" yet had "reached their peak." They were still not bad investments, as they were predicted to remain stable for years, but they were decidedly inferior to the First grade of neighborhoods. Third grade/C/yellow neighborhoods were usually described as "definitely declining." Fourth grade/D/red neighborhoods were defined as areas "in which the things taking place in C areas have already happened."[50]

The HOLC's assumptions about neighborhoods conflated physical attributes of the built environment with racial and economic attributes of the people living in the buildings. This model equated physical deterioration and demographic change, and as it included questions about desirable racial and ethnic mixes, the mere presence of particular undesirable people was enough social pollution to downgrade an entire neighborhood as an unfit investment. A single Jewish resident could prevent a neighborhood from becoming First grade; a single African American resident could relegate a neighborhood to Fourth grade. On a map, such an area would be colored red, thus the practice of classifying neighborhoods housing African Americans as declining became known as "redlining." In every HOLC office in the United States, maps were available to clearly and quickly identify the "red" and undesirable areas in the local vicinity. These maps allowed the HOLC and Federal Housing Authority (FHA) to efficiently grant insured mortgages to white people living in racially exclusive developments of new, clean homes.[51]

The effects of this systematic racism were slow to come during the moribund housing market of the late 1930s and World War II. Once, however, the war was over and the suburban housing boom began, the racist mortgage insurance system reshaped the racial map of American settlement patterns. By the early 1950s, whites throughout American metropolitan areas had rushed to the suburban periphery, owning new homes with the aid of federally insured mortgages. The federal government subsidized a great boom in individual prosperity, as these homes indeed kept and built upon their value, generating wealth not only for those who were prosperous before the war but also elevating many working-class whites into a middle class that was the largest in the nation's history.[52]

This prosperity came at a great price. The cities left behind lost a massive tax base to their suburban fringes, and the people who could not get loans in the new suburbs had to make do with either older housing stock left behind or move into newer public housing that the FHA created in recognition that housing problems persisted in aging cities. Being black in the wake of these policies determined not only where you could live but what the value of your neighborhood was. Although the mortgage insurance maps were developed in the mid-1930s, they endured well after the war. On November 19, 1948, Assistant FHA Commissioner W. J. Lockwood could write that FHA "has never insured a housing project of mixed occupancy" because of the expectation that "such projects would probably in a short period of time become all-Negro or all-white," and even after the Supreme Court ruled against the legality of race-based lending in 1948, the real estate practices that both shaped the policies and that were transformed by them continued to discriminate against African Americans.[53]

The lasting damage done by the national government, Jackson argues, was that it legitimized ethnic and racial discrimination and developed policies encouraging white abandonment of large sections of older, industrial cities owing to both the demography and built environment of these areas. The model became a self-fulfilling prophecy;

without cooperation from the government and the private lending institutions that depended upon the government for stability, capital fled these "declining" areas, putting them in decline. To banks, integrated urban neighborhoods were poor investments, so the residents in areas with any African American residents grew poorer, and their properties increasingly blighted. By the 1960s, sociologists and historians could observe the creation of large ghettoes within most cities.[54] Thus cities had decayed, dirty buildings populated by black people, and residential suburbs featured white homeowners in new houses fleeing fears of urban grime and racial diversity. One white resident of Chicago's Kenwood neighborhood told Marjorie Echols in the mid-fifties, "We're moving because the sun is setting in this neighborhood."[55]

Zoning

Aside from the changes in residential financing and mortgage insurance, another regulatory tool influenced the spatial patterns of race and waste in American communities. Zoning, the practice of designating areas of a municipality specifically for residential, commercial, or industrial use, became a popular tool of American cities in the 1920s. New York City enacted the first comprehensive zoning ordinance in the United States in 1916; by 1932, 766 cities had followed suit.[56]

Zoning adopted the urban ecological models of the Chicago School and attempted to rationalize urban systems and processes. By rationalizing space, municipal zoning could minimize threats to health, children, and neighbors by waste-generating and waste-dealing businesses and other nuisance industries. In the seven years after New York City established zoning, Philadelphia and Chicago enacted zoning regulations to regulate where scrap yards and junk shops could be located, forbidding them in residential areas. In doing so, the Philadelphia Bureau of Health's Division of Housing and Sanitation explained, regulation was put "upon those persons handling waste without any respect for sanitary law or for the health and comfort of their employees."[57]

In 1923, at the beginning of Chicago reform Democratic mayor William Dever's sole term, the city passed a zoning ordinance banning scrap businesses from operating in residential neighborhoods. The zoning ordinance intended for nuisance industries to operate in industrial areas, away from residential neighborhoods. Yet enforcement of the new regulation did not eliminate waste management, storage, and trading in urban residential neighborhoods so much as it racially segregated it.

Initially, African American newspapers welcomed the advent of zoning. Reporting on 1922 plans to institute zoning in Chicago, the *Chicago Defender* exclaimed there was a time when a landowner could do anything he wished with his property, even using his land as "a garbage dump, even though it were situated between two houses," but nuisance laws had sought to control such abuses, and zoning would further strengthen the state's ability to regulate unwanted activities.[58]

In practice, zoning regulations were at best erratically enforced in Chicago (at worst, as in the case of racial covenants restricting home ownership, they were de jure racism) and other cities, exacerbating racial inequalities.[59] Although waste handling and dumping were prohibited in residential neighborhoods, police rarely attended to waste dumping in African American neighborhoods. Despite zoning prohibitions, residents of Cleveland protested the siting of a junkyard next to the largely African American Central High School in 1937. This situation was in stark contrast with white schools, protestors explained, where rubbish and scrap iron would not be tolerated.[60]

After pressure from a neighborhood volunteer committee in 1945, Pittsburgh Fourth District Highways and Sewers supervisor John L. Mullen pledged to send ten garbage trucks into the Hill District to remove the "hokey piles" of rubbish that had amassed in the neighborhood, and local politicians remarked on the possibility of requiring landlords to provide adequate rubbish disposal to tenants in an effort to clean up the Hill.[61] Despite these pledges, residents of the Hill District continued to complain about trash; five years later, the chairman of the Mayor's Committee for a Cleaner City, James F. Hillman, complained that the Hill's situation was "critical" and a problem that time was not healing. Mayor David L. Lawrence pledged to cooperate with neighborhood groups to develop more comprehensive trash collection and properly enforce ordinances relating to public health and sanitation.[62] Over the next three years, the city sponsored annual cleanup campaigns each May; in one such campaign, Public Works Director James S. Devlin announced that city crews had picked up 1,500 tons of rubbish and debris over one week in the neighborhood.[63]

Special collections occasionally alleviated acute problems, but chronic lack of regular collection plagued African American neighborhoods in several cities during the second half of the twentieth century. Often complaints to the police would go ignored, or legal action would be inadequate to correct negligent behavior. Chicago landlords in the 1940s and 1950s could be fined $5 for not providing regular collection, far less than the cost to employ private collection services.[64] Inadequate garbage collection was one of the grievances that spurred a successful voter registration drive and the election of Harold Washington as Chicago's first African American mayor in 1983.[65]

Hispanic New York City residents reported similar conditions. A 1949 investigation of Puerto Rican living conditions in East Harlem found streets full of garbage despite residents being personally clean and tidy because landlords did not keep up maintenance and collection. Elizabeth Ridder of the Casita Maria settlement house said: "The Puerto Rican women are instinctively clean and are tidy housekeepers. It only takes a small number of garbage throwers to spoil the appearance of an entire community."[66]

Decades of poor sanitation services combined with worsening economic conditions to make it difficult for urban residents to maintain clean homes. Unequal sanitation services occasionally led to legal action. In 1969, lawyers from the National Association for the Advancement of Colored People Legal Defense and Educational Fund argued on behalf of the African American residents of Shaw, Mississippi, that they deserved equal services. In a town of 25,000 people, the complaint read, the 1,500 African American residents received "sharply lower levels" of public services, including fewer modern sewers and less garbage collection. A federal appeals court ruled in favor of the plaintiffs in 1971.[67]

African Americans noticed the unequal concentration of waste handling businesses in their neighborhoods. An editorial in the *Chicago Defender* complained about the prevalence of junk dealing in African American neighborhoods. "A close scrutiny of these junk carts reveals that they do most of their business in our neighborhoods; their shops are always in close proximity to where we live, and they ply their wagons up and down our alleys and streets from day to day; buying from us the commodities which they market."[68] Junkyards could be used as fronts for other illicit operations, including gambling, prostitution, and drug dealing.[69]

In 1969, Chicago public housing residents protested inadequate garbage collection of the piled up garbage at their homes on the city's South and West Sides by dumping the piles of waste into the street.[70] Tenants at one South Side building reported that garbage had been collected only twice between October 1968 and February 1969 and that uncontrolled vermin was also a problem. Over sixty years after Upton Sinclair had deplored the "great open sewer" of waste plaguing Chicago's residents, African Americans in the city continued to suffer from inadequate sanitary conditions owing to neglect from municipal services.[71]

Waste and Race Reordered

In the years between 1915 and 1960, urban spaces across the United States had been reorganized with race as a primary organizing factor. In the words of the historian Lillia Fernandez, "Race had been inscribed into the very geography of the [American] city, and urban space reflected and reinforced the city's polarized racial relations and inequalities."[72]

Racial polarization in Chicago was dramatic, worsening over the twentieth century. The demographers Nancy Denton and Douglas Massey observed in their book *American Apartheid* that residential segregation in Chicago intensified after World War I to the point that neighborhoods on the city's South and West Sides were composed of over 80 percent African American residents in the late twentieth century. The areas, commonly referred to as the "Black Belt" as early as the 1920s, spanned over thirty city blocks in length.[73]

This ghetto—more populous, larger in area, and more segregated than Chicago's earlier slums—concentrated the city's poverty, conflating race with class. The "Black Belts" were also areas of selective law enforcement. After Republican mayor "Big Bill" Thompson regained the office in 1927, Chicago's South and West Sides became famous for hosting speakeasies, prostitution, numbers running, and other illegal activities with the tacit approval of the police and City Hall. Scrap dealing was not as glamorous as those other vices, but scrap continued to be desired by steel fabricators and continued to be disposed of by Chicago's residents. After the 1923 ordinance, Chicago's scrap firms moved into industrial areas on the South Side, but they also moved into the residential Black Belt on the city's South and West Sides. Over the next forty years, the African American population of these neighborhoods became more concentrated as dilapidated tenements and houses were replaced by high-rise public housing developments located near freeways and industrial areas.[74]

The junk shops, scrap yards, and peddlers whom Progressives considered such blights upon the city did not disappear after zoning was enacted, and their activities could not be eliminated from residential areas, especially since peddlers depended on contact with residents to collect their materials. After 1923, these businesses survived by exploiting the regulatory inequalities produced by the economic and racial segregation that grew in most American metropolitan areas between World War I and the 1950s. Smaller yards and shops persisted in poorer inner-city neighborhoods, where they were close to post-consumer sources of scrap and might be overlooked by lax zoning enforcement. As mass migration of African Americans to Northern cities during World War II combined with mass suburbanization of whites after the war to expand ghettos, these establishments concentrated in African American neighborhoods.

The concentration of the ferrous scrap trade in the Black Belt was so conspicuous that it moved scholars of business to take note. The geographer Gerald A. Gutenschwager wrote a dissertation at the University of Chicago in 1957 about the city's ferrous scrap industry. Much of the dissertation focused on economic and technical matters, and he included a map of the location of scrap and junk shops in 1919. The concentration of scrap businesses in African American neighborhoods was so great that he was moved to draw a series of maps describing the relationship.

Gutenschwager's maps, entitled "Relation of Junk Shops to Redevelopment and Negro Population in Chicago," over a series of dates between 1919 and 1956, linked junk shops listed in the *Waste Trade Directory* with residential areas of at least 25 percent African American population in the year 1950. The vast majority of junk shops within the city limits were located in the areas on the South and West Sides that Gutenschwager identified as being at least one-quarter African American. In 1957, Gutenschwager had identified a significant environmental inequality in Chicago.[75]

If anything, Gutenschwager's analysis was conservative. The neighborhoods he described as having "at least 25 percent Negro population" were in fact much more segregated by 1957. By the time of his study, the effects of mass suburbanization under federal mortgage insurance laws that effectively prohibited African Americans from purchasing homes in new neighborhoods (and effectively prohibited any prospective homeowner from purchasing homes in neighborhoods that housed African Americans) were noticeable. The process of white residents abandoning older neighborhoods and being succeeded by African Americans had been observed in Chicago since the Great Migration; after World War II, it accelerated as whites made an exodus to the suburban periphery, leaving larger areas on the South and West Sides to African American residents. By 1980, Chicago's African American population was (to use Denton and Massey's term) hypersegregated at over 80 percent. That is to say that African Americans lived in neighborhoods that were at least 80 percent African American, a concentration unseen in earlier ethnic enclaves such as Greektown or Ukrainian Village or in Mexican American barrios in Los Angeles or in Cuban American neighborhoods in southern Florida.[76]

Chicago was not unique in the racial reorganization of residential space. In communities throughout the country, from New York City to Los Angeles and from Detroit to Miami, African American residents clustered into unusually concentrated, homogenous neighborhoods between 1945 and 1980. All of the thirty metropolitan areas with the largest African American populations in 1980 featured unusually high levels of residential segregation; Denton and Massey observed sixteen with hypersegregated African American populations averaging more than 83 percent concentration (Atlanta, Baltimore, Buffalo, Chicago, Cleveland, Dallas, Detroit, Gary, Indianapolis, Kansas City, Los Angeles, Milwaukee, New York, Newark, Philadelphia, and St. Louis). These sixteen metropolitan areas housed over one-third of the African American population of the United States in 1980.[77]

Some regional variations existed. Denton and Massey found that while black neighborhoods in the South were isolated, they (with the notable exception of Atlanta) were less likely to be part of larger enclaves than was the case in Northern cities.[78]

In these enclaves, visible concentration of waste handling businesses developed. Gutenschwager's study of the scrap iron industry of Chicago was not focused on racial inequities, but he could not help but observe the pattern that had developed since World War I. This pattern was not simply due to location near heavy industrial customers to scrap businesses. The concentration of junk shops did not conform with proximity to the Gary Steel Works; few shops could be found on Chicago's Southeast Side. Nor were shops distributed throughout areas where sources of scrap could be found, although a case could be made that the slum clearance in western and southern neighborhoods could produce scrap from demolition and construction sites. The strongest correlation to junk shop siting in 1957 was the presence of African American residents in the area. As with prostitution, gambling, and other vices cities sought to limit, public officials pushed scrap dealing into areas with little political power rather than eradicating the activity within the city limits.

The new spatial patterns of scrap business location produced new social effects. Chicago's African American and Hispanic populations became increasingly important sources of new yard labor and small-scale scrap collecting between World War I and 1960 as scrap recycling businesses recruited workers from the surrounding neighborhoods. African Americans and Hispanics did not simply replace European-born scrap workers; the children of the immigrant Jews who founded many businesses continued as owners and managers of yards. But increasingly, the workers in the yards sorting, cutting, and hauling scrap metal were African Americans and Hispanics.

The work of sorting and processing scrap metal involves handling jagged materials, possibly contaminated with corrosive substances. In yards that process automobiles, cutting and shredding automobile bodies released hazards into the ground, and residue from shredded automobile bodies could contaminate the water table. These hazards combined with the traditional hazards of noise pollution, explosions, and injuries from shears and jagged metal to make scrap work among the most dangerous in American industry in the late twentieth century. Insurance premiums in scrap yards exceeded those of mills and mines as early as the 1950s; in Chicago, the people doing this work were part-time employees performing dangerous jobs without health insurance.

The Spatial Characteristics of Waste

Chicago's experience with waste and race reordering its geography is especially well documented, though not especially unique in American urban history. The general trend of American demographic distribution between 1945 and 1970 was an exodus of white people from urban centers to suburbs. Among the appeals of the suburbs was an embrace of nature—controlled, sanitized, planned nature—and separation from the grime and smog of the central city. When the dream of pristine suburban living was disturbed by pollution, suburbanites organized environmental responses. In the post-war era, existing organizations such as the Sierra Club and Audubon Society had grown during the post-war era, and suburbanites founded new groups such as the Environmental Defense Fund and National Resources Defense Council. Metropolitan development during the twentieth century, in the words of the historian Christopher Sellers, was shaped by the "suburban quest for nature."[79]

As middle-class whites decamped to suburbs, divestment of capital from central cities caused crises of funding for services such as police, fire, and sanitation. Industry continued to produce pollution for the air, land, and water, with deindustrialization beginning to produce further wastes of abandoned buildings in some cities by the end of the 1960s. The presence of municipal zoning regulations did not prevent waste disposal or processing near residential areas, nor did the expansion of municipal services provide African American or Hispanic neighborhoods with adequate sanitary services.

Gutenschwager's study indicated that, while large clusters of Chicago's ferrous scrap firms were located on the city's South Side, they were not necessarily located near large industrial scrap customers such as U.S. Steel in northwestern Indiana. Gutenschwager's conclusion that there was a strong correlation between the location of scrap firms and African American residential concentration indicates that selective enforcement of the 1923 zoning ordinance had a significant effect on the spatial pattern of the local scrap trade.

The placement of scrap businesses in residential areas produced growing environmental inequalities between World War I and the end of the 1950s. Within forty years of the establishment of municipal zoning, most of the Chicago's small and medium-sized scrap businesses had relocated to the Black Belt, exposing residents to the sounds, smells, and sights of processing old metal. This reorganization in Chicago produced elevated concerns about waste and nuisance in African American neighborhoods that were also facing concerns about dilapidated housing and insufficient city services, such as garbage collection. African American communities in other cities experienced the same effects of residential segregation and worries over inadequate help keeping their neighborhoods clean. The resulting environmental inequalities would endure and have consequences for the ways in which people of color lived and worked after 1960. At the same time, the descendants of European immigrants who had worked in waste handling occupations in the early twentieth century were among those who migrated from city neighborhoods to suburban peripheries. Residential relocation was part of an assimilation into white American identity that involved putting increasing distance between the assimilated people and waste.

PART IV

Assimilation and Resistance

7

Out of Waste into Whiteness

Environmental burdens on African Americans and Hispanics grew heavier over the course of the twentieth century, but many Americans who had borne the brunt of environmental inequalities at the turn of the century managed to escape them in the second half of the century. How and why they were able to do so indicates both the permeability of white identity and the enduring power of whiteness to inform waste burdens.

At the end of World War II, the United States embarked on a period of intense debate over what race meant in the Land of the Free. Less than two years after V-J Day, Jackie Robinson, the first African American major league player since baseball instituted the color line in the 1880s, took the field for the Brooklyn Dodgers. Chief Counsel Thurgood Marshall of the National Association for the Advancement of Colored People (NAACP) shepherded the landmark *Brown v. Board of Education* case to the U.S. Supreme Court. In 1954, the justices determined that separate educational facilities could not be equal. If *Brown v. Board of Education* did not overturn the doctrine of separate but equal established by the 1896 *Plessey v. Ferguson* decision, it did establish a legal precedent for challenging the color line. The social and legal challenges that came during the 1950s and 1960 forced the United States to examine race and white privilege in ways the nation had not done since Reconstruction.

Rise of the "White Ethnics"

Whiteness evolved during World War II, as evident in federal policy. In 1940, the Immigration and Naturalization Service designated European immigrants' race as "white" on application forms instead of designating the racial categories previously used on immigration records. The historian Eric Goldstein cited public opinion polls carried out just after the war that showed that Americans had far less of a tendency after the war to identify Jews as a race rather than an ethnic group, which was the general sentiment before the war.[1]

The years after World War II saw millions more Americans achieve white identity than they had before the war. This assimilation was not immediate—American views of who could and could not enjoy the privileges of white society were more restricted in 1950 than they would be at century's end. Exclusive clubs and subdivisions still discriminated against Jews in 1950, as one of America's most famous comedians, Groucho Marx, pointed out. Groucho often told the story that when his daughter Melinda was prevented from swimming in a pool with friends at a country club that excluded Jews, he wrote a letter to the club president: "Since my little daughter is only half-Jewish, would it be alright if she went in the pool only to her waist?"[2]

Melinda Marx was born in 1946, so Groucho's story was likely set between 1950 and 1955. Groucho's logic was (as was often the case with Groucho) intentionally ridiculous; segregating a pool by ethnicity or race is ridiculous, so why not challenge the restriction based on fractions? But the club president would also find Groucho's logic ridiculous because of the logic of pollution. A little pollution contaminates the entire body. It was not enough for Melinda's mother to be a white Christian, her father had to be as well. Groucho's Jewish identity— independent of the fame and wealth he had accrued by the 1950s— tainted the whole of his daughter's body, just as having one Jewish parent or grandparent made a person subject to imprisonment or execution under the Nazis. Just as Americans classified people of mixed African and European descent as mulattoes and octoroons, all those so identified were, with the proliferation of Jim Crow laws, subject to the same disenfranchisement of those classified as Negroes—unless they somehow could pass for white. The illogic of racial pollution was at once absurd and prevalent.

Melinda Marx, happily for her, grew into a world where she would not face such outward discrimination based on her father's heritage. Indeed, her very identity as a person with a Jewish father and Christian mother indicated a tolerance for intermarriage between the two religions. Conversely, bans on marriage between black and white Americans remained law in several states until 1967, an indication of where the flexibility of white identity in the United States ended.

Participation in World War II helped the transition to white ethnic status of Southern and Eastern Europeans. Access to home loans and the GI Bill (not available to African Americans but accessible to Jews, Italians, and Slavs) for returning veterans greatly improved economic mobility, allowing Italian Americans to purchase homes and attend universities at rates approaching the national norms for native-born whites. The broad demographic portrait of the American city in 1960 was a dilapidated and dirty central city populated primarily by African Americans with a suburban ring of clean, new middle-class homes populated by white people.

White ethnics melted into the new middle-class suburban subdivisions eating up countryside on the peripheries of cities. The novelist Philip Roth critiqued suburbanization in his biographical stories of Jews leaving Newark for suburban New Jersey. By the 1960s, suburbanites could look back with nostalgia on their immigrant roots, which both gave some distinction amid a broad identity of the mass middle class and measures of pride in the victorious narrative of enterprising families: "My grandfather was a junk peddler. Now look at us!"

The divide separating blacks from whites—including the "white ethnics" who enjoyed dramatic socioeconomic mobility after World War II—inspired academic explanations. Most famous was a study the sociologists Nathan Glazer and Daniel Patrick Moynihan conducted in New York City. Their 1963 book *Beyond the Melting Pot: The Negroes, Puerto Ricans, Jews, Italians, and Irish of New York City* became a remarkably widely read study that seemed to explain why some groups were thriving and others stayed mired in poverty and violence. The book was criticized even at its release for scant primary sources and trading in stereotypes, but it also proved influential in policy circles for prescribing economic solutions to the ills of the ghetto without actually addressing acute residential segregation levels or racially restricted lending practices. Most of the criticism of *Beyond the Melting Pot* came from civil rights groups. Floyd McKissick concluded that the report detailed pathologies particular to the Negro and "then seems to say that it's the individual's fault when it's really the damn system that needs changing."[3]

The historian and *Uprooted* author Oscar Handlin praised *Beyond the Melting Pot* in a 1963 review for the *New York Times*. Handlin identified its great accomplishment as recognizing that "ethnicity is a permanent quality of the American society, particularly cities. The expectations of a half-century ago that a melting-pot process would ultimately fuse the American population into a single homogenous product have not been realized. Instead, although immigration has ended and today's Jews, Italians, and Irish are far different from their European parents and grandparents, groups derived from the original experience of immigration have persisted." Although Handlin critiqued the sections on Jews, Italians, and the Irish as falling back on "flimsy generalizations and intuitive guesswork" to interpret the scant primary sources on those groups, he praised their analysis of African Americans and Puerto Ricans in particular and the book overall as a substantial accomplishment.[4]

By 1970, Glazer's introduction to the second edition of *Beyond the Melting Pot* worried that American society seemed to be moving away from a variety of groups into "a new set of categories, black and white, and that is ominous." Glazer's concern was the rise of black militants rejecting white liberalism. What he witnessed was the successful assimilation into whiteness by many who had previously been marginalized. As the historian Nell Irvin Painter put it, what the "white ethnics" now had in common "was not being black," and that distinction had significance for where one lived, where one worked, and what one's social experiences were.[5]

"Not being black" had great benefits to the white ethnic groups in post-war America. The Jewish experience changed markedly, to the point that anthropologist Karen Brodkin titled her book *How Jews Became White Folks and What That Says about Race in America*. Brodkin argued that Jews achieved upward economic and social mobility after World War II as explicitly anti-Semitic prejudice declined, allowing greater access to residential neighborhoods, schools (as quotas limiting Jewish students declined), places of employment, and swimming pools in the 1950s and 1960s. The idea of keeping Jews out of affluent suburbs in New York City or Chicago was standard practice in 1930; it was antiquated by 1980.

If the immigrant experience of the era of mass migration included shaping the modern waste management industry of the nation, the white ethnic experience involved removing the burdens of handling wastes from the children and grandchildren of the founders. By the end of the 1960s, veteran scrap dealers lamented the difficulty of getting their children involved in running the family businesses. Having provided the next generation with college educations and graduate educations in law and management, they found that their children often opted to choose work in fields other than managing the scrap businesses. Lacking heirs, scrap business owners often opted to sell the family business to corporations. Consolidation of the scrap recycling and waste management trades occurred, with a few companies—notably the scrap metal firms Luria Brothers, Schiavone Bonomo, and David J. Joseph and the waste-hauling firms Waste Management, Inc., and Browning-Ferris Industries—purchasing dozens of smaller businesses. Some of the larger companies themselves were purchased by holding companies, testament to the profitability of waste management and scrap recycling in a consumptive era.[6]

Furthermore, the structure of the businesses handling wastes had changed to reflect the quest for white identity by these businesses' founders. As David Roediger argued in *Working toward Whiteness*, workers from Eastern and Southern Europe fought to achieve white identity over the first half of the twentieth century, a fight that was largely won by the end of World War II. In the post-war era, Jews and Italians gained access to the jobs, communities, and amenities most white Americans enjoyed.[7]

Out of Waste

The achievement of whiteness had complicated interactions with the ways Jews and Italians handed waste management. On the surface, a study of the American scrap industry in 1960 would find few changes from 1920. Most of the scrap businesses—large or small—throughout the nation remained urban in their setting and remained owned by Americans of Jewish or Italian heritage. In many cases, businesses were in their second or third generation of family ownership.

Yet important changes had occurred. Though scrap firms remained situated in large cities, their location within the cities now had strong racial dimensions. Furthermore, the firms themselves had changed. Many had grown, requiring new layers of specialization and bureaucracy. A firm owner might be joined by accountants, lawyers, and managers coordinating the business and might no longer handle wastes as he did when the firm was a one-man operation. Blue-collar workers employed by family-owned firms actually handled the materials. The divide between white- and blue-collar work increased, and with it a racial divide.

Among the distinctive developments were a few private enterprises growing much larger and the structure of large- and medium-sized businesses becoming more corporate with modern management. The image of a small entrepreneur who was a one-man business became a historical artifact. Leading scrap metal firms had originated as family-owned operations from Jewish and Italian immigrants. They grew in the post-war era, with descendants of the founders specializing in management positions. The work of actually handling and processing scrap metal was left to blue-collar yard labor.

The management structure of Luria Brothers evolved from a one-man operation at the end of the nineteenth century to a large, diversified, and highly educated management team after World War II. In 1949, *Fortune* magazine profiled the firm, noting it grew from one Reading, Pennsylvania, scrap yard to the largest ferrous scrap operation in the United States, including operations in sixteen cities. The business remained in the Luria family (though in a few years it would be sold to the Ogden Corporation). In addition to the largely retired Alex Luria (son of the founder Hirsch Luria) as the head of the firm, his son-in-law Joel Claster served as executive president, and Hirsch's Yale-educated grandsons served as president (Herbert Luria), vice president (Henry Luria), and secretary (Mortimer Luria). Treasurer William F. Luria studied at the Babson Institute, and Vice President David Luria attended Lehigh and Oxford. The children and grandchildren of the firm's founder enjoyed the status and safety of white-collar work half a century into the firm's history, work that was substantially different from what the workers at Luria's scrap yards experienced daily. The labor of doing the most dangerous and dirty work was no longer done by Jewish family members but by seasonal labor hired from the neighborhoods surrounding the scrap yards.[8]

The transition out of waste handling was one of a series of transitions into white identity during the post-war era. Jews and Italians successfully distanced themselves from the stigma of waste through moving out of urban slums, alternately growing waste handling businesses to the point where management was white-collar work or by getting out of the waste trades altogether.

The distancing had spatial consequences. In the Chicago metropolitan area, portions of the South and West Sides that had been centers of Jewish, Italian, Polish, Irish, and Slavic residential life in the early twentieth century lost their white ethnic populations largely to suburban development after World War II. The Slavs who had populated the Back of the Yards neighborhood around the slaughterhouses gave way to Mexican Americans beginning in the 1920s. Chicago's first aldermanic ward on the near South Side was largely Italian American before the war; by the 1980 Census, it was plurality African American. Lawndale and the near West Side were pockets of heavy Jewish settlement in 1900. Jewish merchants established the famous Maxwell Street Market, which would be a local institution of bartering and haggling until the University of Illinois at Chicago bulldozed it to install parking lots in 1994. By that point, the Jews had long left the area, and the surrounding residents were almost entirely African American.[9]

Italian Americans migrated to western suburbs such as Cicero and Oak Lawn; Jews populated the near North Side, and the Hyde Park and South Shore neighborhoods on the South Side. Hyde Park retained a Jewish community in part because of the presence of the University of Chicago; between 1970 and 2000, however, Jews departed from South Shore and that neighborhood became mostly African American. By the end of the century, Chicago's Jews were largely suburban, with Skokie and Highland Park north of the city being the most prominent settlements. The historian Irving Cutler estimated in 1996 that four times as many Jews left Chicago for the suburbs than came into the city.[10]

From Rags to Riches: The Narrative of Upward Mobility

The immigrant story of upward mobility was celebrated in the scrap industry by those businesses that became successful. The pages of the *Waste Trade Journal* and *Scrap Age* in the twentieth century and *Recycling Today* and *Scrap* in the twenty-first regularly look back at the industry's rich immigrant heritage, and leaders in the industry are often the children, grandchildren, and great-grandchildren of immigrant junkmen. That is certainly a narrative of successful enterprise in America.

White ethnic recollections of their backgrounds in the waste trades in the late twentieth century revised the image for both nostalgia and progress. The junk collector became the primitive, an anachronism no longer burdening Jewish American identity as the Dickensian Fagin archetype had before the war. The institutional memory of the scrap industry revealed an ambiguous pride in the trade's history. Edwin C. Barringer, head of the Institute of Scrap Iron & Steel, Inc., one of the two major recycling trade associations, championed the industry's immigrant roots in his 1954 history *The Story of Scrap*: "There is a tradition that scrap as an organized industry first put its roots down into the soil of healthy and energetic but destitute immigrants from Northern and Eastern Europe. . . . These honest but poor immigrants lacked a trade and a background in agriculture. . . . Into New England, New York, New Jersey, and Eastern Pennsylvania these immigrant peddlers made forays, at first with sacks on their backs but as soon as they had accumulated a little capital, by horse and wagon."[11]

Charles H. Lipsett, for decades the chronicler of industry dealings in his *Waste Trade Journal*, published the second edition of a history-cum-memoir of American scrap dealing in 1974. Entitled *100 Years of Recycling History: From Yankee Tincart Peddlers to Wall Street Scrap Giants*, Lipsett's history at once took pride in and distanced contemporaries from the industry's humble origins. His book described a literal rags-to-riches story of the industry that Lipsett witnessed: "I saw the general junk dealer, who originally may have been a peddler, gradually transformed into a specialist operating exclusively in either scrap iron or metal, or rubber, or waste paper." The industry, in his eyes, transformed from "picturesque and colorful" characters to a modern, professionally managed industry.[12]

Lipsett collected dozens of recollections from the veteran scrap dealers he interviewed. For the 1955 edition, he quoted the veteran scrap dealer Marvin S. Plant, who gave a representative account of the industry's progress. Plant recalled that, when he first started in the trade, "The scrap dealer was considered as a person who drove a horse and wagon, or a small two-wheeled cart peddler who roamed around the streets picking up various scrap materials from which his living could be derived. . . . Today, 1955, our role in the National Economy is certainly the No. 1 role—or very close to it, and one that is absolutely necessary to the steel mill, and is regarded as a very prominent part of the National Economy."[13]

By 1974, the idea of recycling as an environmental virtue had taken hold in the United States. Concern over the consequences of solid waste had led to the creation of both grassroots efforts and public attempts to divert materials out of landfills and back into industrial production. Middle- and upper-class Americans now actively recycled as an environmental ethic.

Lipsett seized upon this rather new handling of waste materials as virtue to claim that the old junk peddlers who traversed city streets by the thousands and who spread out across the countryside were pioneering environmentalists. Lipsett and the Institute of Scrap Iron & Steel (ISIS), the major scrap recycling trade association, identified junk dealers as "The Original Recyclers"—now progressives rather than the bane of Progressive urban reformers (as they had been in the early twentieth century).

If junk collectors were the original recyclers, in Lipsett's story, they were also historical artifacts. The peddlers were no more for Lipsett. The idea of a solitary man with a sack or buggy collecting scraps had given way to modern corporate scrap firms with university-trained management, investments in cutting-edge technology, and operations fitting within accepted zoning regulations and social norms. The scrap industry had come a long way from its immigrant roots, and while 1974's scrap firms claimed to be environmentalists all along from those roots, the contemporary environmentalist was a far cry from the primitive immigrant.

The Institute of Scrap Iron and Steel encouraged this simultaneous embrace and distancing of the scrap trade's heritage. In 1977, its monthly trade periodical *Scrap Age* published a special bicentennial edition celebrating the industry's history in the now two-century-old United States. While taking pride in the stories of immigrants who went from rags to riches in the late nineteenth and early twentieth centuries, it firmly brought the trade into the modern age, boasting of how modern and complex operations had become over the years.[14]

A variant on that story is the successful Jew who has achieved in a field distinct from his family's humble roots in the waste trades. In this story, waste is worth a nostalgic look back by an individual who has escaped it for a more glamorous life. A narrative featuring a hard-working immigrant raising his family up from the mire so his children could achieve greater things was a particularly literal version of the rags-to-riches story.

In 1966, the journalist Harry Golden, reacting to a critical biography of the Hollywood film producer Louis B. Mayer, argued that Mayer's rise from junk dealer to Hollywood film producer was the story of Jewish American success and not something to be mocked. "I think the time has come," Golden wrote, "to stand up and applaud these ex-junk dealers, ex-trouser pressers, and ex-glove salesmen because in the industry they created no one was killed; no strikers were shot down in cold blood . . . and no ten-year-old children were trained to . . . fix the looms as they were in the Anglo-Saxon cotton mills of the old South."[15]

Far from seeing them as a badge of shame, Jewish celebrities like the actors Mandy Patinkin and Kirk Douglas reveled in their families' humble origins. Writing in 1998, Patinkin told of his grandfather Max's early life in a Polish shtetl interrupted by having to flee the czar's army in 1905. With nothing but "a pack on his back" he booked passage to New York City and ultimately made his way to Chicago. There, he invested his savings in a horse and wagon and became a junk peddler, a business he would grow into People's Iron and Metal Company. Patinkin remembers the family firm with pride, noting it "was an important part of the recycling business and employed many relatives, including my father [Lester]." His pride in the family business was evident in 1998, but by then Mandy and his brother Sheldon had long traded scrap for lives in the theater.[16]

Kirk Douglas placed his family heritage front and center, titling his 1988 autobiography *The Ragman's Son*. The title underlined his personal struggle coming from humble beginnings as Issur Danielovich Demsky, the Russian-Jewish son of an illiterate ragpicker in Amsterdam, New York, who began acting in high school and, through hard work at university, in summer stock theater, and in the Navy, rose from poverty to become Broadway and Hollywood star Kirk Douglas. If Douglas sounds less proud of his father's work than Patinkin, his pride stems from his achievements in leaving waste behind. By the end of the twentieth century, Patinkin and Douglas were unusual in their celebrity but not the general trajectory of their lives; it was not at all unusual for Jewish families to have had an ancestor in the waste trades.[17]

The stories Douglas and Patinkin told of their families were mirrored by the stories told by industry leaders. Aaron Levinson recounted that his grandfather was a junk peddler who went through the streets of Pittsburgh with a horse and wagon collecting scrap metal in the 1920s. Aaron's father and uncles took over the business and transitioned it into Levinson Steel, one of the largest steel fabrication businesses in Pittsburgh. The waste trades were a first step up the socioeconomic ladder, a step taken by forefathers for the benefit of their children fortunate enough to not have to get their hands dirty.[18]

Dirty . . . and White?

Enduring stereotypes of dirty work as both physically unsanitary and morally corrupt complicated this narrative of upward mobility. Glazer and Moynihan drew upon these allegations in *Beyond the Melting Pot*, noting that a "major theme in the Italian-American role in New York politics is involvement with crime," and they identified an "Italian-American superiority in organized crime."[19]

This infamous stereotype drew in associations between the dirty work of handling waste materials and the dirty work of organized crime. A series of hearings by the Senate Select Committee on Improper Activities in Labor or Management (also known as the McClellan Committee, after its chairman, Senator John L. McClellan of Arkansas) on organized crime in the late 1950s made connections between Italian American organized crime figures and garbage handling in the New York metropolitan area explicit.

In 1958, the committee invited U.S. Bureau of Narcotics Agent Martin F. Pera to testify about these ties. Under questioning from Committee Chief Counsel Robert F. Kennedy, Pera claimed that Vincent J. Squillante, allegedly part of Carlo Gambino's organization (and a man who had been under investigation for allegedly murdering rival organized crime boss Albert Anastasia's underboss Frank Scalise), had developed a reputed $50 million operation in garbage-hauling services in Manhattan, Queens, and Westchester County. Squillante's Greater Cartmen's

Association of New York, Pera charged, was "gaining a practical monopoly in the garbage removal field."[20]

Subsequent federal investigations connected organized crime to several of New York City's borough-based trade associations, with the Genovese family linked to the Kings County Trade Waste Association and the Greater New York Waste Paper Association and the Gambino family linked to the Association of Trade Waste Removers of Greater New York and the Queens County Trade Waste Association. The direct impact of the hearings on Squillante was his 1960 indictment on extortion charges, which led to him going missing shortly thereafter. He was last seen that September 23, with the Gambino family suspected of killing him to avoid testifying. The broader implications of the McClellan Committee's activities were public associations between New York–area waste management operations and Italian American organized crime.[21]

The novelist Mario Puzo referenced both *Beyond the Melting Pot* and the 1958 Senate hearings in his portrayals of Italian Americans. In a review of *Beyond the Melting Pot*, Puzo gave a favorable reading of the book's depiction of Italian American upward mobility, agreeing with Glazer and Moynihan that alleviating social problems in the ghettoes would put residents on the same track of socioeconomic mobility as the "white ethnics" who rose before them. Puzo also noted that Frank Sinatra and other prominent figures had founded the American Italian Anti-Defamation League and the Jewish Anti-Defamation League to combat obsolete stereotypes.[22] (Other Italian Americans were more critical of the book. When Moynihan ran for New York City Council president in 1965, Paul P. Rau, Jr., of the United Italian American League assailed the book as a "mass of twisted facts, contorted conclusions, and hearsay statements," focusing on Italian American ties to organized crime.)[23]

Puzo's 1969 novel *The Godfather* referenced both the use of garbage hauling by Mafia families (in the novel, the Bocchicchio family) and Francis Ford Coppola's 1974 sequel to the film version explicitly referenced the 1958 Senate hearings, inserting Michael Corleone into the proceedings. The links between organized crime, waste hauling, and Italian American identity were unfortunately sufficiently iconic to merit inclusion in Puzo's epic.[24]

The enduring criminal stereotyping that had plagued the waste trades before World War II complicated the narrative of progress into white

American identity. Notably, such stereotyping did not stop it. Both Jews and Italians enjoyed upward mobility after the war, including relocating to the suburbs surrounding New York City, Boston, Philadelphia, Cleveland, and Detroit. In many places where economic downturns reduced the employment base, white ethnics did not merely leave the inner city but the metropolitan area itself, moving into the Sun Belt rather than the suburbs. Many of the smaller communities in South Florida became retirement enclaves where colloquial Yiddish or Italian was common by the 1960s. By the end of the century, white ethnics in the suburbs were the norm rather than rarities, indication of the success these ethnic groups had achieved assimilating into white society.[25]

Unmeltable Americans

In Melinda Marx's lifetime, Jews, Italians, and Southern and Eastern Europeans gained acceptance into white society. By the time she became an adult, housing discrimination and federal mortgage insurance practices no longer denied her relatives access to home ownership in particular neighborhoods. These people had made the transition to "white ethnics," with the privileges and opportunities of white identity. By the end of the 1960s, this assimilation was sufficient that people descended from Southern and Eastern European immigrants could feel safely nostalgic about their origins. By the late 1960s, pride in European roots was amplified and, as the University of Chicago historian Arthur Mann concluded in 1969, "It is now 'in' to be ethnic." The reverend Andrew Greeley noted that the increased consciousness of white ethnics was in response to heightened black consciousness and that white ethnic identity was often formed in response to economic insecurity (compared with both whites and blacks) and that ethnic identification involved "demands of white ethnic groups for control over their own destiny."[26]

A century after arriving in the United States, Americans of Eastern European and Southern European heritage had largely achieved whiteness. Though jokes and stereotypes about Italians and Jews still remained in popular culture, Italians and Jews enjoyed the benefits of whiteness, including home ownership in the suburbs, access to good education and employment, and the legal ability to marry others considered white. Sociological studies in the wake of Gunnar Myrdal's indictment of

American racism referred to these people as "white ethnics," rather than as other races; *Beyond the Melting Pot* concluded that, as ethnic groups, they were able to achieve upward socioeconomic mobility.[27]

"White ethnics" achieved success in corporate boardrooms and in politics. In the 1930s, Chicago elected Bohemian American mayor Anton Cermak (in an explicitly racist electoral campaign in which Southern and Eastern Europeans backed the Democrat and African Americans backed the Republican), and New York City elected Italian American mayor Fiorello LaGuardia. In addition to serving as governor of New York State during the 1920s, Italian American Al Smith was the Democratic nominee for president in 1928. Jewish politicians had served in the U.S. Senate as early as 1845; between 1949 and 1970, Jews represented Alaska, Connecticut, Oregon, and New York in the Senate. New York had the bipartisan Jewish achievement of having Republican Jacob Javits win the 1956 election to succeed retiring Democratic Senator Herbert Lehman. The presidency remained in white Anglo-Saxon Protestant hands throughout the twentieth century, but white ethnics found many electoral paths to success by 1970.

Among non-white Americans, African Americans were clearly more "unwhite" than anyone else. Nat King Cole's experience testing racial boundaries in southern California was scarier than Groucho's. After Cole purchased a house in an all-white Los Angeles neighborhood in 1948, the Ku Klux Klan placed a burning cross on his lawn. Although Cole stayed in the house, his experience indicated that acceptance by white society was more open to Jews than to African Americans.[28]

Which is not to say that Jews were on completely equal footing with white, Anglo-Saxon Protestants in 1950. Jews, were, however, penetrating social barriers with some success and would continue to do so. The same could be said about Italians, Slavs, and other second- and third-generation immigrant families who were identified by themselves and by others as white Americans.

African American gains were limited. Financial success during the period largely involved businesses catering to African Americans, including the Johnson Publishing Company (publishers of *Ebony* and *Jet* magazines) and Madame C. J. Walker's cosmetics company. The African Americans elected to the U.S. House of Representatives were limited to those representing hypersegregated districts. A large city did not elect an African American mayor until Carl Stokes became mayor of Cleveland in 1967. Shortly thereafter, national media decried the terrible pollution in Cleveland by publishing photographs of the burning Cuyahoga River. River fires had been periodic for decades, but the national outrage followed fears of what Stokes's election might mean to the city.[29]

Mobility came as the new white ethnics were able to largely shake free of the stigma of waste. Many of the waste firm owners had sold out their interests to corporations by 1970, opting to work in more respected fields. Even many who stayed in waste focused on white-collar aspects of managing the businesses rather than handling wastes. The businesses located in areas zoned industrial or in ghettoes distant from the white residential communities Italians and Jews now had the ability to reside in. In just about every respect, the "low, degraded people" with "a penchant for scow trimming" had transcended the stigma of waste and had become white Americans.

Though this upward mobility represented a great change from the early twentieth century, one important continuity remained—the burdens of waste management fell unduly upon people not considered white. As the newly deemed "white ethnics" enjoyed the benefits of whiteness, people still classified as other races found waste shaping their communities, their employment, and their health. The stark inequalities that resulted were too glaring to ignore or to forgive away.

The Waste Labor Market: 1950–1970

Leaving waste behind was an important facet of achieving whiteness. If the Jewish junk peddler was an iconic figure in the late nineteenth-century American city, the image was a historical artifact at the end of the twentieth century. Many Jews transitioned out of the trade when better, more respectable options came open. Others saw the next generation opting out in search of better work.

Jews still participated in the scrap metal industry in large numbers, yet the terms of this participation had changed. Rare was the scrap firm in 1980 employing Jews as yard labor. Jews remained prevalent as owners and in managerial roles in scrap businesses, but they were less common among the people who regularly handled the materials.

Many Jews sold their ownership of firms to corporations between 1950 and the end of the century, starting with the largest scrap firm of all, Luria Brothers, which was sold to the Ogden Corporation in 1953. In many of these cases, the corporation agreed to keep the previous owners on as executives, since the experienced scrap dealers had built up decades of networks and professional relationships. Yet now the trade more resembled the mainstream of American corporations than the immigrant operations that cities attempted to zone away as nuisances earlier in the century. The Jewish junk peddler remains an important part of the scrap recycling industries' heritage, yet the work and social status of the fourth- and fifth-generation of Jewish scrap barons' families had changed. These changes were to the benefit of the immigrants' descendants; an example of the American Dream providing opportunity to newcomers.

Analysis of occupational category by racial category in the Integrated Public Use Microdata Series (IPUMS) samples of the U.S. population for 1950, 1960, and 1970 indicates that workers in most waste handling occupations became progressively less white between 1950 and 1970, with African American and Hispanic workers represented in these occupations well above their representation in the general population. The percentage of African Americans in the general population of the United States was 10 percent in 1950, 10.5 percent in 1960, and 11.1 percent in 1970, and the percentage of Hispanic Americans in the general population was 2.1 percent in 1950, 3.2 percent in 1960, and 4.4 percent in 1970. The percentage of non-Hispanic whites in the general population was 87.5 percent in 1950, 85.4 percent in 1960, and 83.5 percent in 1970.[30]

The share of workers in "sanitary industries" (comprising waste hauling, salvage, and related services) became increasingly African American and Hispanic between 1950 and 1970. In 1950, 22.4 percent of workers in sanitary industries were African American, 3.2 percent were Hispanic, and 74.4 percent were white and not Hispanic. In 1960, 24.8 percent of workers in sanitary industries were African American, 5 percent were Hispanic, and 69.6 percent were white and not Hispanic. In 1970, 27.9 percent of workers in sanitary industries were African American, 5.8 percent were Hispanic, and 65.6 percent were white and not Hispanic. African American representation in the sanitary industries

"The AFSCME Collection: D.C. Sanitation: Sanitation workers and members of Local 2091 empty Washington, D.C.'s trash, May 1974." Walter P. Reuther Library, Archives of Labor and Urban Affairs, Wayne State University, Detroit, Michigan.

in 1950 was more than twice their representation in the general population, and African Americans increased their share of the sanitary labor force over the next twenty years.

This facet of the industry had great variance in public and private ownership, as well as levels of unionization. Since the 1920s, San Francisco has been distinctive in that its waste management operations are managed by a collectively owned association of the small immigrant-founded scavenging operations found in most cities at the turn of the twentieth century. African American, Asian American, and Hispanic scavengers found entry into the association difficult for decades, but by the late 1970s, those three groups combined to account for roughly 40 percent of the Bay Area's scavengers. New York City's sanitation services were run by the city, and the workers successfully unionized in 1956, with wages and safety precautions being relatively good for the industry (albeit with hazards on the job still well beyond that of most occupations). New York City's Department of Sanitation resident anthropologist Robin Nagle estimates that, in the early twenty-first century, the department's more than 10,000 members were roughly a quarter African Americans, with slightly fewer than a fifth being Hispanic. More than half were white ethnics, though "within that category are many who make a sharp distinction between Irish and Italian."[31]

As the number of middle-class homeowners in the United States increased, more Americans could afford private housekeepers. Between 1950 and 1970, the share of private housekeepers working in American homes became more African American and (in lesser numbers) more Hispanic. In 1950, 24.3 percent of enumerated private housekeepers in the United States were African American, 1.7 percent were Hispanic, and 73.5 percent were white and not Hispanic. In 1960, 26.9 percent of private housekeepers were African American, 3 percent were Hispanic, and 69.2 percent were white and not Hispanic. In 1970, 39 percent of private housekeepers were African American, 4.5 percent were Hispanic, and 55 percent were white and not Hispanic. African Americans worked in housekeeping at more than twice their representation in the 1950 Census and almost four times their representation in the 1970 Census.

Roughly one-third of American laundry workers in the United States were African American during the period between 1950 and 1970, a share that remained static while the percentage of Hispanic laundry workers progressively grew. In 1950, 32.6 percent of enumerated laundry workers in the United States were African American, 3.6 percent were Hispanic (mostly Mexican American), and 62.5 percent were white and not Hispanic. In 1960, 31.9 percent of laundry workers were African American, 6 percent were Hispanic, and 60.1 percent were white and not Hispanic. In 1970, 31.2 percent of laundry workers were African American, 7.2 percent were Hispanic, and 59 percent were white and not Hispanic. African American participation in laundry work remained approximately three times their representation in the general population, though the industry went into decline after the successful mass marketing of washing machines made mechanized laundry services common in middle-class American homes between 1950 and 1970.[32]

Janitorial work was an outlier in the sanitary workforce, as non-Hispanic whites actually grew as a percentage of the workforce between 1950 and 1970. In 1950, 29.2 percent of janitors and sextons in the United States were African American, 2.4 percent were Hispanic, and 67.9 percent were white and not Hispanic. In 1960, 25.9 percent of janitors and sextons were African American, 3.4 percent were Hispanic, and 69.6 percent were white and not Hispanic. In 1970, 21.4 percent of janitors and sextons were African American, 4.9 percent were Hispanic, and 72.3 percent were white and not Hispanic. This occupation is an example of the representation of African Americans shrinking over time, from almost three times their representation in the general population to slightly over double their representation between 1950 and 1970.

One factor that may account for the increase in white participation in this occupation is that janitors were more likely to be unionized than other waste handling workers. The 1921 founding of the Service Employees International Union (SEIU) by Chicago janitors was followed by a national expansion of the union between 1921 and 1980. Its strongest core represented workers in New York City and Chicago office buildings. The sociologist Ray Gold estimated that the income of the average Chicago janitor was $385 per month in 1952, an income often higher than many of the janitor's tenants. Prior to setbacks in the 1980s, SEIU had achieved gains in wages and benefits beyond those of most waste trade workers (with the exception of some local sanitary workers who had also unionized).[33]

Service unions such as the American Federation of State, County and Municipal Employees (AFSCME) had successfully organized public sanitation workers in a few northern municipalities (most notably New York City), and the Congress of Industrial Organizations (CIO) had attempted to unionize workers at a few scrap yards between the 1930s and 1950s. Even with those efforts, unionization rates among sanitary workers were low, with reluctance to organize non-white workers being one barrier to higher rates of organization.[34]

The experience of janitors aside, the demographic portrait of waste handling workers in the post-war period was one of African Americans being represented at two to four times their representation in the general population and Hispanic Americans gaining in both the general population and representation in relevant occupations. Whites who were not Hispanic consistently were represented below their numbers in the general population. While accurate enumeration of the third- and fourth-generation descendants of people who had immigrated to the United States before 1920 is difficult, anecdotal evidence strongly suggests that many of the "white ethnics"—including Jews and Italians—who had participated in the waste trades prior to World War II transitioned out of these occupations after the war.

The separation of "white ethnics" from waste handling had two components. In many cases, Jews who operated scrap and waste businesses moved into more reputable occupations. One example is the scrap iron business Abe Levinson operated in Pittsburgh. When his sons took over the business, they converted it from scrap to steel production. After World War II, Levinson Steel was one of the largest steel producers in the United States.[35]

A second way out of waste was subtle but used often. Existing waste firms changed their operations, creating more specialized job descriptions and placing a divide between white-collar and blue-collar work, in which the latter workers handled wastes while the former workers managed the business. The seasonal nature of scrap yard employment after World War II makes quantitative assessment of African American participation in the scrap industry difficult. Many firms paid workers strictly on a cash basis without written records. Furthermore, the Census underreports African American participation in the industry because many individuals participated on a part-time basis in order to supplement their income. Thus an individual listed as a steelworker or gas station attendant might have collected scrap or worked in a scrap yard for decades without ever having been enumerated as such in the Census.

Anecdotal evidence suggests that African American participation in scrap handling was widespread by 1960—but only at the lowest rungs of the industry. Though many African Americans worked for scrap firms, African American ownership of processing yards or brokerages did not exist in most cities, likely owing to racism among customers and other dealers. African Americans faced barriers to upward mobility in the industry beyond those that Jewish entrepreneurs were able to overcome. Cleveland scrap dealer Leonard Tanenbaum recalled several instances of buyers and sellers abusing his African American employees in the 1950s if they drove his truck into customers' businesses. In this way, the color line facing African Americans in 1960 was substantially harder than any barriers to whiteness that Jewish immigrants faced during the twentieth century. The racial inequalities that concentrated scrap yards in African American neighborhoods also acted to deny African Americans the opportunity to realize profits from these businesses. African Americans could participate in the industry as labor doing the dirtiest and most dangerous work, but racism from the large industrial customers that scrap firms depended upon prevented African Americans from rising to the level of owner or manager of scrap firms.[36]

Asserting Whiteness through Hygiene

Transitioning out of waste handling was one part of the complex assimilation into white identity. Though it brought new opportunities, it also sparked concerns about cultural loss. Speaking on an American Historical Association panel with Moynihan in 1964, Yeshiva University Professor Irving Greenberg declared that rapid assimilation was destroying Jewish identity and identified secular education as a particular problem: "The college setting is particularly destructive to Jewish culture and . . . 80 percent of the eligible Jews now go to college."[37]

The fears of complete assimilation were joined by racial resentments. By 1964, a conservative racial backlash against African Americans within white ethnic groups became visible; New York Times reporter William Lee Miller noted opposition to the Civil Rights movement and recalled hearing the following arguments repeatedly: "We Italians had to work our own way up—why can't they?" One Irish American man told Miller, "Equal opportunities, eh? We didn't have that when I was startin' out."[38]

Securing white identity often involved attacks against people of color. In The History of White People, Nell Irvin Painter quoted one Italian American remembering an invitation to attack African Americans during the 1943 Harlem riot. "They'd say, 'let's beat up some niggers.' It was wonderful. It was new. The Italo Americans stopped being Italo and started becoming Americans. We joined the group. Now we're like you guys, right?"[39]

This often involved racially antagonistic politics by white ethnics against African Americans. Newark, New Jersey, politician Tony Imperiale's stump speeches including disparaging neighborhoods that had become majority black, presenting a fifteen-year-old photograph of a clean neighborhood back when it was majority white, then lamenting, "Look at it now, with garbage in the streets." (The reporter who investigated then found the streets were actually clean.)[40]

Imperiale's rhetoric explicitly associated African Americans with garbage, and he was accused of ties with the Ku Klux Klan. New Jersey Grand Dragon John Behringer claimed to have initiated Imperiale into the secret society in 1967, though Imperiale denied it, instead claiming alliance with the John Birch Society. The accusations did not prevent Imperiale from winning a seat on the Newark City Council or subsequent elections to the New Jersey State Assembly and State Senate. He narrowly lost a 1974 race for governor.[41]

If Imperiale's campaigning in Newark represented a particularly virulent example of a new form of white supremacy, his rhetoric was consistent with an effective appeal to disenfranchised whites by the end of the 1960s. The following year, former vice president Richard M. Nixon capped a remarkable political comeback by defeating sitting vice president Hubert H. Humphrey using a campaign imploring America's "silent majority" to embrace proposed "law and order" crackdowns on crime and dissent. In his speech accepting the presidential nomination at the 1968 Republican Convention in Miami Beach, Nixon refuted any associations between his "law and order" platform and racism.[42]

Nixon's denials did not diminish allegations of racism. The *New York Times* quoted Gloria Marquez, executive board member of the Northern Westchester branch of the NAACP critiquing Nixon's rhetoric: "Nixon's appeal for law and order has a special meaning when he uses it. I'm all for law and order, but he is trying to get the support of the white backlash people around the country."[43]

Even after the Supreme Court's *Loving v. Virginia* decision found bans on interracial marriage that emerged after the Civil War unconstitutional, sitting president Nixon expressed revulsion at the idea of interracial unions. In a discussion with White House Special Counsel Charles Colson about the recent *Roe v. Wade* Supreme Court decision, Nixon remarked that sometimes abortion was necessary, for example, "when you have a black and a white." In 1973, President Nixon's intolerance of black-white unions belied his 1968 denials of racist intent. White fears of interracial sex polluting white purity endured, remaining a concern in the White House.[44]

Cleaner and Whiter

By the end of the 1960s, Americans of Southern and Eastern European descent had largely achieved the identities of "white ethnics," with all the privileges whiteness offered. Many had reaped economic rewards from waste handling businesses; to fully embrace whiteness, most moved into management roles or transitioned to other occupations. Homes in the clean suburbs, college educations, and opportunities in white-collar jobs became greater possibilities. Those who remained in waste handling industries had the opportunities to become a managerial class. The children of successful waste managers had the options to become managers themselves or to take the wealth and educational opportunities from their parents' achievements and transition into cleaner, less stigmatized occupations. Waste handling was a nostalgic trope among white ethnics, an important dimension in recounting humble family origins. In some cases, these narratives were quite literally ones from rags to riches.

Regrettably, one aspect of the assimilation into white identities involved tarring other Americans with the stigma of dirt. The people who handled sanitary services increasingly were the people not deemed white in the post-war era, particularly African Americans. The people who bore these inequalities found new ways to resist, shaping how Americans would understand environmental racism in the late twentieth century.

"We Are Tired of Being at the Bottom"

The noxious relationship between race and waste had been evident to those affected by it between the Civil War and 1960s. Laundry workers initiated strikes. Residents complained to politicians about poor sanitary services. Booker T. Washington sought to improve African American status with uplifted standards of hygiene. But the late twentieth century brought new consciousness and modes of resistance to the doctrine of clean and white that shaped the conversation at the end of the twentieth century.

This consciousness was made most explicit through a conflict shaped by Henry Loeb III of Memphis, Tennessee. Loeb's life embodied the achievement of the American dream. Born Jewish in the South in 1920, he epitomized successful assimilation into white privilege. His grandparents were German Jews who migrated to Memphis in the 1860s, and Loeb's family grew prosperous through a laundry business founded by his grandfather Henry Loeb, Sr., in 1887. Moving into public service, Henry Loeb III was the Memphis city commissioner who oversaw the Public Works Department's management of sewage, drainage, streets, and sanitation services. His rewards included prosperity and victory in two mayoral elections. Henry Loeb enjoyed the power and privilege of a white man in a Southern town.[1]

Keeping Memphis Clean

These benefits came from the complex ways in which Loeb and his family benefited from environmental inequalities in a city greatly concerned with sanitation. Effective sanitation services are vital to all cities, but the Sanitation Department in Memphis has a special place in that city's history. Hot and humid Memphis suffered from epidemic diseases as it grew. Yellow fever almost wiped the city off the map in the 1870s; after thousands died, more fled, and almost every person who stayed became infected in 1878. In response, the state of Tennessee repealed the city's charter. The creation of the Sanitation Department under Col. George E. Waring, Jr., in order to build modern sewers, pick up garbage, keep the streets clean and reduce the presence of infectious materials in the community as much as possible truly saved Memphis in the 1880s.

Memphis was the central city of a vast rural hinterland where impoverished African Americans lived and worked. Many of the sanitation workers had worked fields in Mississippi in abject poverty with few rights and had come to the city for better wages. Collecting garbage and yard waste was in many ways a step up, but the work was dangerous, brutal, and ill paid. The workers were not respected by their employers or by many of the residents and businesses who benefited from waste removal. Aside from the hazards the trucks posed, sanitation workers had to handle all sorts of materials from tree limbs to broken glass to biological wastes that could infect, poison, or injure them. In the Memphis summers, this work was conducted under temperatures regularly exceeding 90 degrees, often without shade or breaks to get water. Sanitation workers could be maimed at any time, and crippling injuries were common. Once disabled on the job, a worker had little recourse for compensation and was vulnerable to a life of poverty.

The tensions over waste and race that had increased throughout the twentieth century culminated in a Memphis confrontation, and the focal point of that confrontation was Mayor Henry Loeb III. The family business, Loeb's Laundry Cleaner Company, employed African American women to do the hard work of cleaning clothes at low wages. This arrangement made the Loeb family prosperous. Henry Sr. passed the laundry business on to his son William, ensuring that young Henry III lived a comfortable life. He attended Phillips Academy prep school and Brown University. His friends included John F. Kennedy (who, like Henry, served on a patrol boat during World War II), and Loeb's service in World War II later made him attractive to the Memphis electorate.[2]

Coming home from the war, Loeb began managing Loeb's Laundry Cleaner Company in 1946. There, twenty-six-year-old Henry resisted efforts from black workers to organize unions, kept wages and overhead low, and continued to keep the enterprise profitable.[3]

In 1951, Loeb married Mary Gregg, the 1950 queen of the Memphis Cotton Carnival (a celebration of the Cotton South and the Confederacy).

His wife belonged to the Episcopalian Church, which he joined in 1963. Loeb's civic participation included raising money as chairman of the American Legion's Red Cross fund.[4]

A tall man referred to in the sympathetic local press as handsome, jovial, and independent of the infamous Crump political machine, Loeb began his political career by winning a race for the Memphis City Commission in 1955. Many blacks supported him for suggesting during his campaign that, as a Jew, Loeb would be sympathetic to black Memphians' needs. Each of the four elected commissioners ran a department of the municipal government with great latitude, and Loeb had control over the Public Works Department. The department's responsibilities included road maintenance, repairing city vehicles, and (continuing the work of George Waring) ensuring that sewage and drainage functioned effectively, as well as handling the city's garbage.[5]

Loeb changed the name of the Garbage Department to the Sanitation Division. Although the focus of the department was removing waste as a hazard, Loeb embraced the battle of waste as inefficiency, gaining a reputation for carefully looking at the bottom line and transforming the department into a paragon of honesty (in reaction to Mayor E. H. Crump's legendary graft and corruption). During the 1950s, Loeb pledged that Memphis's Public Works Department would benefit blacks and whites alike, and indeed road repairs, garbage collection, and sewage maintenance improved throughout the city.

An argument could be made that Loeb thought himself a benevolent manager of the Public Works employees. If, like John C. Calhoun, he thought them to be inferior, he also at times used his authority to help them. Public Works employee and labor organizer Thomas "T. O." Jones remembered that during the time Loeb ran Public Works between 1956 and 1960, "he did many good things for the men. . . . He was the first commissioner to bring vacations to them and he also was the first commissioner to allow them sick time, when a man was actually sick, and he could bring in a statement and he would be paid for it." Compared to previous management, Loeb corrected many things in the department because "he would come down and he would talk to the men and he wouldn't allow the foremens to say that 'I'll take care of this situation,' and things like that. He would hear from the men."[6]

The Emerging Environmental Inequalities of Memphis Sanitation

Keeping those efforts in mind, Loeb's management of the Public Works Department put undue burdens on African Americans. Loeb's management of municipal services was influenced by his success in the laundry business—keeping costs down at the expense of black workers. Far and away, the majority of workers in the department were African American men, and Loeb's transformation of the department forced the workers to work much harder while he held down wages and failed to invest in the repair and replacement of obsolete equipment. Under Henry Loeb, the Public Works Department became a more dangerous place to work.[7]

When a white resident reported that black sanitation workers were selling some of the scrap metal, rags, and bottles they collected, Loeb charged them with infringing upon the city's "right to contract." In response, he forced them to work an additional hour each day without pay.[8]

Workplace discrimination was a problem. Former Mississippi sharecropper L. C. Reed began working for the Public Works Department in 1954. When workers were not needed, the department sent black men home without pay. "They never sent white men home, only black men," he said. While the black men were sent home, the white men would "just sit there . . . they didn't have no one to work . . . they just sit there till four o'clock and then get up and go home [and draw their pay]."[9]

Ed Gillis, who worked primarily in the asphalt division of the Public Works Department, experienced racial discrimination on a regular basis. The black workers were subservient to the white workers, both in authority and wages. The most dangerous and dirty work was done by black workers under orders from "truck drivers [who] get out there, and they're white, they want to dictate, they want to boss."[10]

This explicit realization of environmental inequalities had benefited Loeb's family for years, and it also bolstered his political career as an example of his incorruptible passion for clean government. City services without theft, without organized labor, and without bribery were thus efficient services providing the best value to the taxpayer. That these services also were performed by impoverished African Americans was not a problem. Indeed, that, too, may have extended Loeb's popularity among the white electorate.

Mayor Loeb's White Privilege

As Commissioner Loeb set his sights on higher office, he embraced racist politics. Running for mayor in 1959, he declared: "I would fight any integration court order all the way." This stance worked. White Memphians elected Loeb mayor in 1959 with the largest number of votes in the city's history. The electorate was racially divided; though Candidate Loeb had sought the black vote in 1955, he made no effort to do so in 1959. His share of the black vote in the commissioner's election of 1955 was 12 percent; in the mayoral election of 1959 it was 2 percent.[11]

In his first term, the racial employment record of his time as commissioner continued throughout the city, with African Americans having few prospects for well-paying jobs. Only 42 of Memphis's 1,200 police officers were black, whereas almost all of the 1,300 Public Works employees were black. The exposure to injury and disease associated with the work fell exclusively on the African American community despite the entire metropolitan area contributing to the wastes that had to be managed. As Loeb became mayor, William "Bill" Farris succeeded him as commissioner overseeing Public Works. Farris continued the harsh treatment of organized labor Loeb had established in the 1950s. After Jones and some of his colleagues began their attempts to organize, Farris's manager Jimmy Cole brought them into the office to inform them their work was not satisfactory. The workers refused to accept the forms stating this, and they were fired on June 27, 1963. Jones informed Cole that they knew they were being fired for being active in the attempts to establish a union rather than any job-related performances.[12]

Despite the racist campaign and harsh working conditions, the black workers of the Public Works Department attempted to work with Mayor Loeb. As Loeb's first term neared its end, T. O. Jones attempted to meet with him to discuss the labor problems. Jones later remembered the mayor telling him "Tom, this is a matter that you have to talk with Bill Farris on. He's the commissioner." But the commissioner claimed he had no authority to recognize a union, a stance in keeping with Mayor Loeb's history.[13]

Enjoying his success, Loeb entertained a bid for Tennessee governor in 1962, but he became mired in conflicts with the city commissioners as he sought to impose his authority on them despite their having a history of autonomy. This conflict spilled into the media. As Loeb faced increasing criticism from the *Memphis Commercial Appeal* and *Memphis Press-Scimitar*, he sought to limit their access by vowing to respond only to written questions instead of unscripted interviews. Failing that, he planned to hold daily televised press conferences, but the local television stations declined to participate. In the wake of mounting public opposition, Loeb briefly engaged in a re-election campaign during the late summer of 1963. That September, however, Frederic Thesmar, who managed Loeb's Laundry, died of a heart attack. Loeb's mother and brother William urged Loeb to leave public office and run the family business. Complying, he resigned in October, one month before the 1963 election.[14]

Upon receiving news of Mayor Loeb's resignation, the African American newspaper *Tri-State Defender* blasted the outgoing mayor for "afford[ing] himself the folly of dreaming the clock back to Ante Bellum days," and hoped the resignation would end Loeb's political career.[15]

Marginal Improvements between Loeb's Terms

With that, Henry Loeb returned to private life. As was the case in 1946, Loeb's management of the family laundry business was profitable. The more moderate mayor William B. Ingram was elected and took office January 1, 1964. Pete Sisson became the commissioner overseeing Public Works. Memphis remained anti-union, but the Public Works Department employees found the new administration more receptive to talking. Workers felt conditions improved somewhat; although all of the foremen remained white men, Gillis recalled that the new mayor and commissioner improved labor conditions, established an oral grievance procedure, and invested in new equipment. "Pete Sisson said if he got elected he'd take the tubs off the colored men's hands. Well, he did that. He got them little scooters there for them to put the tubs in and push 'em and roll 'em, and then he got them other little scooters with the tractors on them for the men to put the garbage on."[16]

AFSCME prepared a charter to create Local 1733 in Memphis, and the workers held a dedication ceremony on November 13, 1964.[17] The city still did not formally recognize the workers' right to organize, but informally did negotiate with labor representatives. Jones, Sisson, and

Ingram negotiated an agreement in 1966 on labor relations. The department had people working from 7 a.m. to 5 p.m. on irregular days of the week. This agreement was never signed, but Jones remembered it was put into effect: "The mechanics were used, and it was helpful, very helpful." However, Jones believed that someone—perhaps at the Chamber of Commerce—pressured Sisson not to sign the agreement. "He would be impeached, so he said." That said, the terms were observed through 1966 and 1967.[18] After the threatened strike, Commissioner Sisson provided the workers with new rain gear; union representatives remarked that Sisson was "the first, the only commissioner that gave rain gear."[19]

The Public Works employees had made moderate progress, but their old adversary was planning his return to public life. Having arranged for his brother William to manage the laundry business, Loeb decided to run for mayor again in 1967, declaring he had done what he needed to do to run the family business, "and now I'm free to do what I please. I want to run for mayor." If opposition to integration had defined his 1959 campaign, the 1967 run was even more racially charged. Running against moderate incumbent William Ingram, Loeb used slogans like "Law and Order" and "Be Proud Again" in catering to white voters. The gambit succeeded; Loeb defeated Ingram in a November runoff, carrying more than 90 percent of the white vote. Loeb came into office in January 1968 "over the determined opposition of practically the entire black community," remembered Reverend Benjamin Hooks.[20]

A Confrontational Loeb Returns

As Loeb began his second term as mayor, Local 1733 struggled to survive. T. O. Jones had only about forty dues-paying members out of nearly 1,300 sanitation workers in the Public Works Department. The city intimidated workers away from the union, and that worsened under Loeb. Jones and fellow organizer Joe Warren, desperate, came to Loeb over the summer of 1967 and pledged to support his campaign if he'd support their right to organize. He refused. Warren remembers Loeb saying "I want all of you to go fishing on election day, I'm gonna win anyway," and when Warren threatened the workers would strike under Mayor Loeb, Loeb responded: "You'll be the first one fired."[21]

Although Mayor Loeb was a self-styled sanitation expert who prided himself on being aware of the best practices for the department, his refusal to listen to labor representatives alienated the workers. Although he claimed to have an open-door policy to listen to any worker's problems, in practice this did not work. A man who has worked eight hours on a garbage truck, Jones recounted, would have to visit the mayor's office. A worker could not do that without changing into clean clothes, and he may not have time to do that. Furthermore, the mayor's open house was only on Thursdays, and a worker with grievances had to wait in line to see the mayor. "He's got a problem, and he goes in and he discusses it with the mayor, and the mayor tells him, says, 'Well, I'll take care of this for you,' you know. Alright. This gripe, or this grievance continues to linger on, linger on, linger on. It steadily builds up. The foreman is still possibly doing the same thing he was doing at first. No relief from the mayor."[22]

This was the policy under Mayor Loeb's first term, and it was the policy in his second. Upon regaining office in January 1968, he immediately commanded public works employees to extend their hours repairing roads and collecting garbage without overtime pay. The discriminatory decisions to send black workers home without pay continued. Ed Gillis remembered the reasonable dialogue that had occurred with former Commissioner Sisson immediately ended. Sisson was better about letting workers work and paying workers when it rained than Farris was, then when Loeb came in again as mayor, he would call workers in out of the weather and not pay them.[23]

Two weeks after Loeb returned to office, drainage worker L. C. Reed remembered, he went to work at 7:15 a.m. "There come a shower of rain that morning, and it rained about half an hour after we checked in and worked, and they told us to wait awhile. And after then . . . Superintendent Stanley Smith [in the drainage department] cut the crews, and before the crew leaves the barn the sun would be shining pretty, but still go home."[24]

Twenty-two men were sent home without pay. They complained to Jones, who got Public Works director Charles Blackburn down to the sewage and drainage department on High Street to discuss the situation. Jones demanded Blackburn pay the workers for four hours because they reported to work and they were asked to work and they were willing to work. Two weeks after the discussion, the workers discovered they had been paid for two hours. Jones demanded four hours; ultimately, those workers were paid for two hours.[25]

The workers felt sending sewage and drainage workers home in wintry conditions was more about saving money than working conditions. Jones said if the men of the garbage collecting division had been sent home, "I could've kinda seen it, cause garbage freezes in cans without no tops and water's there. It won't come out. The men have to turn it up and beat on the can. Sometimes they have to get a stick and pries [pry] it out, you know, because it's frozen. But this situation was in the sewer and drainage department."[26]

Not only did the workers feel the decision was about saving money, it was made at the expense of black workers. Jones estimated that Public Works had 50 whites and approximately 150 blacks in that sewage and drainage area and recounted that "we never had but one white man— two white men—who actually had membership in Local 1733, from the time it was chartered. And therefore, it *was* a racial thing, because we didn't have one white man from at that installation . . . no whites were sent home, period."[27]

An Enraged Workforce Walks Out

Although Local 1733 had had difficulty organizing members of the Public Works Department, the situation with the sewage and drainage workers' pay infuriated them. Jones contacted Jerry Wurf with the national American Federation of State, County and Municipal Employees (AFSCME) union to send organizer P. J. Ciampa into Memphis so that Jones and Loeb could resume dialogue with the mayor.

A committee was designated by the membership to go with Jones to Director Blackburn's office, where the representatives relayed the labor concerns about wages and working conditions. Jones recalled that Blackburn had "nothing to offer us. And he really didn't show us that he wanted to be cooperative about anything. . . . He said that they mayor wouldn't let him do it."[28]

The astoundingly small stakes involved in the pay dispute provide evidence that the Public Works Department's goal was less fiscal responsibility than dominating a disrespected workforce. No workers with the title "foreman" or "crew chief" were black; positions of authority and higher pay were exclusively given to white workers.[29] Had the four-hour pay issue been settled in the workers' favor, there might not have been a walkout. The money involved—two dollars per man, for a total of $44—might have prevented the strike.[30]

Public works employee Ed Gillis saw the pay issue as racial:

If they can pay a white man $33 and $34 a day to sit up on that roller and roll asphalt, and he works about 40 minutes a day at the least, that's the most he works—40 minutes a day—they could give us a raise, see.

[Mayor Loeb] could have did that. He was just stubborn, low-down, contrary. "Let the garbage pile up on top to the top of one of these buildings, wouldn't make no difference."[31]

These were the stakes when Ciampa and Jones met with Blackburn. They established a dialogue that was to continue via a letter to the city from Ciampa. Jones then accompanied Ciampa to the airport so Ciampa could fly back to Washington. As Jones was leaving the airport, he saw that one of the men who had been working under Blackburn's direction was in a city car going to the Democrat Road installation, which led from the airport. Jones recalled, "I followed him in. He was driving so fast and everything, you know, so I wanted to know what was wrong. And he said, 'You hadn't heard?' and I said, 'No. Heard what?'" And he told me these two men were killed in this packer."[32]

The two workers, Echol Cole and Robert Walker, had been killed on a garbage truck. They were riding on the back of the truck as was procedure in Memphis's Department of Public Works. In a pouring rain, the two men tried to take cover as best they could by climbing onto a perch between a hydraulic ram used to compact the garbage and the inner wall of the truck. Somewhere along the drive, the ram activated, crushing the two men to death. One had tried to escape, but the mechanism caught his raincoat and pulled him back to his death.

Deaths had been anticipated, as workers had complained about the dangerous, malfunctioning equipment. The garbage collectors said it was "a disgrace and a sin, that they shouldn't've continued to use that particular piece of equipment." Complaints had been filed about several trucks' motors and brakes were failing. The complaints went unheeded until the tragedy occurred.[33]

The deaths infuriated the workers. Already angered about the pay issue, they gathered with local clergy (including the reverend James Lawson) and union activists to demand safer work conditions, better pay, the right of union representation, and a measure of respect. The issue of respect was vital, as the workers equated the city's treatment of them to the treatment of sharecroppers. As Jones put it, "You could say that a man is against a man because he's a Negro, and then you could say, on the other hand, that a man is against a man because he's a Negro and wants to upgrade himself."[34]

Cole and Walker's deaths were the culmination of decades of subjugation, made worse by the recent worsening treatment by the mayor's office. The subjugation was not simply of working people, but of African Americans. In Memphis, African Americans effectively *were* the sanitation department—1,300 black workers, some who grew up in the city, others who had left the crushing poverty of the cotton fields in Mississippi to pick up the garbage and yard wastes of all Memphians.

The sanitation workers had been complaining about dangerous work conditions in the meeting about the sewage and drainage workers' pay. They had reported equipment problems to the city, and this concern was among the grievances Ciampa was to follow up with via the letter to Blackburn.

Workers had frequently expressed concerns to Jones about the safety of the equipment they used, and he in turn would relay those concerns to the director of Public Works. The problem with the particular truck that had killed Cole and Walker was what was called a "weenie (or wiener) barrel packer," which was used for compacting garbage and, in this case, had a faulty motor. Instead of repairing or replacing the faulty motor, the department's response to complaints about it was to start it up in the morning and feed it gasoline throughout the day so it would not shut off. After several complaints about the motor, Jones had gone to the yard where the sanitation workers' trucks were, and the compactor with the faulty motor would be running.[35]

"Faulty equipment, that's all," Jones remembered in 1970. "Well, if they turn it off, they had to boost it off to start it again. I think it would have been cheaper to have boosted the thing off. And we would possible have had two men living today. "[36]

After the deaths, Jones got in touch with Blackburn, who said he was sorry that the tragedy had happened and that the city was going to correct it. But by this point, Blackburn's labor force was enraged. There had been no progress on wages or improvement on the pathetic state of the equipment they had to use, and now two men were dead. When Jones and the delegates returned to the 900 waiting men after the meeting with Blackburn to inform them of the negotiations, and even though the letter to Blackburn had not yet been written, the workers decided to walk out immediately. Mayor Loeb, for his part, stubbornly said: "You've got my back against the wall and I'm not the kind of mayor to budge."[37]

Jones recalled that "the decision was made by the men, and we had to report back to them, because before we left they said point blank, 'If he gives us nothing, we give him nothing for it . . .' meaning they were going to withhold their services. We didn't strike. We just withheld our services." He emphasized the choice was that of the rank and file, not the leadership. The union worried that without planning, without developing a strike fund, and without coordination, a walkout would fail. Jones said, "I asked them not to withhold their services and they told me no!"[38]

This was work white people in Memphis considered beneath them. The city found this out the hard way when it tried to recruit whites to fill the jobs during the strike. In Memphis, the necessary, vital work of keeping the neighborhoods clean was not respected by the government or by most of the citizens. It was dirty work, done by inferiors as far out of sight and out of mind as possible. Even as garbage piled up, the city did not negotiate. Mayor Loeb and Director Blackburn did not believe the walkout would succeed. The fact that a walkout happened at all stunned Loeb, who didn't believe it possible. "These men of 1968, who are the same persons on the job, are not the men of 1958 that I begun with," he said.[39]

For his part, Mayor Loeb framed his position as benevolent leader for the greater good, and he characterized his disappointment at the workers' decision as one that threatened public health: "As mayor, I represent the whole city. First, I represent these men, and have been available, and will be available, to discuss their problems. Second, and most important, I represent the public, whose health is endangered, and this cannot be tolerated."[40]

Waste and the Rhetoric of Civil Rights

Although the mayor claimed that the tasks of the sanitation department were crucial to local public health, he did not characterize the workers who performed those tasks as anything other than servile to the city. As the city demeaned the workers as infantile and disrespectful, the workers seized upon a proud, defiant slogan: I AM A MAN!

The slogan was shouted and repeated on hundreds of signs in marches, refuting the paternalism Mayor Loeb expressed toward the workers. As all residents of Memphis quickly learned, the sanitation workers' efforts were necessary to their quality of life, and tensions rapidly escalated just days into the standoff.

The strike quickly moved beyond a simple demand for better working conditions as it neatly defined the frustration of the city's African American community had in living with the existing forms of segregation. Passion for the strike built in the churches, and the sanitation workers' cause was seen in town as a civil rights issue.

This consciousness has roots in the Civil Rights era. The fight for social justice had produced several results by the winter of 1968. Fourteen years earlier, the U.S. Supreme Court had ruled unanimously in *Brown v. Board of Education* that racial segregation in public schools was unconstitutional. The decision opened the door for further challenges to the *Plessy v. Ferguson* doctrine of separate but equal that had allowed Jim Crow laws to flourish for seventy years. Following *Brown*, ten years of demonstrations culminated in a March on Washington in the summer of 1963. Accomplishments to this point included successfully desegregating transportation systems and challenging the color line in universities, restaurants, and a variety of public accommodations. By the summer of 1965, President Lyndon Johnson had signed the Civil Rights Act of 1964 and the Voting Rights Act of 1965, both intended to dismantle racial segregation across the United States.[41]

Many challenges lay ahead. Residential settlement patterns in the United States were more segregated in 1965 than they had been in 1920. Thirty years of mortgage insurance policies favoring new construction and white settlement on the suburban periphery (and making investment in areas with any African Americans difficult) had drained capital from urban neighborhoods across the United States and exacerbated racial segregation.

Martin Luther King, Jr., watched the movement grow with great interest. After a period of historic accomplishments, he had encountered two years of great frustration. Riots in Watts and Detroit in 1965 amplified the need to address segregation and economic inequality in Northern and Western cities. A march through Chicago's Marquette Park neighborhood to protest racial segregation in Northern cities had achieved nothing. Dr. King, after being hit with a rock in the face, remarked he had never seen "mobs as hostile and hate-filled as I've seen in Chicago. I think the people from Mississippi ought to come to Chicago to learn how to hate."[42]

In early 1968, Dr. King's campaigns had expanded beyond breaking the color line in the South to attempting desegregation in the urban North and to oppose the American presence in Vietnam. His vision of equality increasingly incorporated economic issues and the rights of poor people. The criticism Dr. King received for these stances was fierce, and media coverage even among the outlets that had given sympathetic perspectives on the civil rights marches in the South began to echo the J. Edgar Hoover accusations that Dr. King was a Communist and subversive.

Frustrated with a lack of progress on racial equality (despite the 1964 Civil Rights Act, violence in several cities between 1965 and 1967 underlined the continued racial and economic inequalities that plagued the United States), Dr. King proposed a Poor Peoples' Campaign that would ideally produce "distributive justice" in the form of government programs to abolish poverty by providing poor people enough money to pay for their own housing, education, and necessities. Far from promoting the image of "welfare queens" that Ronald Reagan infamously demonized in 1980, these programs would allow participants to get the training required to get and keep a good job and work one's way out of poverty without being beaten down by perpetual debt while reducing the problems of crime, violence, and substance abuse that accompanied poverty. Dr. King's proposals were not unique at the time, as many politicians and academics proposed similar antidotes for the ills of poverty. Yet the scorn he received for advocating these ideas helped make a sustained campaign difficult. In the winter of 1968, Dr. King made several speeches to build the campaign, yet with few organizational achievements.

For Dr. King the Memphis sanitation workers' strike reflected the injustice he was fighting. Despite conflicts between his staffers at the Southern Christian Leadership Conference (SCLC) and strikers, King urged labor and civil rights activists to work together. The poor working conditions and benefits that this exclusively African American workforce put up with while removing the wastes of the city of Memphis were as apt a setting for King's Poor People's Campaign as any he had found. Imploring his staff to see the strike through, King remarked "the movement lives or dies in Memphis."[43]

The strike quickly became a national focal point for labor activism and civil rights. Memphis's churches and local National Association for the Advancement of Colored People (NAACP) chapter saw it as the launching point to address the systemic ills of segregation plaguing the city. Caught by surprise by the sudden walkout, AFSCME saw it as an opportunity to unionize municipal workers in a city that had resisted unionization. Dr. King saw it as the way to present the Poor People's Campaign to the nation.

On March 18, 1968, Dr. King came to Memphis. Speaking at the Bishop Charles Mason Temple in front of 25,000 people (the largest indoor mass meeting of the Civil Rights movement) he framed the struggle as an issue of justice, declaring: "We are tired of being at the bottom. . . . We are tired of working our hands off and laboring every day and not even making a wage adequate to get the basic necessities of life. We are tired of our men being emasculated so that our wives and daughters have to go out and work in the white lady's kitchen leaving us unable to be with our children and give them the time and attention that they need. We are tired."[44]

The crowd, fully into Dr. King's speech, enthusiastically agreed when he extended the strikers' plight to that of all African American Memphians and asked them all—if the city did not come to terms with the strikers—to have a general work stoppage. The alliances, both local and national, involving labor organizations and civil rights organizations were complex. The local media, sympathetic to the mayor, branded the strikers as shiftless and Communist and national union organizers as unwelcome. White people in Memphis had a bad reaction to Ciampa's presence, running unflattering stories in the newspapers and distributing bumper stickers saying "Ciampa Go Home."[45] The reaction to the national AFSCME presence did not surprise Jones. "This has been a tradition with the Southern white. When someone come in to help the blacks that you're just stirring up trouble, you know. 'We know our own people.'"[46]

Within the movement were complex relationships. Some of the ministers in local African American churches also were workers in the Public Works Department, so the churches were already involved to some degree. Then the Ministers' Alliance got the local to touch base with several people, including black civic leaders and some white labor leaders. The local was receptive to their help, Jones said: "Because we needed community involvement; we could not discard the community."[47]

The involvement of Dr. King and the SCLC brought national attention to the dispute, though the local was concerned that the SCLC's presence would distract from the negotiations. Ultimately, Jones thought their participation distracted from the original intent of the walkout: "A union has always tried to keep an issue as a union issue," Jones recalled, "but where there are as many blacks involved as was there, or there are other blacks involved, it finally becomes to be a racial issue, let's face it. Because, I don't know why—but for some reason the civil rights group is going to get in there. And you cannot tell them no. Especially where you're reading out for support."[48]

Jones had been working in a context of organized labor, with rhetoric and strategies coming from organized labor. When King came in with the rhetoric and strategies of the Civil Rights movement, Jones felt this produced conflict. "Well, a lot of people tie civil rights issues and labor issues together, and I guess they are right. But I say a labor problem is a labor problem and should stay in a labor context. . . . When you get the civil rights people involved . . . it does muddy up things you know. They come in with different ideas, and they want to do different things. And you got your militants that follow certain civil rights groups and all that. So you got problem."[49]

In contrast, Gillis valued the efforts of the ministers, whose emphasis on nonviolence prevented much more bloodshed. The tensions within the movement were the result of an unprecedented set of alliances pushing what had started as a dispute over waste workers' pay and working conditions into a focal point of the national civil rights struggle.[50]

Violent Assertions of White Privilege

Dr. King's participation drew national media attention to the Memphis strike. Despite the national focus, Mayor Loeb held firm in his refusal to negotiate. His truculence sparked a consumer boycott of Memphis businesses, and as tensions escalated, so did the city's willingness to suppress the movement with violence. A march on March 28 erupted in violence and tear gas. Maxine Smith of the Memphis NAACP looked down the line of demonstrators and saw some "very unsavory characters" removing heavy sticks from picket signs. She had never seen picket signs that large—they looked more like clubs.

Signs appeared on the sidewalks: "Damn Loeb—Black Power is here."

Memphis police sought to crush any possible violence from the demonstration with an overwhelming show of violence. When it was over, a sixteen-year-old boy named Larry Payne had been killed at the hands of the police. Six-hundred seventy people were injured, and 155 stores were damaged. Dr. King and James Lawson opposed the confrontation, with King announcing, "I will never lead a violent march, so, please, call it off." But it was too late.[51]

Dr. King's reputation suffered because of this march, with critics mocking his calls for nonviolent activism as hollow. Picketing continued after the march was broken up but under conditions that belied America's reputation as a free society. The city's stance against the strike was literally militant, forcing picketers to march in single file in the presence of overwhelming security forces.

Dr. King regrouped to speak at one more rally at the Mason Temple on April 3, delivering the "I've Been to the Mountaintop" speech, which proved to be his final public address. The speech should be read (or better yet, heard) unabridged to appreciate Dr. King's call to economic

Civil Rights Marchers with "I Am a Man" Signs, Memphis, 1968. The Bettman Archive
BE001140, used under license from Corbis Images.

and nonviolent action, but an important aspect was King's focus the
city's unjust dealings with vulnerable sanitation workers. He lamented
that the press focused on violence rather than the fact that 1,300 sanitation workers were on strike "and that Mayor Loeb is in dire need
of a doctor."[52]

The metaphor of illness to describe white Memphians' behavior was
repeated one more time in the speech. King said this was a struggle that
had to be seen through to the end, and it would be tragic not to stand
up for the workers regardless of the dangers. He referred to the personal
threats on his life, wondering, "What would happen to me from some of
our sick white brothers?" King's choice of words amplified the irony of
Memphis delegating vital sanitation work to African Americans in ways
that corrupted the moral health of the white population.

He concluded by proclaiming to the crowd that he was not afraid of
death, even if he might not live to see the movement through to victory.
Whatever happened to him, he had been to the mountaintop and seen
what progress lay ahead. With that, he inspired the crowd to keep moving toward the Promised Land.

He was killed the following evening. When Americans hear the words "MLK" and "Memphis" together, minds inevitably turn to the details of Dr. King's death. Too often, though, we forget what Dr. King was doing in Memphis—and that his death effectively ended the strike as the city recognized the union's right to exist in the wake of the overwhelming grief and rage that gripped the nation. We forget how the events of early 1968 reflected not only his long-standing campaign for civil rights, but how that concern intersected with the specific injustices of the sanitation workers in ways that compelled Dr. King to work with them.

Aftermath: Justice for Sanitation Workers

In the immediate aftermath of Dr. King's death, his widow Coretta Scott King led a march through the streets of Memphis that attracted international attention. The Public Works Department workers held fast to their demands that Loeb recognize their right to organize. Meanwhile President Johnson implored Mayor Loeb to end the strike. The outrage over Dr. King's death allowed the strikers to win recognition from the city and gain some measure of job security and economic justice.[53]

In some respects, the stakes were small. The money demanded for wages and equipment was a pittance of the city's budget. That it took the killing of a Nobel Peace Prize recipient, the specter of riots across the United States, and pressure from the president of the United States for the city to settle indicates how invested Memphis and Mayor Loeb were in subjugating the black sanitation workers. The dispute was about respect for the workers as valuable guardians of public health doing the work Mayor Loeb took credit for as commissioner and mayor. Loeb positioned himself as the protector of Memphis's hygiene and characterized the workers as ungrateful dupes led astray by forces from outside of Memphis.

Mrs. L. C. Reed, wife of one of the strikers, saw Loeb as condescending and paternalistic, unable to see the workers as men or bargain sincerely with them:

> I believe if Mr. Loeb had taken the men and talked to them and explained to them there wasn't no money and explained to them that he would give them a raise when he could, but still instead he was telling them

like some little child, like you tell a little child, "Go on back to work, I'll give you some candy," or "Stop that!" You [can't] treat them like little children you know, anybody. Men are mens these days, no matter what color they are.

They're men and they's supposed, you know, to look out for themselves. You don't tell men, you know, just talk to them any kind of way. I believe if he had just got them all and talked to them, that they would have gone on back to work and all this would have been, you know, different ways.[54]

T. O. Jones, the man who had worked for eight years to unionize the sanitation workers, who had himself been the target of an incredible amount of threats and physical abuse, tearfully summed up the mood upon ratification of the new union contract. "We have been aggrieved many times, we have lost many things. But we have got the victory."[55]

It was a victory that combined the efforts of civil rights and labor organizers, both local to Memphis and nationwide. Dr. King's involvement and framing of the dispute in moral terms, combined with the tragedy of his assassination, provided the legitimacy to overcome Mayor Loeb's resistance to recognizing the power of his black workers. Jones recognized this, summing up the victory as having happened when "the muscles of the community and the muscles of the nation began to get behind you. Then when the muscles of the President stepped in, these people have a right, you know, and this is what really helped to change the climate tremendously, in my opinion."[56]

It was not, to be sure, a victory that would erase all existing injustices, but it was a victory that would better the lives of hundreds of workers. After 1968, waste handing in Memphis remained the domain of black labor, but at least these workers had won the right to collectively bargain. Their struggle presented the most forceful revolt yet against racial inequality in waste disposal practices.

Environmental Justice beyond the Memphis Strike

The confrontation at Memphis was relevant to the long history of environmental racism in two respects. The first was the role of Mayor Henry Loeb III. Mayor Loeb was the descendant of Jewish immigrants who had gained wealth through a chain of laundry businesses. The chain employed mostly African American women to do the labor as the family reaped the wealth. Loeb enjoyed an elite education and mingled with elite whites in Memphis, even converting to the Episcopal Church. He had achieved the full measure of white privilege and used this status to win elections. Once in power, he managed Memphis's sanitation department as he had managed the family business. His confrontational, paternalist approach toward the workers provoked the walkout and the tragic violence that ensued.

The Memphis strike was also important for what the strikers accomplished. The words "environmental justice" did not pass through any sanitation worker's lips in 1968. The terminology and expressed goals of that movement were more than a decade away from coming into existence. Yet the consciousness of organizing non-white workers who were performing the dirty work to keep the city clean and framing that organization as an issue of justice was an important precedent for the ways in which environmental racism would be addressed.

The immediate aftermath of the Memphis action saw momentum for organized labor and its alliance with the Civil Rights movement. Under pressure from President Johnson, Mayor Loeb negotiated a contract with AFSCME. Subsequently, the national union worked to organize sanitation workers in other cities. In the months after the Memphis strike concluded, T. O. Jones left his post as president of the local and worked with the national AFSCME to organize other locals of sanitation workers, including ones in Tampa and Saint Petersburg, Florida, Baltimore, and Spring Valley, New York. The union sent Jones to Washington, DC, with the instruction to assist SCLC in any way that they could.[57]

When the Memphis Public Works employees allied first with local churches and then the national Civil Rights movement, their cause shifted from being a labor grievance to a more complex definition of their plight as demeaned black waste workers seeking social justice. The city's paternalism and inequitable working conditions that placed the dirtiest jobs in black hands shaped that definition. The burdens of waste and race had become a nationally recognized civil rights issue.

The conflict between Mayor Loeb and the Public Works employees was a conflict between those who enjoyed the privileges of racialized hygiene and those made vulnerable by the environmental burdens of racialized hygiene. The conflict consumed the city, left an American icon dead, and triggered strife across the United States. It also produced an articulated resistance that joined waste handling workers, organized labor, African American churches, and the people and organizations of the Civil Rights movement in fighting the status quo. It led to an immediate victory in recognizing the workers' right to organize and negotiate their working conditions. This victory was followed by similar victories across the nation.

Although the Memphis sanitation workers won the right to organize, environmental inequalities persisted in the city as well as throughout the United States. The vast majority of laborers charged with handling Memphis's wastes remained African American. The overrepresentation of people of color in waste handling occupations across the United States remained well above their representation in the general population ten years after the Memphis strike.

Members of African American communities across the nation had complained about waste facilities sited in their neighborhoods for decades; in the years after the Memphis strike, these complaints were reframed as violations of civil rights. In 1978, plans to create a landfill in the majority African American middle-class Houston, Texas, neighborhood of Northwood Manor resulted in the attorney Linda McKeever Bullard filing a class-action lawsuit that successfully blocked the landfill. During the trial her husband, the sociologist Robert D. Bullard, completed a study of waste siting in Houston that established that siting was based upon racial characteristics of the chosen areas, regardless of income levels.[58]

In 1982, the state of North Carolina considered how to dispose of 32,000 cubic yards of soil contaminated with toxic PCBs (polychlorinated biphenyls) that had been illegally dumped along the roadways in fourteen North Carolina counties in 1978 by the Raleigh-based Ward Transfer Company. It settled on an area that seemed to have little political capital. Warren County, a rural, mostly African American county in northern North Carolina (closer to Virginia Beach than Raleigh or Charlotte), was selected as the disposal site. In the 1980 Census, Warren County had the highest percentage of African Americans in the state; it was also one of the poorest counties in North Carolina. The precise location of the landfill was Afton, a community that was 84 percent African American. The selection of the site continued a pattern of inequalities that endured because the state reasoned that little political opposition would emerge in poor, rural, black Warren County.[59]

Yet the announced plans drew powerful responses by a coalition resembling the one that came together in Memphis. Local residents organized, forming the Warren County Citizens Concerned About PCBs. National civil rights leaders, black elected officials, environmental activists, and labor leaders joined the local protestors. The reverend Leon White of the United Church of Christ's Commission for Racial Justice, reverends Joseph Lowery and Ben Chavis and Fred Taylor of the Southern Christian Leadership Conference, District of Columbia House Delegate Walter E. Fauntroy, and approximately 500 supporters were able to focus the national limelight on the tiny black town of Afton.

Dr. Charles E. Cobb, director of the United Church of Christ's Commission for Racial Justice, voiced his strong opposition to the landfill and other siting decisions that make blacks and the poor bear a heavier burden than other communities. Cobb's rhetoric framed the waste issue as a matter of civil rights: "We must move in a swift and determined manner to stop yet another breach of civil rights. We cannot allow this national trend to continue. If it means that every jail in this country must be filled, then I say let it be. The depositing of toxic wastes within the black community is no less than attempted genocide."[60]

Their protests did not prevent the trucks from rolling in and dumping their loads. The state began hauling more than 6,000 truckloads of the PCB-contaminated soil to the landfills in mid-September 1982. Just two weeks later, more than 414 protesters had been arrested. The protest demonstrations in Warren County marked the first time anyone in the United States had been jailed trying to halt a toxic waste landfill.[61]

Although the demonstrations in North Carolina were not successful in halting the landfill construction, the protests brought a sharper focus to the convergence of civil rights and environmental rights and mobilized a nationally broad based group to protest these inequities. Many more conflicts based on race and waste would come. With those conflicts came a new strategy informed by the Memphis experience. Waste had become a part of the consciousness of civil rights and racial equity. Those protests followed the Memphis model of discussing the dangers of waste in a civil rights context. In contrast to the environmental movement that developed in the wake of Rachel Carson's *Silent Spring* in the 1960s, the Environmental Justice movement was rooted in the institutions and rhetoric of the Civil Rights movement. The alliances and arguments of Memphis provided a context for these protests and the research that has informed American understanding of environmental justice.

After the 1982 Warren County demonstrations, Fauntroy directed the 1983 U.S. General Accounting Office (GAO) to complete a study of hazardous-waste landfill siting in the region. This study, completed in 1983, observed a strong relationship between the siting of off-site hazardous-waste landfills and race and the socioeconomic status of surrounding communities.[62]

The GAO study identified four off-site hazardous-waste landfills in the eight Southern states in Region IV of the Environmental Protection Agency (Alabama, Florida, Georgia, Kentucky, Mississippi, North Carolina, South Carolina, and Tennessee). It concluded that, although blacks made up about 20 percent of the region's population in the 1980 Census, they constituted the majority population in three of the four communities where the off-site hazardous-waste landfills were located.[63] The facility siting controversy cannot be reduced solely to a class phenomenon because there is no shortage of poor white communities in the region.[64]

The GAO provided broad regional evidence of racial disparities in toxic waste siting. The same year its study was released, the NAACP passed its first resolution on hazardous waste. Subsequent protest actions were instrumental in getting the New York–based Commission for Racial Justice to sponsor its 1987 national study of toxic waste and race. This national study, like the GAO report on the South, found a strong association between race and the location of hazardous-waste facilities. Race was by far the most prominent factor in the location of commercial hazardous-waste landfills, more prominent than household income and home values. The report concluded that

— Race proved to be the most significant among variables tested in association with the location of commercial hazardous waste facilities. This represented a consistent national pattern.

— Communities with the greatest number of commercial hazardous waste facilities had the highest composition of racial and ethnic residents. In communities with two or more facilities or one of the nation's five largest landfills, the average minority percentage of the population was more than three times that of communities without facilities (38 percent vs. 12 percent).

— In communities with one commercial hazardous waste facility, the average minority percentage of the population was twice the average minority percentage of the population in communities without such facilities (24 percent vs. 12 percent).

— Although socio-economic status appeared to play an important role in the location of commercial hazardous waste facilities, race still proved to be more significant. This remained true after the study controlled for urbanization and regional differences. Incomes and home values were substantially lower when communities with commercial facilities were compared to communities in the surrounding counties without facilities.[65]

Following more than a century of environmental inequalities, waste had become a recognized civil rights issue in the United States. Existing environmental inequalities would be articulated as environmental justice issues. A new chapter in American environmental history had begun. The illusion of "clean and white" endured after Memphis, but a new resistance conscious of the illusion's consequences had emerged.

Conclusion

A Dirty History

Waste is a social process, and waste management practices in the United States reveal the constructions of environmental racism. Since the end of the Civil War, American sanitation systems; zoning boards; real estate practices; federal, state, and municipal governments; and makers and marketers of cleaning products have all worked with an understanding of hygiene that assumes that "white people" are clean, and "non-white people" are less than clean. This assumption is fundamental to racist claims of white supremacy, a rhetoric that involves concepts of "race pollution," "white purity," and the "dangers" of non-white sexuality as "miscegenation." It is also fundamental to broad social and environmental inequalities that emerged after the Civil War and that remain in place in the early twenty-first century.

Are Americans unique in our waste handling practices? In some respects, no. Social inequities in waste siting and handling exist throughout human societies. In India, for example, the Hindi caste system evolved over thousands of years to include a lower caste—the untouchable Bhangi—who are charged with handling wastes. By 1912, observer John MacGowan noted that the lowly classes in China had "for ages" settled the issue of fertilizing the nation's fields by collecting "night-soil" (human excrement) and carrying it to the agricultural districts. Although Parisians valued that city's elaborate sewer system when it was constructed, few bragged about the sewer workers who kept it functioning. Work with waste rarely escapes stigma in any corner of the world, and waste handling people are often classified within a particular social group.[1]

The American example, however, has important distinctions— exceptions that reveal much about assumed social and spatial norms in this country. The cultural assumption of white cleanliness has shaped modern American society—and not only during the era of Jim Crow, when facilities ranging from water fountains to restaurants to hospitals were racially segregated to protect white society from racial pollution south of the Mason-Dixon line. American residential settlement patterns were shaped by a cultural understanding of suburbs as cleaner than cities, as refuges of nature available to white people (initially the upper and upper-middle classes, and then, with government assistance, working-class white families after World War II). For most of the twentieth century, these suburban idylls were de jure or de facto exclusive to whites—and to the people who achieved whiteness over time. "White flight" from the dirty cities to the pristine suburbs was so commonplace as to be called a symptom of the urban crisis in the final third of the century. And, as the historian Adam Rome has argued, the modern environmental movement emerged from those white middle-class families who moved to the suburbs and found that the smog from automobiles, watershed destruction from subdivisions, and solid waste management problems from sprawl made their new suburban lives dirtier than they imaged, expected, and had paid for. By 1970, white people expected to have clean bodies and clean clothes and to live in clean neighborhoods, with waste out of sight and out of mind.[2]

Who could blame them? For a century, American waste management systems had been organized to keep white communities clean. From the time that garbage hauling and scrap material recycling had become profitable for private enterprise in the United States in the early twentieth century, these waste management jobs have largely been done by people who were not considered white at the time they were doing these jobs. Historians are thus able to offer a key contribution to our contemporary discussion of racial and environmental problems, for the definitions of whiteness in the United States have evolved over time to include more people, including those of Irish, Italian, and Jewish ancestry. Yet they have not evolved, to the date of this book, to include African Americans; Latino communities are likewise still referred to as people of color. The Environmental Justice movement that emerged in the 1980s grew in recognition that Americans of non-white identities were particularly vulnerable to working in and living near toxic waste sites, and it emerged with the rhetoric and alliances that informed the Memphis sanitation workers' action in 1968.

The inequalities endure, as do the constructions of environmental racism. The corrosive stereotype of "clean and white" affected a watershed moment in American race relations. On January 20, 2009, Barack Obama took the oath of office as president of the United States of America. More than one million people huddled together on the National Mall to witness his inauguration. Days before the big event, the historian Douglas Brinkley declared that the swearing-in of the first black president of the United States "is the culmination of the freedom struggle. It's a national marathon of incremental steps that began with the first slavery revolt, continued through the Civil War, Reconstruction, the Jim Crow era and the civil rights movement."[3]

"There is no way we can overdramatize what is happening," Brinkley stated. "When he takes the oath of office, there will be a healing. If slavery is our original curse and racism is our national disease, Obama is a cultural healing agent." From the moment he captured the nation's attention at the Democratic National Convention in 2004, the young senator from Illinois ably wove his story as part of a grand American narrative, one including not only civil rights leaders but presidents from Jefferson to Lincoln to Roosevelt. The forty-fourth president of the United States offered a rhetoric of unity.[4] After the event, Brinkley exclaimed: "Barack Obama's inauguration stands as the most uplifting public spectacle in contemporary American history since Neil Armstrong walked on the moon."[5]

If the inauguration promised change, it revealed continuities. Standing by the new president's side throughout the festivities on January 20 was his vice president, Joe Biden. Two years earlier, on the day his own bid for the presidency began, Biden attempted to compliment his rival for the Democratic nomination. Speaking to a reporter for the *New York Observer* about the crowded Democratic field, Biden described Obama as "the first mainstream African-American who is articulate and bright and clean and a nice-looking guy."[6]

The comment immediately demolished Biden's presidential campaign. Critics blasted the senator from Delaware for racial insensitivity. The economist and blogger Duncan Black wrote: "Volumes could be written about all that was wrong with what Biden said about Obama, but I believe we've just witnessed the shortest presidential run in history." Josh Marshall of *Talking Points Memo*, responding to reader posts that a missing comma in the transcript may have changed the meaning of Mr. Biden's words, said: "Even with the comma it's really condescending, bordering on racist. And it would still probably mean that Biden's mouth presents a clear and present danger to Democratic electoral prospects no matter what he meant."[7]

Many white observers (reportedly including the outgoing president George W. Bush) were confused that an attempted compliment might get Joe Biden into so much trouble, but African American journalists had little difficulty expounding on Biden's offense. In the *Boston Globe*, columnist Derek Z. Jackson wrote that Biden's comments "sparked a debate about unconscious stereotypes about white people still being shocked in the year 2007 that educated black people can speak, take baths, or aren't running off with your purse."[8]

Jackson's comment about taking baths underlined the truly offensive nature of the comment. Writing in the *Washington Post*, the columnist Eugene Robinson politely admonished the Delaware senator. "I'll leave it to Joe Biden to explain (or figure out) why he used 'clean' as one of a logorrheic string of adjectives describing his Senate colleague Barack Obama. I'm not sure his initial revision and extension of his remarks—that he meant 'clean as a whistle'—get him off the hook."

Robinson noted that Obama's reaction attempted to deflect the most incendiary aspects of the comment, focusing on the misperception of Obama as the first articulate candidate for president. Obama stated: "I didn't take Senator Biden's comments personally, but obviously they were historically inaccurate. African American presidential candidates like Jesse Jackson, Shirley Chisholm, Carol Moseley Braun, and [Al Sharpton] gave a voice to many important issues through their campaigns, and no one would call them inarticulate." As Robinson noted, Obama did not reference the "clean" remark at all, nor did he address its implications.[9]

Biden's choice of words implied that Obama's oratorical skills were certainly above average, and while the senator from Illinois had already established himself as a superb speechmaker, in context the compliment implied that most men of African heritage were not good speakers. But why did Biden think to call Obama *clean*? The comment seemed meant to separate an exceptional individual from the norm—a norm where

African Americans were considered less than clean. There is no question as to why Jackson and Robinson drew offense; the question is what prompted Biden to think of the term.

The answer is that, whether conscious or unconscious, Biden's choice of words revealed the troubling history of the United States's particular system of classifying dirt. In this case, Obama was not materially harmed by the comment; the immediate effect damaged Biden's candidacy, and Obama went on to win the presidency. Yet even as Obama moved into the White House, material consequences of the stereotype continue to harm many in the United States. Two months after Biden's comment, the United Church of Christ published an update to its 1987 report. *Toxic Wastes and Race at Twenty, 1987–2007*, concluding that "race continues to be an independent predictor of where hazardous wastes are located, and it is a stronger predictor than income, education, and other socioeconomic indicators." Despite two decades of grassroots organizing and recognition from the U.S. Environmental Protection Agency that environmental justice is a concern, the report's findings "raise serious doubts about the ability of current policies and institutions to adequately protect people of color and the poor from toxic threats."[10]

The material consequences of waste siting persist. The material consequences of racialized waste work also continue to harm workers. Barack Obama rose to fame after winning the Illinois Democratic primary for U.S. Senate on March 16, 2004. Two weeks after the primary, on the morning of April 2, Daniel Valdivia left his home in Cicero and headed east into Chicago to his job at a plastics recycling facility on the city's West Side. Around two o'clock that afternoon, while standing on a platform feeding plastic waste into a reprocessing machine, he lost his footing, fell, and got entangled in the machine's automatic shredder. He was pronounced dead at the scene. Daniel Valdivia was 65 years old.[11]

The facts of this workplace accident were almost not newsworthy. Workers performing the dirty work of managing industrial society's wastes risk injuries and illness every day. The accident took place inside a facility on Chicago's West Side, located in the middle of one of the largest African American communities in the United States. The dead worker was of Hispanic heritage, representative of the ethnic makeup of the material recycling industry's workforce. Rare is the material recycling facility in the Chicago area where the workers on the line are not Hispanic or African American.[12]

The workplace conditions Echol Cole and Robert Walker faced persist. Every day, workers handling wastes are exposed to ear-damaging volumes; particulate matter and fumes; risks of puncture, abrasion, and chemical burns; and even possible explosions. The burdens of waste labor remain racially unbalanced. As I researched this book in 2013, eighteen-year-old worker Luis Carmarillo died when the hydraulic compactor of a paper recycling truck crushed him. His death occurred a brief walk from my office in Brooklyn; the papers that I, a professor, place in my office recycling bin may have been in that truck.[13]

The circumstances that killed Cole and Walker inspired new resistance to environmental racism, but environmental racism continues to imperil American waste workers. Without attention to the cultural constructions of waste and race, and the material consequences of those constructions, the United States will be home to environmental inequalities well into the future. Perhaps reconsidering the history of the nation through the lens of dirt will help Americans attend to these enduring inequalities and enable the United States to live up to Thomas Jefferson's declaration that all its people are created equal, with the ability to enjoy life, liberty, and the pursuit of happiness.

NOTES

INTRODUCTION

1 Douglas, *Purity and Danger*, xi.

2 Chavis, quoted in Di Charo, "Nature as Community," 304; the original quote is from Grossman, "From Toxic Racism," 31. See Commission for Racial Justice, *Toxic Wastes and Race*.

3 Norment, "Ben Chavis," 78.

4 Cole and Foster, *From the Ground Up*, 17.

5 Bernier, *Almost Everything*, 2.

6 Commission for Racial Justice, *Toxic Wastes and Race*. Following the landmark 1987 Commission for Racial Justice study, significant works in this field include Hurley, *Environmental Inequalities*; Bullard, *Dumping in Dixie*; Pulido, "Rethinking Environmental Racism"; Pellow, *Garbage Wars*; Washington, *Packing Them In*; Sze, *Noxious New York*; Honey, *Going Down Jericho Road*; McGurty, *Transforming Environmentalism*; Taylor, *Toxic Communities*; Norton et al., "Race, Wealth, and Solid Waste Facilities"; Maranville, Ting, and Zhang, "An Environmental Justice Analysis."

7 See, e.g., Roediger, *The Wages of Whiteness*; Crenshaw, *Critical Race Theory*; Delgado, *Critical Race Theory*; Gates, *The Concept of "Race"*; Parker, Deyhle, and Villenas, *Race Is—Race Isn't*; Brodkin, *How Jews Became White Folks*; Roediger, *Working toward Whiteness*; Painter, *The History of White People*.

8 Valenčius, *The Health of the Country*.

9 On constructions of white identity and the law in the United States, see López, *White by Law*; Gross, *What Blood Won't Tell*.

10 Sellers, "Thoreau's Body," 486–514.

11 Shoemaker, *A Strange Likeness*, 129–130.

12 In his discussion of biopolitics, Foucault identified four major types of technologies that people use to create power relations. These include technologies of production, "which permit us to produce, transform, or manipulate things"; technologies of sign systems, "which permit us to use signs, meanings, symbols, or signification"; technologies of power, "which determine the conduct of individuals and submit them to certain ends or domination"; and technologies of the self, "which permit individuals to effect by their own means or with the help of others a certain number of operations on their own bodies and souls, thoughts, conduct, and way of being, so as to transform themselves in order to attain a certain state of happiness, purity, wisdom, perfection, or immortality." Foucault argued that these four types of

technologies "hardly ever function separately, although each one of them is associated with a certain type of domination. Each implies certain modes of training and modification of individuals, not only in the obvious sense of acquiring certain skills but also in the sense of acquiring certain attitudes" (Michel Foucault, "Technologies of the Self," 18).

CHAPTER 1. THOMAS JEFFERSON'S IDEAL

1 Quoted in Ellis, *American Sphinx*, 345–346; citation of Thomas Jefferson to Roger C. Weightman, June 24, 1826, found in Ford, *The Writings of Thomas Jefferson*, 390–392. The handwritten draft, with its multiple cross-outs and revisions, is reproduced in Ellis, *Passionate Sage*, 207.

2 Randall, *Thomas Jefferson*, 585–595; Ellis, *American Sphinx*, 344–346.

3 Jefferson, *Notes on the State of Virginia*, query 19, 276–277; Thomas Jefferson to Benjamin Rush, 1800, in Lipscomb and Bergh, *The Writings of Thomas Jefferson*, 10:173.

4 Letter to Baron Geismer, Paris, September 6, 1785, in Jefferson, *Memoir, Correspondence, and Miscellanies*, 311–312.

5 Jefferson to James Madison, 1787, in Jefferson, *The Papers of Thomas Jefferson*, 12:442.

6 Jefferson to John Melish, 1813, in Lipscomb and Bergh, *The Writings of Thomas Jefferson*, 13:207; Jefferson to Benjamin Austin, 1816, in ibid., 14:389.

7 Jefferson to William Short, 1823, in ibid., 15:469.

8 Jefferson to James Jay, 1809, in ibid., 12:271.

9 Jefferson, *Notes on the State of Virginia*, 169.

10 Ibid., 280.

11 Ibid., 290.

12 Ibid., 259.

13 U.S. Bureau of the Census, "Population and Housing Unit Counts" (1990), CPH-2-1, table 46.

14 Hoy, *Chasing Dirt*, 4.

15 April 29, 1798, in Latrobe, *The Journal of Latrobe*, 92–98.

16 Hoy, *Chasing Dirt*, 4.

17 Duffy, *The Sanitarians*, 33.

18 Wood, *The Radicalism of the American Revolution*, 51.

19 United States Congress, "An act to establish an uniform Rule of Naturalization" (March 26, 1790), Ch. 3, 1 Stat. 103; López, *White by Law*, 1.

20 Lewis, "Industrial Slavery."

21 Shoemaker, *A Strange Likeness*, 129.

22 Ibid., 129–130; Jordan, *White over Black*; Smedley and Smedley, *Race in North America*; Painter, *The History of White People*.

23 Foote, *Black and White Manhattan*, 97–98.

24 Painter, *The History of White People*, 111–112.

25 Jefferson, *Memoir, Correspondence, and Miscellanies*, 229–230.

26 Jefferson, *Notes on the State of Virginia*, 270.

27 Ibid., 266.

28 Act of March 26, 1790, Ch. 3, 1 Stat. 103.

29 Jefferson, *Notes on the State of Virginia*, 229.

30 Ibid., 149; emphasis added.

31 Ibid., 229–230.

32 Ibid., 230–231.

33 Ibid., 273.

34 Jefferson to Doctor Walter Jones, March 31, 1801, in Washington, ed., *The Writings of Thomas Jefferson*, 4:392–393.

35 Jefferson to William A. Burwell, January 28, 1805, in Ford, ed., *The Works of Thomas Jefferson*, 126–127.

36 Berlin, *Generations of Captivity*, 168.

37 Taylor, *The Internal Enemy*, 408.

38 Jefferson to John Holmes, April 22, 1820, in Washington, ed., *The Writings of Thomas Jefferson*, 7:159–160.

39 Jefferson, *Notes on the State of Virginia*, 291.

40 Letter to Baron Geismer, Paris, September 6, 1785, in Jefferson, *Memoir, Correspondence, and Miscellanies*, 311–312.

41 Randall, *The Life of Thomas Jefferson*, 3:278.

CHAPTER 2. THE DECAY OF THE OLD

1 John Quincy Adams was the first president to use the term "representative democracy"; see Parsons, *John Quincy Adams*, 176.

2 North, *The Economic Growth of the United States*; Koeppel, *Bond of Union*.

3 Anbinder, *Nativism and Slavery*, ix; Hurt, "The Rise and Fall of the 'Know Nothings.'"

4 Duffy, *The Sanitarians*, 305.

5 Ibid., 52

6 Ibid., 99.

7 On Cole, who went from New York City to visit the Catskills, see Stradling, *Making Mountains*, 59–75.

8 Hoy, *Chasing Dirt*, 26.

9 Griscom, *The Sanitary Condition of the Laboring Population*, 14.

10 Ibid., 55.

11 Massachusetts Sanitary Commission et al., *Report of a General Plan*, 428.

12 Ibid., 521.

13 Ibid., 271.

14 Duffy, *The Sanitarians*, 99.

15 Melosi, *Garbage in the Cities*, 21–22; Rosenberg, *The Cholera Years*, 5.

16 Einhorn, *Property Rules*.

17 Beecher, *A Treatise on Domestic Economy*, 15, 16.

18 Hoy, *Chasing Dirt*, 15.

19 Ibid., 17.

20 "The New York Labor Market: Female House Servants," *Harper's Weekly* 1 (July 4, 1857): 418–419; Juneiana, *Talks on Women's Topics*, 45; Hoy, *Chasing Dirt*, 15.

21 President Thomas Jefferson's confidential message to Congress concerning relations with the Indians, January, 18, 1803, Record Group 233, Records of the United States House of Representatives, HR 7A-D1, National Archives. On removal efforts in the eighteenth century, see Warren, *The Worlds the Shawnees Made*, 15–16.

22 Andrew Jackson, "Second Annual Message to Congress," December 7, 1830, in *Congressional Serial Set*, quoted passage on 20.

23 Foreman, *Indian Removal*; Green, *The Politics of Indian Removal*.

24 Calhoun, "Speech on the Abolition Petitions."

25 Gould, *The Mismeasure of Man*, 102.

26 Ibid., 102–103.

27 Massachusetts Sanitary Commission et al., *Report of a General Plan*, 411.

28 Matt Wray, *Not Quite White*, 41.

29 Ibid., 23.

30 De Tocqueville, *Democracy in America*, 426. On de Tocqueville's discussion of race in America, see Painter, *The History of White People*, 124–128.

31 Dickens, *Household Words*, 3–4. Dickens was not immune to racializing waste-trade workers; his *Oliver Twist* character Fagin is the most famous Shylock character in literary history, a hook-nosed Jewish "receiver of stolen goods" who corrupts children. This stereotype, present in England at mid-century, became a common identifier of Jewish scrap dealers by the early twentieth century.

32 Trollope, "Washington to St. Louis."

33 Valenčius, *The Health of the Country*, 256.

34 Berlin, Reidy, and Rowland, *Freedom's Soldiers*.

35 Kramer, "Effect of the Civil War," 456.

36 Forman, *The Western Sanitary Commission*, 4.

37 Kramer, "Effect of the Civil War"; 455.

38 Hamilton, "Our Surgeons upon the Field."

39 Forman, *The Western Sanitary Commission*, 29–33.

40 Stillé, *History of the United States Sanitary Commission*; U.S. Surgeon General's Office et al., *The Medical and Surgical History*; Kramer, "Effect of the Civil War," 457.

41 Duffy, *The Sanitarians*, 118.

CHAPTER 3. SEARCHING FOR ORDER

1 Wiebe, *The Search for Order*.

2 Balser, ed., *Abraham Lincoln*, 796–802.

3 Neil Fligstein, *Going North*; Bodnar, *The Transplanted*; Melosi, *Garbage in the Cities*, 14.

4 Balser, *Abraham Lincoln*, 796–802.

5 Woodward, *The Strange Career of Jim Crow*, 22–23.

6 López, *White by Law*.

7 Ngai, *Impossible Subjects*, 3.

8 Soennichsen, *The Chinese Exclusion Act*.

9 Melosi, *The Sanitary City*, 103–204.

10 Wade, *The Urban Frontier*; Cronon, *Nature's Metropolis*.

11 McShane and Tarr, *The Horse in the City*, 26.

12 Joel A. Tarr, "Railroad Smoke Control."

13 McShane and Tarr, *The Horse in the City*, 30.

14 Melosi, *Garbage in the Cities*, 14.

15 Stead, *If Christ Came to Chicago!* 18–19.

16 Sinclair, *The Jungle*, 24–26.

17 Ibid., 32–36.

18 Hering, "Disposal of Municipal Refuse"; H. de B. Parsons, "Disposal of Municipal Refuse"; Melosi, *Garbage in the Cities*, 146–147.

19 Melosi, *Garbage in the Cities*, 15.

20 Layton, *The Revolt of the Engineers*, 3, 13–14, 53–68; Schultz and McShane, "Pollution and Political Reform"; Tarr, "Searching for a 'Sink'"; Stradling, *Smokestacks and Progressives*, 85–107.

21 Mrs. Wagner, "What the Women Are Doing," 35.

22 Addams, *Twenty Years at Hull-House*, 281–287.

23 Zimring, *Cash for Your Trash*, 37–80.

24 Jacobson, *Waste Management*, 48–49.

25 U.S. Bureau of the Census, *General Statistics of Cities: 1909*, 133.

26 Zimring, *Cash for Your Trash*, 37–58.

27 Hoy, *Chasing Dirt*, 92–103; Mason, "Mary McDowell and Municipal Housekeeping; Platt, "Jane Addams and the Ward Boss Revisited."

28 Bushnell, *The Social Problems at the Chicago Stock Yards*, 73; Sinclair, *The Jungle*; Slayton, *Back of the Yards*; Jablonsky, *Pride in the Jungle*, 19–20; Washington, *Packing Them In*, 78–79.

29 Walker, "Chicago Housing Conditions."

30 Riis, *How the Other Half Lives*, 22.

31 Ibid., 105.

32 Melosi, *Garbage in the Cities*, 22.

33 Tarr, "Historical Perspectives on Hazardous Wastes"; Leighton, "Industrial Wastes and Their Sanitary Significance."

34 Melosi, *Garbage in the Cities*, 24–25.

35 Ibid.

36 Picchi, *The Five Weeks of Guiseppe Zangara*; Millard, *Destiny of the Republic*; Miller, *The President and the Assassin*.

37 Taylor, *The Principles of Scientific Management*, 5–6.

38 Unger, *Fighting Bob LaFollette*; Melosi, *Garbage in the Cities*, 91.

39 Hoy, *Chasing Dirt*, 59–86.

40 Roosevelt, "Opening Address by the President," 12.

41 Zimring, *Cash for Your Trash*, 12–36.

42 Misa, *A Nation of Steel.*

43 Henri, *Black Migration*; Fligstein, *Going North*; Grossman, *Land of Hope*; Alexander, "Great Migrations."

44 U.S. Department of Commerce, "Table No. 27."

45 Foner, *Reconstruction*, 289.

46 Ibid., 293–294.

47 Ibid.

48 Ibid., 314–315.

49 Pascoe, *What Comes Naturally*, 7.

50 Ibid., 9.

51 Ibid., 13.

52 Ibid., 115.

53 Foner, *Reconstruction*, 340; McPherson, *The Political History of the United States*, 380–381; John D. Van Buren to Horatio Seymour, September 5, 1868, New-York Historical Society, American Historical Manuscript Collection, Horatio Seymour letters, 1860–1869, folder 4 of 6; Wood, *Black Scare*, 126–128.

54 Foner, *Reconstruction*, 342.

55 Ibid., 438; Trelease, *White Terror*, 89, 124, 294; Howard, *Death at Cross Plains.*

56 Byrd, *The Senate*, 565.

57 Foner, *Forever Free*, 217–218.

58 "Report of the Imperial Kligrapp (secretary) at the 1924 Klonvokation," quoted in Jackson, *The Ku Klux Klan in the City*, 15; Maury Zimring, interview with the author, June 22, 1993.

59 Foner, *Forever Free*, 220–223.

60 "Ideals of the Ku Klux Klan," pamphlet, n.d., National Museum of American History, Archives Center, Warshaw Collection of Business Americana, collection 60, box 1, "Ku Klux Klan General Works," folder 1, "Pamphlets."

61 Woodward, *The Strange Career of Jim Crow*, 69–70.

62 Wiebe, *The Search for Order*, 301.

CHAPTER 4. "HOW DO YOU MAKE THEM SO CLEAN AND WHITE?"

1 Franklin, *Reconstruction after the Civil War*; Foner and Mahoney, *America's Reconstruction.*

2 Cronon, *Nature's Metropolis*; Miller, *City of the Century.*

3 "All About a Nigger. A Laboratory Analysis of Our Brother in Black," *Columbus Enquirer-Sun*, September 26, 1886, 5; "News of the Northwest," *Portland Morning Oregonian*, May 27, 1886, 6.

4 "Mr. Yaple; Intelligent," *Jackson Citizen Patriot*, October 13, 1886, 2.

5 Katznelson, *When Affirmative Action Was White*, 80–84.

6 Mingus, *Beneath the Underdog*, 46.

7 Ibid., 52, 65.

8 Wright, *The Messenger*, 39, 138, 144; Gates, *Colored People*, 73.

9 Moore, *Booker T. Washington*, 107.

10 Wiebe, *The Search for Order*; Hale, *Making Whiteness*; Grossman, "Review of Grace Elizabeth Hale, *Making Whiteness*."

11 Hale, *Making Whiteness*, 6–8.

12 Tarr and Zimring, "The Struggle for Smoke Control."

13 Addams, *Twenty Years at Hull-House*, 51–52.

14 Ibid., 284.

15 Roediger, *Working toward Whiteness*, 190.

16 Examples of these terms used to describe members of specific groups may be found in newspapers of the time, e.g., "Cave; Shylock; Congress," *Indianapolis American Nonconformist*, January 18, 1894, 4; "Thorne and the Lawyers," *Miami Herald*, July 8, 1918, 4; "John Lind; Mexican; Greaser," *Portland Morning Oregonian*, November 21, 1914, 6; "Why Mexicans Call Us Gringos," *Philadelphia Inquirer*, March 14, 1915, 8; "They Ask Damages," *Dallas Morning News*, December 2, 1931, 2.

17 See, e.g., the variety of disciplines described in Gould, *The Mismeasure of Man*, 105–150.

18 Roediger, *Working toward Whiteness*, 53–54.

19 Ross, *The Old World in the New*, 146.

20 Ibid., 213.

21 Ibid., 215–216.

22 Ibid., 291.

23 Ibid., 293.

24 Spitzka, quoted in Gould, *The Mismeasure of Man*, 120.

25 Greenberg, "Class Culture and Generation Change," 75–77, quoted in Roediger, *Working toward Whiteness*, 192–193.

26 Sinclair, *The Jungle*.

27 Useful overviews of the history of print advertising include Marchand, *Advertising the American Dream*; Lears, *Fables of Abundance*.

28 Ruffins, "Mythos, Memory, and History."

29 Trollope, "Washington to St. Louis," 414; Hale, *Making Whiteness*, 162–163.

30 National Museum of American History (NMAH) Archives Center, Warshaw Collection of Business Americana, collection 60, box 7, folder 14, "Proctor & Gamble—Ivory Soap—Booklets, Consumer."

31 NMAH Archives Center, Warshaw Collection of Business Americana, collection 60, oversize box 187, folder 2, "Soap"; box 7, folder 14, "Proctor & Gamble—Ivory Soap—Booklets, Consumer"; oversize box 58, folder 8, "Envy."

32 NMAH Archives Center, Warshaw Collection of Business Americana, collection 60, oversize box 58, folder 19, "Fairbanks, N.K. & Co.—Fairy Soap."

33 NMAH Archives Center, Warshaw Collection of Business Americana, collection 60, box 2, folder 9, "David's Prize Soap."

34 NMAH Archives Center, Warshaw Collection of Business Americana, collection 60, oversize box 58, folder 18, "Fairbanks, N.K. & Co.—Fairy Soap."

35 NMAH Archives Center, Warshaw Collection of Business Americana, collection 60, box 2, folder 9, "Soap."

36 NMAH Archives Center, Warshaw Collection of Business Americana, collection 60, box 3, folder 22, "Kendall Manufacturing Company"; box 7, folder 19, "Pyle, James—Pearline."

37 NMAH Archives Center, Warshaw Collection of Business Americana, collection 60, box 4, folder 3, "James Kirk and Company."

38 NMAH Archives Center, Warshaw Collection of Business Americana, collection 60, box 7, folder 11, "Proctor & Gamble—Ivory Soap."

39 NMAH Archives Center, Warshaw Collection of Business Americana, collection 60, box 4, folder 9, "Larkin, J.D. and Company."

40 Wohlman, *Playing the Races*, 69, 119; emphasis in original.

41 Willard, "The Juvenile Street-Cleaning Leagues."

42 Hering and Greeley, *Collection and Disposal*, 38–39; the survey is also quoted in Melosi, *The Sanitary City*, 177.

43 McPherson, *The Abolitionist Legacy*, 368–393.

44 Washington, *Up from Slavery*, 38.

45 Ibid., 75.

46 Washington and Scott, *Tuskegee and Its People*, 29–30.

47 Colored Home and Hospital Sixty-Fifth Street and First Avenue, *Forty-Eighth Annual Report*, 21.

48 Colored Orphan Asylum and Association for the Benefit of Colored Children in the City of New York, *Fifty-Second Annual Report*, 6.

49 The Nashville Institute for Negro Christian Workers, pamphlet, 1913, NMAH Archives Center, Warshaw Collection of Business Americana, collection 60, box 2, folder 17, "Articles by and about African Americans." On the Hamburg cholera epidemic of 1892, see Evans, *Death in Hamburg*.

50 "Curd soap" is "soap separated as curds by addition of salt during saponification." In the *Courier* article, users were instructed to "wet the toothbrush, rub lightly on the soap, dip in prepared chalk, and brush the teeth well; rinse with tepid water." See "Soap Good for the Teeth," *Pittsburgh Courier*, December 16, 1911, 1.

51 "Keep Healthy by Dr. A. Wilberforce Williams," *Chicago Defender*, May 3, 1913, 3.

52 "Dr. A. Wilberforce Williams Talks on Preventative Measures First Aid Remedies Hygienics and Sanitation," *Chicago Defender*, April 4, 1914, 8.

53 Ibid., March 3, 1917, 9.

54 Ibid., March 30, 1918, 16.

55 Ibid., December 10, 1921, 16.

56 "An Address before the Negro Organization Society," 169.

57 Ibid.

58 "Observe Health Week," *Pittsburgh Courier*, April 16, 1932, A2; "Along the Main Beat," *Chicago Defender*, February 24, 1951, 6; Work, "Tuskegee Institute More than an Educational Institution"; Brown, "The National Negro Health Week Movement.

59 Foucault, *Technologies of the Self*.

CHAPTER 5. DIRTY WORK, DIRTY WORKERS

1 Hoy, *Chasing Dirt.*
2 Blumin, *The Emergence of the Middle Class.*
3 Horowitz, *The Morality of Spending Attitudes*; Strasser, *Waste and Want.*
4 U.S. Department of Commerce, Series D 152–166, 138.
5 U.S. Department of Commerce, Series D 233–682, 138.
6 Ibid., 144.
7 Ibid.
8 Ibid.
9 Sinclair, *The Jungle*; Bell, *Out of This Furnace*; Roediger, *Working toward Whiteness.*
10 On national employment patterns, see Gregory, "The Southern Diaspora."
11 Waldinger, *Through the Eye of the Needle*, 19–47.
12 Perry, *Collecting Garbage.* On constructions of "dirty work" as unethical and stigmatized labor, see Goffman, *Stigma*; Hughes, "Good People and Dirty Work."
13 Stansell, *City of Women*, 51.
14 Koukol, "A Slav's a Man for A' That"; Drake and Cayton, *Black Metropolis*, 26.
15 Population analysis from Ruggles et al., *Integrated Public Use Microdata Series.* The following IPUMS samples of the U.S. Census of Population were used in this chapter and chapter 7: 1 percent samples from 1870 (N = 383,358), 1910 (N = 923,153), 1920 (N = 1,050,634), 1940 (N = 1,351,732), 1950 (N = 1,922,198), 1960 (N = 1,799,888), and 1970 (N = 2,030,276); 5 percent samples from 1900 (N = 3,852,852) and 1930 (N = 6,103,822); and 10 percent sample from 1880 (N = 5,882,038). Confidence level for all samples: 95 percent. Occupation codes used for 1870–1900 include 037 (janitors), 040 (launderers and laundresses), 114 (traders and dealers in junk), and 229 (ragpickers). Occupation codes used for 1910–1930 include 114 (traders and dealers in junk), 804 (garbage men and scavengers), 910 (charwomen and cleaners), 918 (janitors and sextons), 922 (launderers and laundresses—not in laundry), 926 (laundry operatives: laborers), and 970 (cleaners and renovators—clothing, etc.). Occupation codes used for 1940–1970 include 597 (sanitary services), 643 (laundry and dry cleaning operatives), 710 (laundresses, private household), 753 (charwomen and cleaners), and 770 (janitors and sextons). Each occupation code was analyzed by nativity, with categories including native born of native-born parents, native born of native-born mother and foreign-born father, native born of foreign-born mother and native-born father, native born of two foreign-born parents, and foreign born. Each occupation code was analyzed by race, with relevant categories for the time period, including White, Non-Hispanic White, Negro/Black, American Indian or Alaskan Native, Chinese, Japanese, Other Asian or Pacific Islander, and Hispanic (Mexican, Puerto Rican, Cuban, and Other Hispanic). Code 114 (traders and dealers in junk) was also analyzed by native tongue of the individual and of the individual's parents in the 1920 sample.
16 Swierenga, *Dutch Chicago*, 586–588.

17 Newspaper clippings of the Philadelphia Housing Association, 1917–1919, 3/II/133, box 22, "Sanitary Curb a Farce, Says Housing Chief," *Philadelphia Public Ledger*, November 23, 1918, 40.

18 Melosi, *Garbage in the Cities*, 173. On San Francisco garbage collectives, see Perry, *Collecting Garbage*.

19 Perry, *Collecting Garbage*, 15.

20 Ibid., 15–16.

21 Kaztauskis, "The Life Story of a Lithuanian."

22 "The Refuse of the City," *New York Times*, December 4, 1881, 2.

23 Waring, *Street-Cleaning*, 74.

24 Melosi, *Garbage in the Cities*, 123; "Some Hazards of City Housecleaning," *Survey*, April 14, 1917, 42.

25 Bernstein, *Next to Godliness*.

26 Smith, "New Paths to Power."

27 Van Raaphorst, *Union Maids Not Wanted*; May, *Unprotected Labor*.

28 Taylor, "Blacks and Asians in a White City."

29 Coulter, *Take Up the Black Man's Burden*, 74–75.

30 Gold, "Janitors versus Tenants," 487.

31 Ibid., 488.

32 Strasser, *Waste and Want*, 140–153; Le Zotte, "Not Charity, but a Chance."

33 Weissbach, *Jewish Life in Small-Town America*, 109.

34 Ibid., 110.

35 Zimring, *Cash for Your Trash*; McNeill and Vrtis, "Thrift and Waste in American History"; Brownell, "Negotiating the New Economic Order."

36 Clapperton, *The Paper-Making Machine*, 45–53, 115–253; McGaw, *Most Wonderful Machine*, 39–40.

37 Misa, *A Nation of Steel*; Rogers, *An Economic History*.

38 Melosi, *Garbage in the Cities*, 71–72.

39 Nasaw, *Children of the City*, 88; Strasser, *Waste and Want*, 110–116.

40 Edward Schlezinger, interviewed by Judy Blair, recorded May 14, 1985, Columbus Jewish Historical Committee's Oral History Project, Columbus, Ohio.

41 Maury Zimring, interview with the author, June 22, 1993.

42 Nasaw, *Children of the City*, Stansell, *City of Women*, and Strasser, *Waste and Want*, all suggest that scavenging was common to recent immigrants in American cities. For more on the demographic structure of the waste trades in the 1880 and 1920 IPUMS samples, see Zimring, "Recycling for Profit," 64–102.

43 Watkins, "Background," 25–26.

44 MacLeish, *Jews in America*, 9.

45 "Tenement-Houses," *Chicago Daily Tribune*, September 20, 1874, 10; emphasis in the original.

46 Pollack, "Success from Scrap and Secondhand Goods."

47 Kraut, "The Butcher, the Baker."

48 Pollak, "The Jewish Peddlers of Omaha." The number of "hucksters and peddlers" enumerated in the Census declined from 77,000 in 1900 to 57,000 in 1930. U.S. Department of Commerce, Series D 233–682, 142.

49 "Receivers of Stolen Goods," *New York Times*, July 6, 1866, 2.

50 Ibid.

51 More precisely, 46 percent of individuals trading in junk in 1920 had a native tongue of "Jewish," Yiddish, or Hebrew, and 12 percent had a native tongue of Russian. For a more detailed demographic breakdown of this occupational category in the 1920 Census, see Zimring, "Recycling for Profit," 90–100.

52 For additional anecdotes, see Fleming, *History of Pittsburgh and Environs*, 323–324.

53 Lipsett, *100 Years of Recycling History*, 22–28; "The Scrapmen," *Fortune*, January 1949, 86–91, 134–139.

54 Lipsett, *100 Years of Recycling History*, 188.

55 Oberman, *Encyclopedia of Scrap Recycling*, 51–52.

56 Joe Brenner, Trading as Reliable Junk Company and the Ocean Accident and Guarantee Corporation, Ltd. v. Toba Brenner and Mary Brenner, 127 Md. 189, 96 A. 287, 1915 Md. LEXIS 20, December 2, 1915, decided.

57 Alexander, "Sales of Scrap Materials."

58 Letter from Principio Forge Co. to John S. Wirt, September 16, 1895, Manuscripts Department, Maryland Historical Society Library, Baltimore, George P. Whitaker Co., MS 1730.1.

59 On the construction of the Chinese laundry man in the United States, see Takai, *A Different Mirror*; and Yu, *Thinking Orientals*.

60 Chew, "Life Story of a Chinaman"; Foo, "The Chinese in New York."

61 Siu, *The Chinese Laundryman*, 52, 119–123.

62 Chew, "Life Story of a Chinaman," 292–293.

63 Ibid., 296; Ong, "Chinese Laundries as an Urban Occupation," 69, 70, 74; Nee and Nee, *Longtime Californ'*, 22; Chew, "The Chinaman in America."

64 Drake and Cayton, *Black Metropolis*, 249–250.

65 "A Resistant Mayor: Henry Loeb," *New York Times*, April 17, 1968, 24; Hunter, *To 'Joy My Freedom*, 56.

66 Hunter, *To 'Joy My Freedom*, 105, 120.

67 Ibid., 85–89.

68 Ibid., 89–91, 131.

69 Drake and Cayton, *Black Metropolis*, 250.

70 Cowan, *More Work for Mother*.

71 Kelley, "Building Bridges."

CHAPTER 6. WASTE AND SPACE REORDERED

1 Jackson, *Crabgrass Frontier*.

2 McDowell, quoted in Heuchling, *City Club Bulletin*.

3 Sandburg, *The Chicago Race Riots*, 9–10.

4 Ibid.

5 Carter et al., *Historical Statistics of the United States*; U.S. Bureau of the Census, "United States Summary: 2010," 20–26.

6 Melosi, *Garbage in the Cities*.

7 McShane and Tarr, *The Horse in the City*.

8 Tarr, "Sewerage"; Melosi, *The Sanitary City*, 235.

9 Stradling, *Smokestacks and Progressives*; Stradling and Thorsheim, "The Smoke of Great Cities"; Uekötter, *The Age of Smoke*.

10 Tarr and Zimring, "The Struggle for Smoke Control."

11 Melosi, *Garbage in the Cities*.

12 Barringer, *The Story of Scrap*; Zimring, *Cash for Your Trash*.

13 On the emergence of the middle class and its consumptive patterns, see Blumin, *The Emergence of the Middle Class*; Kasson, *Rudeness and Civility*; and Strasser, *Waste and Want*.

14 Franklin and Schweninger, *Runaway Slaves*, 219–223.

15 Veblen, *The Theory of the Leisure Class*.

16 Strasser, *Waste and Want*, 161–202.

17 On expanding shopping options between the late nineteenth and mid-twentieth centuries, see Benson, *Counter Cultures*, 12–30; Cohen, *Making a New Deal*; Longstreth, *The American Department Store Transformed*; Deutsch, *Building a Housewife's Paradise*.

18 Hoy, *Chasing Dirt*, 87–122.

19 Addams, "The Subtle Problems of Charity"; Grigg and Haynes, *Junk Dealing and Juvenile Delinquency*, 50.

20 Jackson, *Crabgrass Frontier*.

21 Sandburg, *The Chicago Race Riots*.

22 Grossman, *Land of Hope*.

23 Bodnar, Simon, and Weber, *Lives of Their Own*; Bodnar, *The Transplanted*; Trotter and Smith, *African Americans in Pennsylvania*; Berlin, *The Making of African America*.

24 "Race Discrimination in Chicago," *Chicago Defender*, October 3, 1914, 1; Spear, *Black Chicago*, 48.

25 Spear, *Black Chicago*; Philpott, *The Slum and the Ghetto*; Nelli, *Italians in Chicago*; Cutler, "The Jews of Chicago"; Grossman, "African American Migration to Chicago"; Casuso and Camacho, "Latino Chicago"; Pacyga, "Chicago's Ethnic Neighborhoods"; Guglielmo, *White on Arrival*; Fernandez, *Brown in the Windy City*.

26 Chicago Commission on Race Relations, *The Negro in Chicago*, 184.

27 Ibid., 642.

28 James "Jack" Isbell, interview with Timuel E. Black, Jr., conducted July 30, August 1, and August 19, 1991. In Black, *Bridges of Memory*, 281–282.

29 *Property Owner's Journal*, December 13, 1919, cited in Chicago Commission on Race Relations, *The Negro in Chicago*, 121.

30 Denton and Massey, *American Apartheid*.

31 Li, *Ethnoburb*, 19.
32 Park et al., *The City*, 27.
33 Ibid., 28.
34 Ibid., 122.
35 Drake and Cayton, *Black Metropolis*, 70.
36 Ibid., 301–302.
37 Ibid., 366.
38 Ibid., 576.
39 Sugrue, *The Origins of the Urban Crisis*, 3.
40 Jackson, *Crabgrass Frontier*, 8.
41 Ibid., 70.
42 Stevenson, *Park Maker*; Rosenzweig and Blackmar, *The Park and Its People*; Taylor, *The Environment and the People*, 251–295.
43 Rome, *The Bulldozer in the Countryside*.
44 Jackson, *Crabgrass Frontier*, 178.
45 Babcock, *The Appraisal of Real Estate*, 71.
46 Jackson, *Crabgrass Frontier*, 198.
47 Hoyt, *One Hundred Years*, 226.
48 Ibid., 316–317.
49 Jackson, *Crabgrass Frontier*, 196–197.
50 Ibid., 197–198.
51 Ibid., 198.
52 Ibid., 206.
53 Ibid., 208–209.
54 Ibid., 217; Freund, *Colored Property*.
55 Marjorie Echols and Harvey Echols, interview with Timuel E. Black, Jr., conducted May 6, 1995. In Black, *Bridges of Memory*, 536.
56 Babcock and Bosselman, "Suburban Zoning and the Apartment Boom"; Babcock, *The Zoning Game*; Sze, *Noxious New York*, 41.
57 "City Regulation of Junk Shops," *American City*, July 1918, 24–25.
58 "Chicagoans Get First Chance to Study Preliminary Zoning Chart," *Chicago Defender*, October 14, 1922, 14.
59 Silver, "The Racial Origins of Zoning."
60 "Clevelanders Kick on Junk Yard Next to Central Hi School," *Pittsburgh Courier*, March 20, 1937, 5.
61 "Hill Gets Action on Collection of 'Hokey Piles', Back Rubbish," *Pittsburgh Courier*, March 3, 1945, 3.
62 "Mayor Indicates He Will Help Group Attempting Hill Cleanup," *Pittsburgh Courier*, November 25, 1950, 1.
63 "Clean-up Drive Enters 3rd Ward," *Pittsburgh Courier*, May 17, 1952, 1.
64 "Lanlord [sic] Fined," *Chicago Defender*, March 27, 1948, 6; "Breaks Sanitary Law," *Chicago Defender*, September 16, 1950, 23; "Slum Operators Appear in Court," *Chicago Daily Defender*, August 4, 1958, 4.

65 Grimshaw, *Bitter Fruit.*

66 Grutzner, "City Puerto Ricans Are Found Ill-Housed."

67 "Court Rules Miss. Town Must Provide Services Equally," *New Pittsburgh Courier*, February 13, 1971, 7.

68 "This Is Interesting," *Chicago Defender*, November 22, 1930, 14.

69 "Chicago Policy Barons Becoming Jittery: Fear Outcome of Skidmore Investigation," *Chicago Defender*, August 19, 1939, 6.

70 "Tenants Stage Garbage 'Dump In,'" *Chicago Daily Defender*, February 13, 1969, 1.

71 "South Side Tenants Act in Garbage Rift: 3 Buildings Involved in Demonstration," *Chicago Daily Defender*, February 13, 1969, 3.

72 Fernandez, *Brown in the Windy City*, 4.

73 Denton and Massey, *American Apartheid*, 74–78.

74 Hirsch, *Making the Second Ghetto*; Hunt, *Blueprint for Disaster.*

75 Gutenschwager, "The Scrap Iron and Steel Industry."

76 Denton and Massey, *American Apartheid*, 74–78.

77 Ibid., 78.

78 Ibid.

79 Sellers, *Crabgrass Crucible*, 135–136, 292.

CHAPTER 7. OUT OF WASTE INTO WHITENESS

1 Goldstein, *The Price of Whiteness*, 192–193.

2 Anecdote recounted in Duignan and Gann, *The Rebirth of the West*, 668. Among the many times Groucho told the story was on Mike Douglas's TV show; see the dialogue quoted in Douglas, Kelly, and Heaton, *I'll Be Right Back*, 118–119. See also the recap of his 1972 Carnegie Hall performance in Kanfer, *Groucho*, 5, 152. The anecdote was a sufficiently significant part of Marx's oeuvre that it was included in his *New York Times* obituary. See "Groucho Marx, Comedian, Dead," *New York Times*, August 20, 1977, 1.

3 Meehan, "Moynihan of the Moynihan Report."

4 Handlin, "All Colors."

5 Glazer and Moynihan, *Beyond the Melting Pot*, p. xvi; Painter, *The History of White People*, 381–382.

6 "Exclusive Interview Morton Plant President ISIS 1980," *Scrap Age* 37, no. 2 (February 1980): 67, 69, 71, 73, 75; Institute of Scrap Recycling Industries, "Our Heritage."

7 Roediger, *Working toward Whiteness.*

8 "The Scrapmen," *Fortune*, January 1949, 86–91, 134–139.

9 David K. Fremon, *Chicago Politics Ward by Ward*, 23–28; Cutler, *The Jews of Chicago*, 68–72.

10 Cutler, *The Jews of Chicago*, 267–269.

11 Barringer, *The Story of Scrap*, 78–80.

12 Lipsett, *100 Years of Recycling History*, 11, 13.

13 Ibid., 181.

14 Oberman, *Encyclopedia of Scrap Recycling.*

15 Golden, "A Former Junk Dealer."

16 Patinkin, "My Story As an American Jew.

17 Douglas, *The Ragman's Son.*

18 Selavan, *My Voice Was Heard*, 77–78.

19 Glazer and Moynihan, *Beyond the Melting Pot*, 196, 210.

20 U.S. Senate Select Committee on Improper Activities in the Labor or Management Field, "Hearings before the Select Committee," 12232.

21 Jacobs, Friel, and Radick, *Gotham Unbound*, 85; Jacobs, *Mobsters, Unions, and Feds*, 67.

22 Puzo, "The Italians, American Style.

23 Apple, "Moynihan Scored on Ethnic Views."

24 Puzo, *The Godfather*, 265, 286, *Godfather Part II.*

25 Prell, "Triumph, Accommodation."

26 Mann quoted in Lukas, "Rise in White Ethnic Emphasis Is Studied by 200 Specialists"; Greeley quoted in Wolfe, "Ethnics Carve Out Place for Themselves in U.S. Way of Life."

27 Bertellini, "Black Hands and White Hearts"; Myrdal, *An American Dilemma*; Glazer and Moynihan, *Beyond the Melting Pot.*

28 Levinson, *September in the Rain*, 89.

29 Moore, *Carl B. Stokes*; Stradling and Stradling, "Perceptions of the Burning River."

30 Gratton and Gutmann, *Historical Statistics of the United States*, 1–177 to 1–179; Ruggles et al. *Integrated Public Use Microdata Series.* Integrated Public Use Microdata Series samples of the 1950, 1960, and 1970 U.S. Census of Population are used in this chapter. For codes, sample sizes, and confidence intervals used, see note 15 in chapter 5.

31 Perry, *Collecting Garbage*, 239; Nagle, *Picking Up*, 27.

32 Hoy, *Chasing Dirt*, 169–170, 181.

33 Gold, "Janitors versus Tenants," 487; Lerner, "Black and Brown"; Luff, "Justice for Janitors"; Stillman, *Stronger Together.*

34 Kelley, "Building Bridges."

35 Levinson, *If Only Right Now Could Be Forever.*

36 Tanenbaum, *Junk Is Not a Four-Letter Word*, 163–167.

37 Franklin, "Historians Joust over Effects."

38 Miller, "Analysis of the 'White Backlash.'"

39 Quoted in Painter, *The History of White People*, 363.

40 Goldberger, "Tony Imperiale Stands for Law and Order."

41 Ibid.; Halbfinger, "Anthony Imperiale, 68, Dies."

42 "Transcripts of Acceptance Speeches by Nixon and Agnew to the G.O.P. Convention," *New York Times*, August 9, 1968, 20.

43 Johnson, "Negro Leaders See Bias."

44 Old Executive Office Building 407–18; January 18, 1973; White House Tapes, Richard Nixon Presidential Library and Museum, Yorba Linda, CA; Savage, "On Nixon Tapes, Ambivalence."

CHAPTER 8. "WE ARE TIRED OF BEING AT THE BOTTOM"

1 "A Resistant Mayor: Henry Loeb," *New York Times*, April 17, 1968, 24.

2 Honey, *Going Down Jericho Road*, 33.

3 Ibid., 35.

4 Evans, *The Provincials*, 279.

5 Honey, *Going Down Jericho Road*, 34.

6 Crider, "Rousing Fight Nears End in Free Memphis Election; T. O. Jones, interview by Joan Beifuss and David Yellin, January 30, 1970, Sanitation Strike Archival Project, University of Memphis, tape number 229, series II, 2 of 3, 1.

7 Sivananda, "Henry Loeb III as Public Works Commissioner."

8 Ibid.

9 Mr. and Mrs. L. C. Reed, interview by Bill Thomas, July 15, 1968, Sanitation Strike Archival Project, University of Memphis, tape number 143, series 1 of 1, 5–6.

10 Ed Gillis, interview by David Yellin and Bill Thomas, June 2, 1968, Sanitation Strike Archival Project, University of Memphis, tape number 61, series 2 of 2, 6.

11 Sivananda, "Controversial Memphis Mayor Henry Loeb III," 76–77.

12 T. O. Jones, interview by Joan Beifuss and David Yellin, January 30, 1970, Sanitation Strike Archival Project, University of Memphis, tape number 228, series II, 1 of 3, 14.

13 Ibid., 29.

14 Dowdy, *Crusades for Freedom*, 93–94; "Loeb Quits Race—May Quit Job," *Memphis Press-Scimitar*, October 3, 1963, 1–2.

15 Honey, *Going Down Jericho Road*, 45; "Loeb's Resignation Is Best for Memphis' Future," *Tri-State Defender*, October 12, 1963, 6.

16 Ed Gillis, interview by David Yellin and Bill Thomas, June 2, 1968, Sanitation Strike Archival Project, University of Memphis, tape number 61, series 2 of 2, 7–8.

17 "AFSCME prepared a charter for Local 1733—a number chosen by the workers to recognize the thirty-three men who had been fired in 1963—and the workers held a charter dedication ceremony on November 13, 1964, at the historic W.C. Handy Theater." The city refused to recognize or bargain with the new chapter. See Honey, *Going Down Jericho Road*, 71.

18 T. O. Jones, interview by Anne Trotter and Jack Hurley, May 9, 1968, Sanitation Strike Archival Project, University of Memphis, tape number 92, series I, 1 of 1, 6.

19 T. O. Jones, interview by Joan Beifuss and David Yellin, January 30, 1970. Sanitation Strike Archival Project, University of Memphis, tape number 228, series II, 1 of 3, 37.

20 "Memphis: Loeb to Run for Mayor," *Kingsport News*, July 18, 1967, 4; Honey, *Going Down Jericho Road*, 98.

21 Honey, *Going Down Jericho Road*, 99.

22 T. O. Jones, interview by Anne Trotter and Jack Hurley, May 9, 1968, Sanitation Strike Archival Project, University of Memphis, tape number 92, series I, 1 of 1, 5.

23 Ed Gillis, interview by David Yellin and Bill Thomas, June 2, 1968, Sanitation Strike Archival Project, University of Memphis, tape number 61, series 2 of 2, 27.

24 Mr. and Mrs. L. C. Reed, interview by Bill Thomas, July 15, 1968, Sanitation Strike Archival Project, University of Memphis, tape number 143, series 1 of 1, 4.

25 T. O. Jones, interview by Joan Beifuss and David Yellin, January 30, 1970, Sanitation Strike Archival Project, University of Memphis, tape number 229, series II, 2 of 3, 18–19.

26 Ibid., 20.

27 Ibid., 22.

28 T. O. Jones, interview by Anne Trotter and Jack Hurley, May 9, 1968, Sanitation Strike Archival Project, University of Memphis, tape number 92, series I, 1 of 1, 11–12.

29 Ibid.

30 T. O. Jones, interview by Joan Beifuss and David Yellin, January 30, 1970, Sanitation Strike Archival Project, University of Memphis, tape number 229, series II, 2 of 3, 26–27.

31 Ed Gillis, interview by David Yellin and Bill Thomas, June 2, 1968, Sanitation Strike Archival Project, University of Memphis, tape number 61, series 2 of 2, 32.

32 T. O. Jones, interview by Joan Beifuss and David Yellin, January 30, 1970, Sanitation Strike Archival Project, University of Memphis, tape number 229, series II, 2 of 3, 11–12.

33 Ibid., 34.

34 T. O. Jones, interview by Joan Beifuss and David Yellin, January 30, 1970, Sanitation Strike Archival Project, University of Memphis, tape number 228, series II, 1 of 3, 17.

35 T. O. Jones, interview by Joan Beifuss and David Yellin, January 30, 1970, Sanitation Strike Archival Project, University of Memphis, tape number 229, series II, 2 of 3, 14–15.

36 Ibid., 16.

37 "Garbage Team At Work," *Kingsport Times*, February 11, 1968, 2.

38 T. O. Jones, interview by Joan Beifuss and David Yellin, January 30, 1970, Sanitation Strike Archival Project, University of Memphis, tape number 229, series II, 2 of 3, 30–31.

39 Ibid., 43–44.

40 "Memphis Mayor Demands Sanitation Workers Return to Jobs," *Kingsport Times*, February 13, 1968, 4.

41 Lovey, *The Civil Rights Act of 1964*.

42 "Dr. King Is Felled by Rock," *Chicago Tribune*, August 6, 1966, 1–2; Cohen and Taylor, *American Pharaoh*, 396.

43 Honey, *Going Down Jericho Road*, 381.

44 Transcript of Dr. Martin Luther King, Jr's Mason Temple speech, March 18, 1968, 6–7, box 22, file 121, Mississippi Valley Collection, University of Memphis.

45 T. O. Jones, interview by Joan Beifuss and David Yellin, January 30, 1970, Sanitation Strike Archival Project, University of Memphis, tape number 230, series II, 3 of 3, 7.

46 Ibid., 8.

47 Ibid., 10–11.

48 Ibid., 18–20.

49 Ibid., 31–32.

50 Ed Gillis, interview by David Yellin and Bill Thomas, June 2, 1968, Sanitation Strike Archival Project, University of Memphis, tape number 61, series 2 of 2, 40.

51 Oates, *Let the Trumpet Sound*, 477; U.S. House of Representatives, *Investigation of the Assassination of Martin Luther King, Jr.*, vols. 1, 4, 6, and 7; see 1:15–16 and 6:410, 416, 431–432, 451, 473–481.

52 King, *A Testament of Hope*, 279–286.

53 Mr. and Mrs. L. C. Reed, interview by Bill Thomas, July 15, 1968, Sanitation Strike Archival Project, University of Memphis, tape number 143, series 1 of 1, 17.

54 Ibid., 18.

55 Honey, *Going Down Jericho Road*, 493.

56 T. O. Jones, interview by Anne Trotter and Jack Hurley, May 9, 1968, Sanitation Strike Archival Project, University of Memphis, tape number 92, series I, 1 of 1, 4, 18.

57 T. O. Jones, Interview by Joan Beifuss and David Yellin, January 30, 1970, Sanitation Strike Archival Project, University of Memphis, tape number 228, series II, 1 of 3, 2–3.

58 Bullard, Johnson, and Torres, *Environmental Health and Racial Equity*, 2.

59 Bullard, *Dumping in Dixie*, 30; McGurty, *Transforming Environmentalism*.

60 Urban Environment Conference, Inc., *Taking Back Our Health*, 38.

61 "PCB Soil to Be Dumped Today," *Winston-Salem Sentinel*, September 15, 1982, 13; "55 Arrested in Protest at a Toxic Dump in Carolina," *New York Times*, September 16, 1982, A18; "EPA Official Criticizes Landfill," *Winston-Salem Journal*, September 27, 1982, 7; "11 Arrested for Blocking PCB Trucks," *Durham Morning Herald*, September 30, 1982, 1B.

62 U.S. General Accounting Office, *Siting of Hazardous Waste Landfills* , 1.

63 Ibid., 3.

64 Bullard, *Dumping in Dixie*, 32.

65 Commission for Racial Justice, *Toxic Wastes and Race*, xiii.

CONCLUSION

1 Sharma, *Bhangi, Scavenger in Indian Society*; Macgowan, *Men and Manners of Modern China*, 273; Esherick, *Remaking the Chinese City*, 45; Reid, *Paris Sewers and Sewermen*.

2 Jackson, *Crabgrass Frontier*; Denton and Massey, *American Apartheid*; Rome, *The Bulldozer in the Country*; Freund, *Colored Property*.

3 Weeks, "In Obama, Americans See Promise of a New Start."

4 Ibid.

5 Brinkley, "The Global President."

6 Horowitz, "Biden Unbound."

7 McElroy, "Blogtalk: Biden Fallout."

8 Jackson, "Obama Makes a Clean Hit."

9 Robinson, "An Inarticulate Kickoff."

10 Bullard et al., *Toxic Wastes and Race at Twenty*, xii.

11 "Man Killed in Fall into Industrial Shredder," *Chicago Tribune*, April 4, 2004, Chicago final ed., Metro section, 3.

12 Anecdotal evidence taken from my visit to Waste Management's Recycle America facilities in Grayslake, Illinois, March 8, 2009. Earlier visits to material recycling facilities in Ohio, Illinois, and Pennsylvania between 2001 and 2009 revealed that, regardless of urban, rural, or suburban location, every single person working to sort and separate waste materials in the material recycling facilities was either African American or Hispanic.

13 Moynihan, "Worker Is Crushed by Garbage Truck Compactor in Brooklyn."

BIBLIOGRAPHY

ARCHIVES AND DATABASES

Archives of Labor and Urban Affairs, Walter P. Reuther Library, Wayne State University, Detroit, MI.

Columbus Jewish Historical Committee's Oral History Project, Columbus, OH.

Manuscripts Department, Maryland Historical Society Library, Baltimore, MD.

Mississippi Valley Collection, University of Memphis, Memphis, TN.

New-York Historical Society, New York, NY.

New York Public Library, New York City, NY.

Philadelphia Housing Association, Philadelphia, PA.

Records of the United States House of Representatives, National Archives, Washington DC.

Ruggles, Steven, J. Trent Alexander, Katie Genadek, Ronald Goeken, Matthew B. Schroeder, and Matthew Sobek. *Integrated Public Use Microdata Series: Version 5.0* [Machine-readable database]. Minneapolis, MN: University of Minnesota, 2010.

Sanitation Strike Archival Project, University of Memphis, Memphis, TN.

Warshaw Collection of Business Americana, National Museum of American History, Archives Center, Washington, DC.

White House Tapes; Richard Nixon Presidential Library and Museum, Yorba Linda, CA.

BOOKS, ARTICLES, AND DISSERTATIONS

Addams, Jane. "The Subtle Problems of Charity," *Atlantic Monthly* 83 (1899): 163–179.

Addams, Jane. *Twenty Years at Hull-House*. New York: Macmillan, 1930. Originally published 1910.

Alexander, J. P. "Sales of Scrap Materials." *Electric Railway Journal*, January 23, 1915, 192–193.

Alexander, J. Trent. "Great Migrations: Race and Community in the Southern Exodus, 1917–1970." Ph.D. diss., Carnegie Mellon University, 2001.

Anbinder, Tyler. *Nativism and Slavery: The Northern Know-Nothings and the Politics of the 1850s*. New York: Oxford University Press, 1992.

Apple, R. W., Jr. "Moynihan Scored on Ethnic Views." *New York Times*, August 10, 1965, 15.

Babcock, Frederick Morrison. *The Appraisal of Real Estate*. New York: Macmillan, 1927.

Babcock, Richard F. *The Zoning Game: Municipal Practices and Policies*. Madison: University of Wisconsin Press, 1966.

Babcock, Richard F., and Fred P. Bosselman. "Suburban Zoning and the Apartment Boom." *University of Pennsylvania Law Review* 111 (1963): 1040–1091.

Balser, Roy P., ed. *Abraham Lincoln: His Speeches and Writings*. Cleveland: World Publishing Co., 1946.

Barringer, Edwin C. *The Story of Scrap*. Washington, DC: Institute of Scrap Iron & Steel, 1954.

Beecher, Catharine E. *A Treatise on Domestic Economy for the Use of Young Ladies at Home and at School*. Boston: Marsh, Capen, Lyon, & Webb, 1841.

Bell, Thomas. *Out of This Furnace*. Boston: Little, Brown & Co., 1941.

Benson, Susan Porter. *Counter Cultures: Saleswomen, Managers, and Customers in American Department Stores, 1890–1940*. Urbana: University of Illinois Press, 1986.

Berlin, Ira. *Generations of Captivity: A History of African-American Slavery*. Cambridge, MA: Harvard University Press, 2003.

Berlin, Ira. *The Making of African America: The Four Great Migrations*. New York: Viking, 2010.

Berlin, Ira, Joseph P. Reidy, and Leslie S. Rowland, eds. *Freedom's Soldiers: The Black Military Experience in the Civil War*. New York: Cambridge University Press, 1998.

Bernier, Carlos J. Correa. *Almost Everything You Need to Know about Environmental Justice*. New York: United Church of Christ, n.d.

Bernstein, Daniel Eli. *Next to Godliness: Confronting Dirt and Despair in Progressive Era New York City*. Urbana and Chicago: University of Illinois Press. 2006.

Bertellini, Giorgio. "Black Hands and White Hearts: Italian Immigrants as 'Urban Racial Types' in Early American Film Culture." *Urban History* 31 (2004): 375–399.

Black, Timuel E., Jr. *Bridges of Memory: Chicago's First Wave of Black Migration*. Evanston, IL: Northwestern University Press, 2003.

Blumin, Stuart M. *The Emergence of the Middle Class: Social Experience in the American City, 1760–1900*. New York: Cambridge University Press, 1989.

Bodnar, John. *The Transplanted: A History of Immigrants in Urban America*. Urbana: University of Illinois Press, 1985.

Bodnar, John, Roger Simon, and Michael P. Weber. *Lives of Their Own: Blacks, Italians, and Poles in Pittsburgh, 1900–1960*. Urbana: University of Illinois Press, 1981.

Brinkley, Douglas. "The Global President." In *Barack Obama: The Official Inaugural Book*, by David Hume Kennerly and Robert McNeely, 182. New York: Five Ties Publishing, 2009.

Brodkin, Karen. *How Jews Became White Folks and What That Says about Race in America*. New Brunswick, NJ: Rutgers University Press, 1999.

Brown, Roscoe C. "The National Negro Health Week Movement." *Journal of Negro Education* 6 (1937): 553–564.

Brownell, Emily. "Negotiating the New Economic Order of Waste." *Environmental History* 16 (2011): 262–289.

Bullard, Robert D. *Dumping in Dixie: Race, Class, and Environmental Quality*. Boulder, CO: Westview Press, 2000.

Bullard, Robert D., Glenn S. Johnson, and Angela O. Torres. *Environmental Health and Racial Equity in the United States: Building Environmentally Just, Sustainable, and Livable Communities*. Washington, DC: American Public Health Association, 2011.

Bullard, Robert D., Paul Mohai, Robin Sana, and Beverly Wright. *Toxic Wastes and Race at Twenty, 1987–2007: A Report Prepared for the United Church of Christ Justice and Witness Ministries*. Cleveland: United Church of Christ, 2007.

Bushnell, Charles J. *The Social Problems at the Chicago Stock Yards*. Chicago: University of Chicago Press, 1902.

Byrd, Robert C. *The Senate, 1789–1989: Addresses on the History of the United States Senate*. Washington, DC: U.S. Government Printing Office, 1991.

Calhoun, John C. "Speech on the Abolition Petitions, Delivered in the Senate, March 9th, 1836." In *The Works of John C. Calhoun*, edited by Richard Kenner Crallé, 465–490. New York: D. Appleton & Co., 1888.

Carter, Susan B., Scott Sigmund Gartner, Michael R. Haines, Alan L. Olmstead, Richard Sutch, and Gavin Wright, eds. *Historical Statistics of the United States—Millennial Edition*. New York: Cambridge University Press, 2006.

Casuso, Jorge, and Eduardo Camacho. "Latino Chicago." In *Ethnic Chicago: A Multi-cultural Portrait*, edited by Melvin G. Holli and Peter d'Alroy Jones, 346–377. Grand Rapids, MI: Wm. B. Eerdmans Publishing Co., 1995.

Chew, Lee. "Life Story of a Chinaman." In *The Life Stories of Undistinguished Americans as Told by Themselves*, edited by Hamilton Holt, 289–290. New York: James Pott & Co., 1906.

Chew, Ng Poon. "The Chinaman in America." *Chautauquan* 9 (1889): 802.

Chicago Commission on Race Relations. *The Negro in Chicago: A Study of Race Relations and a Race Riot*. Chicago: University of Chicago Press, 1922.

Clapperton, Robert H. *The Paper-Making Machine*. New York: Pergamon Press, 1967.

Cohen, Adam, and Elizabeth Taylor. *American Pharaoh: Mayor Richard J. Daley—His Battle for Chicago and the Nation*. New York: Little, Brown, & Co., 2000.

Cohen, Lizabeth. *Making a New Deal: Industrial Workers in Chicago, 1919–1939*. New York: Cambridge University Press, 1990.

Cole, Luke W., and Sheila R. Foster. *From the Ground Up: Environmental Racism and the Rise of the Environmental Justice Movement*. New York: NYU Press, 2001.

Colored Home and Hospital Sixty-Fifth Street and First Avenue. *Forty-Eighth Annual Report, 1887–8*. New York: Angell's Printing Office, 1888.

Colored Orphan Asylum and Association for the Benefit of Colored Children in the City of New York. *Fifty-Second Annual Report of the Colored Orphan Asylum and Association for the Benefit of Colored Children in the City of New York, for the Year 1888: Asylum, 143d Street, 10th Avenue*. New York: Trow's Printing & Bookbinding Co., 1889.

Commission for Racial Justice, United Church of Christ. *Toxic Wastes and Race in the United States: A National Report on the Racial and Socio-economic Characteristics of Communities with Hazardous Waste Sites*. New York: Commission for Racial Justice, 1987.

Congressional Serial Set. 21st Congress, 2nd sess., 3–27. Washington, DC: U.S. Government Printing Office, 1831.

Coulter, Charles Edward. *Take Up the Black Man's Burden: Kansas City's African American Communities, 1865–1939*. Columbia: University of Missouri Press, 2006.

Cowan, Ruth Schwartz. *More Work for Mother: The Ironies of Household Technology from the Open Hearth to the Microwave*. New York: Basic Books, 1983.

Crenshaw, Kimberlé, ed. *Critical Race Theory: The Key Writings That Formed the Movement*. New York: New Press, 1995.

Crider, Bill. "Rousing Fight Nears End in Free Memphis Election." *Kingsport Times-News*, November 6, 1955, 7-B.

Cronon, William. *Changes in the Land: Indians, Colonists, and the Ecology of New England*. New York: Hill & Wang, 1983.

Cronon, William. *Nature's Metropolis: Chicago and the Great West*. New York: W. W. Norton, 1991.

Cutler, Irving. "The Jews of Chicago: From Shtetl to Suburb." In *Ethnic Chicago: A Multicultural Portrait*, edited by Melvin G. Holli and Peter d'Alroy Jones, 122–172. Grand Rapids, MI: Wm. B. Eerdmans Publishing Co., 1995.

Cutler, Irving. *The Jews of Chicago: From Shtetl to Suburb*. Urbana: University of Illinois Press, 1996.

Daniels, Roger. *Coming to America: A History of Immigration and Ethnicity in American Life*. New York: HarperCollins, 1990.

Delgado, Richard. *Critical Race Theory: The Cutting Edge*. Philadelphia: Temple University Press, 1995.

Denton, Nancy A., and Douglas S. Massey. *American Apartheid: Segregation and the Making of the Underclass*. Cambridge, MA: Harvard University Press, 1993.

Deutsch, Tracey. *Building a Housewife's Paradise: Gender, Politics, and American Grocery Stores in the Twentieth Century*. Chapel Hill: University of North Carolina Press, 2010.

Di Charo, Giovanna. "Nature as Community: The Convergence of Environmental and Social Justice." In *Uncommon Ground: Rethinking the Human Place in Nature*, edited by William Cronon, 298–320. New York: W. W. Norton, 1995.

Dickens, Charles. *Household Words: A Weekly Journal*. London: Bradley & Evans, 1852.

Diner, Hasia R. *A Time for Gathering: Second Migration, 1820–1880*. Baltimore: Johns Hopkins University Press, 1992.

Douglas, Kirk. *The Ragman's Son: An Autobiography*. New York: Simon & Schuster, 1998.

Douglas, Mary. *Purity and Danger: An Analysis of Concepts of Pollution and Taboo*. Routledge Classics ed. New York: Routledge, 2002.

Douglas, Mike, Thomas Kelly, and Michael Heaton. *I'll Be Right Back: Memories of TV's Greatest Talk Show*. New York: Simon & Schuster, 2000.

Dowdy, G. Wayne. *Crusades for Freedom: Memphis and the Political Transformation of the American South*. Jackson: University Press of Mississippi, 2010.

Drake, St. Clair, and Horace Roscoe Cayton. *Black Metropolis: A Study of Negro Life in a Northern City*. Chicago: University of Chicago Press, 1993. Originally published New York: Harcourt, Brace & Co., 1945.

Duffy, John. *The Sanitarians: A History of American Public Health*. Urbana: University of Illinois Press, 1990.

Duignan, Peter, and Lewis H. Gann. *The Rebirth of the West: The Americanization of the Democratic World, 1945–1958*. New York: Rowman & Littlefield, 1996.

Einhorn, Robin. *Property Rules: Political Economy in Chicago, 1833–1872*. Chicago: University of Chicago Press, 1991.

Ellis, Joseph J. *American Sphinx: The Character of Thomas Jefferson*. New York: A. A. Knopf, 1997.

Ellis, Joseph J. *Passionate Sage: The Character and Legacy of John Adams*. New York: A. A. Knopf, 2001.

Esherick, Joseph. *Remaking the Chinese City: Modernity and National Identity, 1900–1950*. Honolulu: University of Hawaii Press, 2002.

Evans, Eli N. *The Provincials: A Personal History of Jews in the South*. Chapel Hill: University of North Carolina Press, 2005.

Evans, Richard J. *Death in Hamburg: Society and Politics in the Cholera Years*. New York: Oxford University Press, 1987.

Fernandez, Lilia. *Brown in the Windy City: Mexicans and Puerto Ricans in Postwar Chicago*. Chicago: University of Chicago Press, 2012.

Fleming, George Thornton. *History of Pittsburgh and Environs, from Prehistoric Days to the Beginning of the American Revolution*. New York: American Historical Society, 1922.

Fligstein, Neil. *Going North: Migration of Blacks and Whites from the South, 1900–1950*. New York: Academic Press, 1981.

Foner, Eric. *Forever Free: The Story of Emancipation and Reconstruction*. New York: A. A. Knopf, 2005.

Foner, Eric. *Reconstruction: America's Unfinished Revolution, 1863–1877*. New York: HarperCollins, 2002.

Foner, Eric, and Oliva Mahoney. *America's Reconstruction: People and Politics after the Civil War*. New York: HarperCollins, 1995.

Foo, Wong Chin. "The Chinese in New York." *Cosmopolitan* 5 (1888): 298.

Foote, Thelma Wills. *Black and White Manhattan: The History of Racial Formation in Colonial New York City*. New York: Oxford University Press, 2004.

Ford, Paul L., ed. *The Works of Thomas Jefferson, Vol. X (in 12 Volumes): Correspondence and Papers, 1803–1807*. New York: Cosimo Classics, 2009. Originally published 1905.

Ford, Paul Leicester, ed. *The Writings of Thomas Jefferson*. Vol. 10, *1816–1826*. New York: G. P. Putnam's Sons, 1899.

Foreman, Grant. *Indian Removal: The Emigration of the Five Civilized Tribes of Indians*. Norman: University of Oklahoma Press, 1932.

Forman, Jacob G. *The Western Sanitary Commission: A Sketch of Its Origin, History, Labors for the Sick and Wounded of the Western Armies, and Aid Given to Freedmen and Union Refugees, with Incidents of Hospital Life.* St. Louis: R. P. Studley & Co., 1864.

Foucault, Michel. "Technologies of the Self." In *Technologies of the Self: A Seminar with Michel Foucault,* edited by Luther H. Martin, Huck Gutman, and Patrick H. Hutton, 16–49. London: Tavistock, 1988.

Franklin, Ben A. "Historians Joust over Effects of the U.S. Melting Pot." *New York Times,* December 31, 1964, 15.

Franklin, John Hope. *Reconstruction after the Civil War.* Chicago: University of Chicago Press, 1961.

Franklin, John Hope, and Loren Schweninger. *Runaway Slaves: Rebels on the Plantation.* New York: Oxford University Press, 1999.

Fremon, David K. *Chicago Politics Ward by Ward.* Bloomington: Indiana University Press, 1988.

Freund, David M. P. *Colored Property: State Policy and White Racial Politics in Suburban America.* Chicago: University of Chicago Press, 2007.

Gates, Henry Louis. *Colored People: A Memoir.* New York: A. A. Knopf, 1994.

Gates, Nathaniel E. *The Concept of "Race" in Natural and Social Science.* New York: Garland Publishing, 1997.

Glazer, Nathan, and Daniel P. Moynihan. *Beyond the Melting Pot: The Negroes, Puerto Ricans, Jews, Italians, and Irish of New York City,* 2nd ed. Cambridge, MA: MIT Press, 1970.

Goffman, Erving. *Stigma.* Englewood Cliffs, NJ: Prentice Hall, 1963.

Gold, Ray. "Janitors versus Tenants: A Status-Income Dilemma." *American Journal of Sociology* 57 (1952): 486–493.

Goldberger, Paul. "Tony Imperiale Stands for Law and Order." *New York Times Magazine,* September 29, 1968, 30–31, 117–122.

Golden, Harry. "A Former Junk Dealer." *Jewish Advocate,* September 15, 1966, 19B.

Goldstein, Eric L. *The Price of Whiteness: Jews, Race, and American Identity.* Princeton, NJ: Princeton University Press, 2006.

Gould, Stephen Jay. *The Mismeasure of Man,* 2nd ed. New York: W. W. Norton, 1996.

Gratton, Brian, and Myron Gutmann. "Hispanic Population Estimates, by Sex, Race, Hispanic Origin, Residence, Nativity, 1850–1990." In *Historical Statistics of the United States: Millennial Edition,* edited by Susan B. Carter, Scott Sigmund Gartner, Michael R. Haines, Alan L. Olmstead, Richard Sutch, and Gavin Wright, 1:1–177 to 1–179. New York: Cambridge University Press, 2006.

Green, Michael D. *The Politics of Indian Removal: Creek Government and Society in Crisis.* Lincoln: University of Nebraska Press, 1982.

Greenberg, Ivan. "Class Culture and Generation Change: Immigrant Families in Two Connecticut Cities during the 1930s." Ph.D diss., City University of New York, 1990.

Gregory, James. "The Southern Diaspora and the Urban Dispossessed: Demonstrating the Census Public Use Microdata Samples." *Journal of American History* 82 (1995): 111–134.

Grigg, Harry H., and George E. Haynes. *Junk Dealing and Juvenile Delinquency*, text by Albert E. Webster. Chicago: Juvenile Protective Association, [1919?].

Grimshaw, William J. *Bitter Fruit: Black Politics and the Chicago Machine, 1931–1991.* Chicago: University of Chicago Press, 1992.

Griscom, John Hoskins. *The Sanitary Condition of the Laboring Population of New York: With Suggestions for Its Improvement.* New York: Harper, 1845.

Gross, Ariella Julie. *What Blood Won't Tell: A History of Race on Trial in America.* Cambridge, MA: Harvard University Press, 2008.

Grossman, James. "African American Migration to Chicago." In *Ethnic Chicago: A Multicultural Portrait*, edited by Melvin G. Holli and Peter d'Alroy Jones, 303–340. Grand Rapids, MI: Wm. B. Eerdmans Publishing Co., 1995.

Grossman, James R. *Land of Hope: Chicago, Black Southerners, and the Great Migration.* Chicago: University of Chicago Press, 1989.

Grossman, James. "Review of Grace Elizabeth Hale, *Making Whiteness: The Culture of Segregation in the South, 1890–1940,*" *Journal of American History* 87 (2001): 1445–1447.

Grossman, Karl. "From Toxic Racism to Environmental Justice." *E Magazine*, May–June 1992, 28–35.

Grutzner, Charles. "City Puerto Ricans Are Found Ill-Housed." *New York Times*, October 4, 1949, 30.

Guglielmo, Thomas. *White on Arrival: Italians, Race, Color, and Power in Chicago, 1890–1945.* New York: Oxford University Press, 2003.

Gutenschwager, Gerald A. "The Scrap Iron and Steel Industry in Metropolitan Chicago." Ph.D diss., University of Chicago, 1957.

Halbfinger, David M. "Anthony Imperiale, 68, Dies; Polarizing Force in Newark." *New York Times*, December 28, 1999, B-9.

Hale, Grace Elizabeth. *Making Whiteness: The Culture of Segregation in the South, 1890–1940.* New York: Pantheon, 1998.

Hamilton, Frank H. "Our Surgeons upon the Field." *American Medical Times* 6 (March 21, 1863): 133–134.

Handlin, Oscar. "All Colors, All Creeds, All Nationalities, All New Yorkers." *New York Times*, September 22, 1963, 3, 23.

Henri, Florette. *Black Migration.* Garden City, NY: Anchor Books, 1976.

Hering, Rudolph. "Disposal of Municipal Refuse: Review of General Practices." *Transactions of the American Society of Civil Engineers* 54 (1904): 278–279.

Hering, Rudolph, and Samuel A. Greeley. *Collection and Disposal of Municipal Refuse.* New York: Mcgraw-Hill, 1921.

Herz, Rachel. *That's Disgusting: Unraveling the Mysteries of Repulsion.* New York: W. W. Norton & Company, 2012.

Heuchling, Fred. "Chicago's Garbage Problem." *City Club Bulletin*, December 20, 1913, 1.

Hirsch, Arnold R. *Making the Second Ghetto: Race and Housing in Chicago 1940–1960.* New York: Cambridge University Press, 1983.

Honey, Michael K. *Going Down Jericho Road: The Memphis Strike, Martin Luther King's Last Campaign.* New York: W. W. Norton, 2007.

Horowitz, Daniel. *The Morality of Spending Attitudes toward the Consumer Society in America, 1875–1940.* Baltimore: Johns Hopkins University Press, 1985.

Horowitz, Jason. "Biden Unbound: Lays into Clinton, Obama, Edwards." *New York Observer*, February 5, 2007, http://observer.com/2007/02/biden-unbound-lays-into -clinton-obama-edwards/, accessed June 12, 2015.

Howard, Gene L. *Death at Cross Plains: An Alabama Reconstruction Tragedy.* Tuscaloosa: University of Alabama Press, 1984.

Hoy, Suellen. *Chasing Dirt: The American Pursuit of Cleanliness.* New York: Oxford University Press, 1995.

Hoyt, Homer. *One Hundred Years of Land Values in Chicago: The Relationship of the Growth of Chicago to the Rise in Its Land Values, 1830–1933.* Chicago: University of Chicago Press, 1933.

Hoyt, Homer. *The Structure and Growth of Residential Neighborhoods in American Cities.* Washington, DC: Federal Housing Administration, 1939.

Hughes, Everett. "Good People and Dirty Work." In *The Other Side*, edited by Howard Becker, 23–26. New York: Free Press, 1964.

Hunt, D. Bradford. *Blueprint for Disaster: The Unraveling of Chicago Public Housing.* Chicago: University of Chicago Press, 2009.

Hunter, Tera. *To 'Joy My Freedom: Southern Black Women's Lives and Labors after the Civil War.* Cambridge, MA: Harvard University Press, 1997.

Hurley, Andrew. *Environmental Inequalities: Class, Race, and Industrial Pollution in Gary, Indiana, 1945–1980.* Chapel Hill: University of North Carolina Press, 1995.

Hurt, Peyton. "The Rise and Fall of the 'Know Nothings' in California." *California History Society Quarterly* 9 (1930): 24–33.

Institute of Scrap Iron & Steel, Inc., *Addresses at the 36th Annual Convention.* Washington, DC: Institute of Scrap Iron & Steel, Inc., 1964.

Institute of Scrap Recycling Industries. "Our Heritage: Next Generation II." Videotape. Washington, DC: Institute of Scrap Recycling Industries, 1986.

Jablonsky, Thomas J. *Pride in the Jungle: Community and Everyday Life in Back of the Yards Chicago.* Baltimore: Johns Hopkins University Press, 1993.

Jackson, Derrick Z. "Obama Makes a Clean Hit." *Boston Globe*, February 14, 2007. www.boston.com/news/nation/articles/2007/02/14/obama_makes_a_clean_hit, accessed August 17, 2009.

Jackson, Kenneth T. *Crabgrass Frontier: The Suburbanization of the United States.* New York: Oxford University Press, 1985.

Jackson, Kenneth T. *The Ku Klux Klan in the City, 1915–1930.* New York: Oxford University Press, 1967.

Jacobs, James B. *Mobsters, Unions, and Feds: The Mafia and the American Labor Movement*. New York: New York University Press, 2006.

Jacobs, James B., Coleen Friel, and Robert Radick. *Gotham Unbound: How New York City Was Liberated from the Grip of Organized Crime*. New York: NYU Press, 1999.

Jacobson, Matthew Frye. *Whiteness of a Different Color: European Immigrants and the Alchemy of Race*. Cambridge, MA: Harvard University Press, 1998.

Jacobson, Timothy. *Waste Management: An American Corporate Success Story*. Washington, DC: Gateway Business Books, 1993.

Jefferson, Thomas. *Memoir, Correspondence, and Miscellanies, from the Papers of Thomas Jefferson*. Edited by Thomas Jefferson Randolph. Vol. 1. Charlottesville, VA: F. Carr & Co., 1829.

Jefferson, Thomas. *Notes on the State of Virginia*. London: John Stockdale, 1787.

Jefferson, Thomas. *The Papers of Thomas Jefferson*. 42 vols. Edited by Julian P. Boyd; associate eds. Lyman H. Butterfield and Mina R. Brian. Princeton, NJ: Princeton University Press, 1950–.

Johnson, Thomas A. "Negro Leaders See Bias in Call of Nixon for 'Law and Order.'" *New York Times*, August 13, 1968, 27.

Jordan, Winthrop D. *White over Black: American Attitudes toward the Negro, 1550–1812*. Chapel Hill: University of North Carolina Press, 1968.

Juneiana, Jennie. *Talks on Women's Topics*. Boston: Lee & Shepard, 1864.

Kanfer, Stefan. *Groucho: The Life and Times of Julius Henry Marx*. New York: A. A. Knopf, 2000.

Kasson, John F. *Rudeness and Civility: Manners in Nineteenth-Century Urban America*. New York: Hill & Wang, 1990.

Katznelson, Ira. *When Affirmative Action Was White: An Untold History of Racial Inequality in Twentieth-Century America*. New York: W. W. Norton, 2005.

Kaztauskis, Antanas. "The Life Story of a Lithuanian." In *The Life Stories of Undistinguished Americans as Told by Themselves*, edited by Hamilton Holt, 9–33. New York: James Pott & Co., 1906.

Kelley, Robin D. G. "Building Bridges: The Challenge of Organized Labor in Communities of Color." *New Labor Forum* 5 (1999): 42–58.

Kiechle, Melanie. "The Air We Breathe: Nineteenth-Century Americans and the Search for Fresh Air." Ph.D. diss., Rutgers University, 2012.

King, Martin Luther, Jr. *A Testament of Hope: The Essential Writings and Speeches of Martin Luther King, Jr.*, edited by James M. Washington. New York: HarperCollins, 1986.

Koeppel, Gerald. *Bond of Union: Building the Erie Canal and American Empire*. Cambridge, MA: Da Capo Press, 2009.

Koukol, Alois B. "A Slav's a Man for A' That." In *The Pittsburgh Survey: Wage-Earning Pittsburgh*, edited by Paul Underwood Kellogg, 61–77. New York: Russell Sage Foundation, 1914.

Kramer, Howard D. "Effect of the Civil War on the Public Health Movement." *Mississippi Valley Historical Review* 35 (1948): 449–462.

Kraut, Alan M. "The Butcher, The Baker, The Pushcart Peddler: Jewish Foodways and Entrepreneurial Opportunity in the East European Immigrant Community, 1880–1940." *Journal of American Culture* 6 (1983): 71–83.

Latrobe, Benjamin Henry. *The Journal of Latrobe: Being the Notes and Sketches of an Architect, Naturalist and Traveler in the United States from 1796 to 1820.* New York: D. Appleton, 1905.

Layton, Edwin T. Jr. *The Revolt of the Engineers.* Cleveland: Case Western Reserve University Press, 1971.

Lears, T. J. Jackson. *Fables of Abundance: A Cultural History of Advertising in America.* New York: Basic Books, 1994.

Leighton, Marshall O. "Industrial Wastes and Their Sanitary Significance." *Reports and Papers of the American Public Health Association* 31 (1905): 29–41.

Lerner, Stephen. "Black and Brown: The United Colors of Low-Wage Workers." *Race, Poverty, and the Environment* 14 (2007): 33–34.

Levinson, Aaron P. *If Only Right Now Could Be Forever.* Hillsboro, OR: Media Weavers, Inc., 1987.

Levinson, Peter J. *September in the Rain: The Life of Nelson Riddle.* New York: Billboard Books, 2001.

Lewis, Ronald L. "Industrial Slavery: Linking the Periphery and the Core." In *The African American Urban Experience: Perspectives from the Colonial Period to the Present,* edited by Joe W. Trotter, Earl Lewis, and Tera Hunter, 35–57. New York: Palgrave Macmillan, 2004.

Le Zotte, Jennifer. "'Not Charity, but a Chance': Philanthropic Capitalism and the Rise of American Thrift Stores, 1894–1930." *New England Quarterly* 86 (2013): 169–195.

Li, Wei. *Ethnoburb: The New Ethnic Community in Urban America.* Honolulu: University of Hawaii Press, 2009.

Lipscomb, Andrew Adgate, and Albert Ellery Bergh, eds. *The Writings of Thomas Jefferson.* Memorial ed., 20 vols. Washington, DC: Thomas Jefferson Memorial Association of the United States, 1903–1904.

Lipsett, Charles H. *100 Years of Recycling History: From Yankee Tincart Peddlers to Wall Street Scrap Giants.* New York: Atlas Publishing Co., 1974.

Longstreth, Richard. *The American Department Store Transformed, 1920–1960.* New Haven, CT: Yale University Press, 2010.

López, Ian Haney. *White by Law: The Legal Construction of Race.* Rev. ed. New York: New York University Press, 2006.

Lovey, Robert D. *The Civil Rights Act of 1964: The Passage of the Law That Ended Racial Segregation.* Albany: State University of New York Press, 1997.

Luff, Jennifer. "Justice for Janitors." In *Encyclopedia of U.S. Labor and Working Class History,* edited by Eric Arensen, 729–731. New York: Routledge, 2007.

Lukas, J. Anthony. "Rise in White Ethnic Emphasis Is Studied by 200 Specialists." *New York Times,* November 19, 1969, 18.

MacGowan, John. *Men and Manners of Modern China.* New York: Dodd, Mead, & Co., 1912.

MacLeish, Archibald. *Jews in America*. New York: Random House, 1936.

Maranville, Angela R., Tih-Fen Ting, and Yang Zhang. "An Environmental Justice Analysis: Superfund Sites and Surrounding Communities in Illinois." *Environmental Justice* 2 (2009): 49–58.

Marchand, Roland. *Advertising the American Dream: Making Way for Modernity, 1920–1940*. Berkeley: University of California Press, 1985.

Mason, Karen M. "Mary McDowell and Municipal Housekeeping: Women's Political Activism in Chicago, 1890–1920." In *Midwestern Women: Work, Community, and Leadership at the Crossroads*, edited by Lucy Eldersveld Murphy and Wendy Hamand Venet, 6–75. Bloomington: Indiana University Press, 1997.

Massachusetts Sanitary Commission, Lemuel Shattuck, Nathaniel Prentiss Banks, and Jehiel Abbott, *Report of a General Plan for the Promotion of Public and Personal Health*. Boston: Dutton & Wentworth, 1850.

May, Vanessa H. *Unprotected Labor: Household Workers, Politics, and Middle-Class Reform in New York, 1870–1940*. Chapel Hill: University of North Carolina Press, 2011.

McElroy, Michael. "Blogtalk: Biden Fallout." *New York Times*, January 31, 2007. http://thecaucus.blogs.nytimes.com/2007/01/31/blogtalk-biden-fallout, accessed August 17, 2009.

McGaw, Judith A. *Most Wonderful Machine: Mechanization and Social Change in Berkshire Paper Making, 1801–1885*. Princeton, NJ: Princeton University Press, 1987.

McGurty, Eileen. *Transforming Environmentalism: Warren County, PCBs, and the Origins of Environmental Justice*. New Brunswick, NJ: Rutgers University Press, 2007.

McNeill, J. R., and George Vrtis. "Thrift and Waste in American History: An Ecological View." In *Thrift and Thriving in America: Capitalism and Moral Order from the Puritans to the Present*, edited by Joshua J. Yates and James Davison Hunter, 508–535. New York: Oxford University Press, 2011.

McPherson, Edward. *The Political History of the United States of America*. Washington, DC: Philp & Sons, 1865.

McPherson, James M. *The Abolitionist Legacy: From Reconstruction to the NAACP*. Princeton, NJ: University of Princeton Press, 1975.

McShane, Clay, and Joel A. Tarr. *The Horse in the City: Living Machines in the Nineteenth Century*. Baltimore: Johns Hopkins University Press, 2007.

Meehan, Thomas. "Moynihan of the Moynihan Report." *New York Times Magazine*, July 31, 1966, 5, 48–50, 54–55.

Melosi, Martin V. *Garbage in the Cities: Refuse, Reform, and the Environment*. Pittsburgh, PA: University of Pittsburgh, 2005.

Melosi, Martin V. *The Sanitary City: Urban Infrastructure in America from Colonial Times to the Present*. Baltimore: Johns Hopkins University Press, 2000.

Millard, Candice. *Destiny of the Republic: A Tale of Madness, Medicine, and the Murder of a President*. New York: Anchor Books, 2011.

Miller, Donald L. *City of the Century: The Epic of Chicago and the Making of America*. New York: Simon & Schuster, 1997.

Miller, Scott. *The President and the Assassin: McKinley, Terror, and Empire at the Dawn of the American Century*. New York: Random House, 2011.

Miller, William Lee. "Analysis of the 'White Backlash.'" *New York Times Magazine*, August 23, 1964, 27, 87–88.

Mingus, Charles. *Beneath the Underdog: His World as Composed by Mingus*. New York, A. A. Knopf, 1971.

Misa, Thomas J. *A Nation of Steel: The Making of Modern America, 1865–1925*. Baltimore: Johns Hopkins University Press, 1995.

Moore, Jacqueline M. *Booker T. Washington, W.E.B. DuBois and the Struggle for Racial Uplift*. Lanham, MD: SR Books, 2003.

Moore, Leonard N. *Carl B. Stokes and the Rise of Black Political Power*. Urbana: University of Illinois Press, 2002.

Moynihan, Colin. "Worker Is Crushed by Garbage Truck Compactor in Brooklyn." *New York Times*, March 16, 2013. www.nytimes.com/2013/03/17/nyregion/man-is -crushed-by-compactor-in-brooklyn.html, accessed March 17, 2013.

Myrdal, Gunnar. *An American Dilemma: The Negro Problem and Modern Democracy*. New York: Harper & Bros, 1944.

Nagle, Robin. *Picking Up: On the Streets and Behind the Trucks with the Sanitation Workers of New York City*. New York: Farrar, Straus, & Giroux, 2013.

Nasaw, David. *Children of the City: At Work and at Play*. Garden City, NY: Anchor Press/Doubleday, 1985.

Nee, Victor G., and Brett de Bary Nee. *Longtime Californ': A Documentary Study of an American Chinatown*. New York: Pantheon Books, 1972.

Nelli, Humbert S. *Italians in Chicago, 1880–1930: A Study in Ethnic Mobility*. New York: Oxford University Press, 1979.

Ngai, Mae M. *Impossible Subjects: Illegal Aliens and the Making of Modern America*. Princeton, NJ: Princeton University Press, 2004.

Norment, Lynn. "Ben Chavis: A New Director, a New Direction at the NAACP." *Ebony* 48, no. 9 (July 1993): 76–80.

North, Douglass C. *The Economic Growth of the United States, 1790–1860*. New York: W. W. Norton, 1966.

Norton, J. M., S. Wing, H. J. Lipscomb, J. S. Kaufman, S. W. Marshall, and A. J. Cravey. "Race, Wealth, and Solid Waste Facilities in North Carolina." *Environmental Health Perspectives* 115 (2007): 1344–1350.

Oates, Stephen B. *Let the Trumpet Sound: A Life of Martin Luther King, Jr*. New York: Harper & Row, 1982.

Obama, Barack. *Dreams from My Father: A Story of Race and Inheritance*. New York: Random House, 1995, 2004.

Oberman, Bobbye, ed. *Encyclopedia of Scrap Recycling: A Special Bicentennial Edition of "Scrap Age: The Voice of the Recycling Industry."* Niles, IL: Three Sons Publishing Company, 1977.

Ong, Paul M. "Chinese Laundries as an Urban Occupation in Nineteenth Century

California." *Annals of the Chinese Historical Society of the Pacific Northwest*, edited by Douglas W. Lee. Seattle, 1983.

Pacyga, Dominic A. "Chicago's Ethnic Neighborhoods: The Myth of Stability and the Reality of Change." In *Ethnic Chicago: A Multicultural Portrait*, edited by Melvin G. Holli and Peter d'Alroy Jones, 604–617. Grand Rapids, MI: Wm. B. Eerdmans Publishing Co., 1995.

Painter, Nell Irvin. *The History of White People*. New York: W. W. Norton, 2010.

Park, Robert Ezra, Ernest Watson Burgess, and Roderick Duncan McKenzie, *The City*. Chicago: University of Chicago Press, 1967. Originally published 1925.

Parker, Laurence, Donna Deyhle, and Sofia Villenas, eds. *Race Is—Race Isn't: Critical Race Theory and Qualitative Studies in Education*. Boulder, CO: Westview Press, 1999.

Parsons, H. de B. "Disposal of Municipal Refuse." *Municipal Journal and Engineer* 35 (November 6, 1913): 625–628.

Parsons, Lynn Hudson. *John Quincy Adams*. Lanham, MD: Rowman & Littlefield, 1998.

Pascoe, Peggy. *What Comes Naturally: Miscegenation Law and the Making of Race in America*. New York: Oxford University Press, 2009.

Patinkin, Mandy. "My Story as an American Jew." *Shofar Magazine*, 1998. http://web .archive.org/web/20121001022650/http://www.mandypatinkin.net/ARTICLES/ shofar.shtm, accessed June 5, 2015.

Pellow, David Naguib. *Garbage Wars: The Struggle for Environmental Justice in Chicago*. Cambridge, MA: MIT Press, 2002.

Perry, Stewart E. *Collecting Garbage: Dirty Work, Clean Jobs, Proud People*. Piscataway, NJ: Transaction Publishers, 1998.

Philpott, Thomas Lee. *The Slum and the Ghetto: Immigrants, Blacks, and Reformers in Chicago, 1880–1930*. New York: Oxford University Press, 1978.

Picchi, Blaise. *The Five Weeks of Guiseppe Zangara: The Man Who Would Assassinate FDR*. Chicago: Academy Chicago Publishers, 1998.

Platt, Harold L. "Jane Addams and the Ward Boss Revisited: Class, Politics, and Public Health in Chicago, 1890–1930." *Environmental History* 5 (2000): 194–222.

Pollack, Jonathan Z. S. "Success from Scrap and Secondhand Goods: Jewish Businessmen in the Midwest, 1890–1930." In *Chosen Capital: The Jewish Encounter with American Capitalism*, edited by Rebecca Kobrin, 93–112. New Brunswick, NJ: Rutgers University Press, 2012.

Pollak, Oliver B. "The Jewish Peddlers of Omaha." *Nebraska History* 63 (1982): 474–501.

Prell, Riv-Ellen, "Triumph, Accommodation, and Resistance: American Jewish Life from the End of World War II to the Six-Day War." In *The Columbia History of Jews and Judaism in America*, edited by Marc Lee Raphael, 114–141. New York: Columbia University Press, 2008.

Pulido, Laura. "Rethinking Environmental Racism: White Privilege and Urban Development in Southern California." *Annals of the Association of American Geographers* 90 (2000): 12–40.

Puzo, Mario. *The Godfather*. Novel. New York: Putnam, 1969.

Puzo, Mario. *The Godfather, Part II*. Film. Directed by Francis Ford Coppola. Hollywood, CA: Paramount Pictures, 1974.

Puzo, Mario. "The Italians, American Style." *New York Times Magazine*, August 6, 1967, 7, 14, 18–22.

Randall, Henry Stephens. *The Life of Thomas Jefferson*. Vol. 3. New York: Derby & Jackson, 1858.

Randall, Willard Sterne. *Thomas Jefferson: A Life*. New York: Henry Holt & Co., 1993.

Reid, Donald. *Paris Sewers and Sewermen: Realities and Representations*. Cambridge, MA: Harvard University Press, 1991.

Riis, Jacob A. *How the Other Half Lives: Studies among the Tenements of New York*. New York: Scribner & Sons, 1890.

Robinson, Eugene. "An Inarticulate Kickoff." *Washington Post*, February 2, 2007, A15.

Roediger, David R. *The Wages of Whiteness: The Making of the American Working Class*. New York: Verso, 1991.

Roediger, David R. *Working toward Whiteness: How America's Immigrants Became White*. New York: Basic Books, 2005.

Rogers, Robert P. *An Economic History of the American Steel Industry*. New York: Routledge, 2009.

Rome, Adam Ward. *The Bulldozer in the Countryside: Suburban Sprawl and the Rise of American Environmentalism*. New York: Cambridge University Press, 2001.

Roosevelt, Theodore. "Opening Address by the President." *Proceedings of a Conference of Governors in the White House*, edited by Newton C. Blanchard. Washington, DC: U.S. Government Printing Office, 1909.

Rosenberg, Charles. *The Cholera Years: The United States in 1832, 1849, and 1866*. Rev. ed. Chicago: University of Chicago Press, 1987.

Rosenzweig, Roy, and Elizabeth Blackmar. *The Park and Its People: A History of Central Park*. Ithaca, NY: Cornell University Press, 1992.

Ross, Edward Alsworth. *The Old World in the New: The Significance of Past and Present Immigration to the American People*. New York: Century Co., 1914.

Ruffins, Fath Davis. "Mythos, Memory, and History: African American Preservation Efforts, 1820–1990." In *Museums and Communities: The Politics of Public Culture*, edited by Ivan Karp, Christine Mullen Kreamer, and Steven D. Lavins, 506–611. Washington, DC: Smithsonian Institution Press, 1992.

Sandburg, Carl. *The Chicago Race Riots, July, 1919*. New York: Harcourt, Brace & Howe, 1919.

Savage, Charlie. "On Nixon Tapes, Ambivalence over Abortion, Not Watergate." *New York Times*, June 24, 2009, A1.

Schultz, Stanley, and Clay McShane. "Pollution and Political Reform in Urban America: The Role of Municipal Engineers, 1840–1920." In *Pollution and Reform in American Cities, 1870–1930*, edited by Martin V. Melosi, 155–172. Austin: University of Texas Press, 1980.

Selavan, Ida Cohen, ed., *My Voice Was Heard*. New York: Ktav Publishing House, 1981.

Sellers, Christopher C. *Crabgrass Crucible: Suburban Nature and the Rise of Environmentalism in Twentieth-Century America*. Chapel Hill: University of North Carolina Press, 2012.

Sellers, Christopher C. "Thoreau's Body: Towards an Embodied Environmental History." *Environmental History* 4 (1999): 486–514.

Sharma, Rama. *Bhangi, Scavenger in Indian Society: Marginality, Identity, and Politicization of the Community*. New Delhi: M.D. Publications Pvt. Ltd., 1995.

Shoemaker, Nancy. *A Strange Likeness: Becoming Red and White in Eighteenth-Century North America*. New York: Oxford University Press, 2004.

Silver, Christopher. "The Racial Origins of Zoning." In *Urban Planning and the African-American Community: In the Shadows*, edited by June Manning Thomas and Marsha Ritzdorf, 24–25. Thousand Oaks, CA: Sage Publishers, 1997.

Sinclair, Upton. *The Jungle*. New York: Harper & Bros., 1905.

Siu, Paul. *The Chinese Laundryman: A Study of Social Isolation*. New York: NYU Press, 1987.

Sivananda, Mantri. "Controversial Memphis Mayor Henry Loeb III, 1920–1992: A Biographical Study." Ph.D dissertation, University of Memphis, 2002.

Sivananda, Mantri. "Henry Loeb III As Public Works Commissioner, 1956–1959." *West Tennessee Historical Society Papers* 66 (2000): 67–80.

Slayton, Robert A. *Back of the Yards: The Making of a Local Democracy*. Chicago: University of Chicago Press, 1986.

Smedley, Audrey, and Brian Smedley. *Race in North America: Origins and Evolution of a Worldview*, 3rd ed. Boulder, CO: Westview Press, 2007.

Smith, Karen Manners. "New Paths to Power: 1890–1920." In *No Small Courage: A History of Women in the United States*, edited by Nancy F. Cott, 375–378. New York: Oxford University Press, 2000.

Smith, Mark M. *Sensory History*. New York: Berg, 2007.

Soennichsen, John. *The Chinese Exclusion Act of 1882*. Santa Barbara, CA: Greenwood, 2009.

Sorin, Gerald. *A Time for Building: The Third Migration, 1880–1920*. Baltimore: Johns Hopkins University Press, 1992.

Spear, Alan. *Black Chicago: The Making of a Negro Ghetto, 1890–1920*. Chicago: University of Chicago Press, 1967.

Stansell, Christine. *City of Women: Sex and Class in New York, 1789–1860*. Urbana: University of Illinois Press, 1987.

Stead, William T. *If Christ Came to Chicago! A Plea for the Union of All Who Love in the Service of All Who Suffer*. Chicago: Laird & Lee Publishers, 1894.

Stevenson, Elizabeth. *Park Maker: A Life of Frederick Law Olmsted*. New York: Macmillan, 1977.

Stillé, Charles J. *History of the United States Sanitary Commission*. New York: Hurd & Houghton, 1868.

Stillman, Don. *Stronger Together: The Story of SEIU*. Washington, DC: Service Employees International Union, 2010.

Stradling, David. *Making Mountains: New York City and the Catskills*. Seattle: University of Washington Press, 2008.

Stradling, David. *Smokestacks and Progressives: Environmentalists, Engineers, and Air Quality in America, 1881–1951*. Baltimore: Johns Hopkins University Press, 1999.

Stradling, David, and Richard Stradling. "Perceptions of the Burning River: Deindustrialization and Cleveland's Cuyahoga River." *Environmental History* 13 (July 2008): 515–535.

Stradling, David, and Peter Thorsheim. "The Smoke of Great Cities: British and American Efforts to Control Air Pollution, 1860–1914." *Environmental History* 4 (1999): 6–31.

Strasser, Susan. *Waste and Want: A Social History of Trash*. New York: Metropolitan Books, 1999.

Sugrue, Thomas. *The Origins of the Urban Crisis: Race and Inequality in Postwar Detroit*. Princeton, NJ: Princeton University Press, 1996.

Swierenga, Robert P. *Dutch Chicago: A History of the Hollanders in the Windy City*. Grand Rapids, MI: Wm. B. Eerdmans, 2002.

Sze, Julie. *Noxious New York: The Racial Politics of Urban Health and Environmental Justice*. Cambridge, MA: MIT Press, 2007.

Takai, Ronald. *A Different Mirror: A History of Multicultural America*. New York: Little, Brown, & Co., 1993.

Tanenbaum, Leonard. *Junk Is Not a Four-Letter Word*. Cleveland: self-published, 1993.

Tarr, Joel A. "Historical Perspectives on Hazardous Wastes in the United States." In *The Search for the Ultimate Sink: Urban Pollution in Historical Perspective*, 341–353. Akron, OH: University of Akron Press, 1996.

Tarr, Joel A. "Railroad Smoke Control: The Regulation of a Mobile Pollution Source." In *The Search for the Ultimate Sink: Urban Pollution in Historical Perspective*, 262–283. Akron, OH: University of Akron Press, 1996.

Tarr, Joel A. "Searching for a 'Sink' for an Industrial Waste: Iron-Making Fuels and the Environment." *Environmental History Review* 18 (1994): 9–34.

Tarr, Joel A. "Sewerage and the Development of the Networked City in the United States, 1850–1930." In *Technology and the Rise of the Networked City in Europe and America*, edited by Joel A. Tarr and Gabriel Dupuy, 159–166. Philadelphia: Temple University Press, 1988.

Tarr, Joel A., and Carl Zimring. "The Struggle for Smoke Control in St. Louis: Achievement and Emulation." In *Common Fields: The Environmental History of St. Louis*, edited by Andrew Hurley, 190–220. St. Louis: Missouri Historical Society, 1997.

Taylor, Alan. *The Internal Enemy: Slavery and War in Virginia, 1772–1832*. New York: W. W. Norton, 2013.

Taylor, Dorceta E. *The Environment and the People in American Cities, 1600s–1900s: Disorder, Inequality, and Social Change*. Durham, NC: Duke University Press, 2009.

Taylor, Dorceta E. *Toxic Communities: Environmental Racism, Industrial Pollution, and Residential Mobility*. New York: NYU Press, 2014.

Taylor, Frederick Winslow. *The Principles of Scientific Management*. New York: Harper & Bros., 1911.

Taylor, Quintard. "Blacks and Asians in a White City: Japanese Americans and African Americans in Seattle, 1890–1940." *Western Historical Quarterly* 22 (1991): 401–429.

Temin, Peter, ed. *Engines of Enterprise: An Economic History of New England*. Cambridge, MA: Harvard University Press, 2000.

de Tocqueville, Alexis. *Democracy in America and Two Essays on America*, translated by Gerald E. Bevan, edited by Isaac Kramnick. New York: Penguin Classic, 2003.

Trelease, Allen W. *White Terror: The Ku Klux Klan Conspiracy and Southern Reconstruction*. New York: Harper & Row, 1971.

Trollope, Anthony. "Washington to St. Louis." Chap. 24 in *North America*, 411–414. New York: Harper & Bros., 1862.

Trotter, Joe W., and Eric Ledell Smith, eds. *African Americans in Pennsylvania: Shifting Historical Perspectives*. State College: Pennsylvania State University Press, 1997.

Uekötter, Frank. *The Age of Smoke: Environmental Policy in Germany and the United States, 1880–1970*. Pittsburgh, PA: University of Pittsburgh Press, 2009.

Unger, Nancy C. *Fighting Bob LaFollette: The Righteous Reformer*. Chapel Hill: University of North Carolina Press, 2000.

Urban Environment Conference, Inc. *Taking Back Our Health: An Institute on Surviving the Toxic Threat to Minority Communities*. Washington, DC: Urban Environmental Conference, Inc., 1985.

U.S. Bureau of the Census. *General Statistics of Cities: 1909*. Washington, DC: U.S. Government Printing Office, 1913.

U.S. Bureau of the Census. "Population and Housing Unit Counts." *1990 Census of Population and Housing*. Washington, DC: U.S. Government Printing Office, 1991.

U.S. Bureau of the Census. "United States Summary: 2010." *2010 Census of Population and Housing, Population and Housing Unit Counts*, CPH-2-5, 20–26. Washington, DC: U.S. Government Printing Office, 2012.

U.S. Department of Commerce. Series D 152–166, "Industrial Distribution of Gainful Workers: 1820 to 1940." In *Historical Statistics of the United States: Colonial Times to the Present, Bicentennial Edition*. Washington, DC: U.S. Government Printing Office, 1976.

U.S. Department of Commerce. Series D 233–682, "Detailed Occupation of the Economically Active Population: 1900 to 1970." In *Historical Statistics of the United States: Colonial Times to the Present, Bicentennial Edition*. Washington, DC: U.S. Government Printing Office, 1976.

U.S. Department of Commerce. "Table No. 27: Population by Sex, Race, Residence, and Median Age: 1790 to 1978." In *Statistical Abstract of the United States: 1979*, 28. Washington, DC: U.S. Government Printing Office, 1979.

U.S. General Accounting Office. *Siting of Hazardous Waste Landfills and Their Correlation with Racial and Economic Status of Surrounding Communities.* Washington, DC: U.S. General Accounting Office, 1983.

U.S. House of Representatives. *Investigation of the Assassination of Martin Luther King, Jr.: Hearings before the Select Committee on Assassinations of the US House of Representatives,* 95th Cong., 2nd sess., 1978.

U.S. Senate Select Committee on Improper Activities in the Labor or Management Field. "Hearings before the Select Committee of Improper Activities in the Labor or Management Field." 85th Congress, 2nd sess., July 1, 1958. Washington, DC: U.S. Government Printing Office, 1958.

U.S. Surgeon General's Office, Joseph K. Barnes, Joseph Janvier Woodward, Charles Smart, George Alexander Otis, and David Lowe Huntington. *The Medical and Surgical History of the War of the Rebellion (1861–65).* Washington, DC: U.S. Government Printing Office, 1879.

Valenčius, Conevery Bolton. *The Health of the Country: How American Settlers Understood Themselves and Their Land.* New York: Basic Books, 2002.

Van Raaphorst, Donna L. *Union Maids Not Wanted: Organizing Domestic Workers, 1870–1940.* New York: Praeger, 1988.

Veblen, Thorstein. *The Theory of the Leisure Class: An Economic Study of Institutions.* New York: Macmillan, 1899.

Wade, Richard C. *The Urban Frontier: The Rise of Western Cities, 1790–1830.* Cambridge, MA: Harvard University Press, 1959.

Wagner, Mrs. C. G. "What the Women Are Doing for Civic Cleanliness." *Municipal Journal and Engineer* 11 (1901): 35.

Waldinger, Roger D. *Through the Eye of the Needle: Immigrants and Enterprise in New York's Garment Trades.* New York: New York University Press, 1986.

Walker, Natalie. "Chicago Housing Conditions." Pt. 10: "Greeks and Italians in the Neighborhood of Hull House." *American Journal of Sociology* 21 (1915): 285–316.

Ward, David. *Cities and Immigrants: A Geography of Change in Nineteenth Century America.* New York: Oxford University Press, 1971.

Waring, George E. *Street-Cleaning and the Disposal of a City's Wastes: Methods and Results and the Effect upon Public Health, Public Morals and Municipal Prosperity.* New York: Doubleday & McClure, 1897.

Warren, Stephen. *The Worlds the Shawnees Made: Migration and Violence in Early America.* Chapel Hill: University of North Carolina Press, 2014.

Washington, Booker T. "An Address before the Negro Organization Society of Virginia, Norfolk, VA, November 12, 1914." In *Booker T. Washington Papers,* vol. 13, *1914–1915,* edited by Louis R. Harlan, Raymond W. Smock, Susan Valenza, and Sadie M. Harlan, 169. Urbana: University of Illinois Press, 1984.

Washington, Booker T. *Up from Slavery: An Autobiography.* New York: Doubleday, Page, 1919.

Washington, Booker T., and Emmett Jay Scott. *Tuskegee and Its People: Their Ideals and Achievements.* New York: Appleton, 1906.

Washington, Henry Augustine, ed., *The Writings of Thomas Jefferson*, vols. 4 and 7. New York: Derby & Jackson, 1859.

Washington, Sylvia Hood. *Packing Them In: An Archaeology of Environmental Racism in Chicago, 1865–1954*. Lanham, MD: Lexington Books, 2005.

Watkins, Susan Cotts, ed. "Background: About the 1910 Census." In *After Ellis Island: Newcomers and Natives in the 1910 Census*, edited by Susan Cotts Watkins, 25–26. New York: Russell Sage Foundation, 1994.

Weeks, Linton. "In Obama, Americans See Promise of a New Start." National Public Radio, January 18, 2009. www.npr.org/templates/story/story.php?storyId=99532472, accessed May 1, 2015.

Weissbach, Lee Shai. *Jewish Life in Small-Town America: A History*. New Haven, CT: Yale University Press, 2005.

Wiebe, Robert H. *The Search for Order, 1877–1920*. New York: Hill & Wang, 1967.

Willard, David. "The Juvenile Street-Cleaning Leagues." In *Street-Cleaning and the Disposal of a City's Wastes: Methods and Results and the Effect upon Public Health, Public Morals and Municipal Prosperity*, by George E. Waring, 177–178. New York: Doubleday & McClure, 1897.

Wohlman, Henry B. *Playing the Races: Ethnic Caricature and American Literary Realism*. New York: Oxford University Press, 2004.

Wolfe, Sheila. "Ethnics Carve Out Place for Themselves in US Way of Life." *Chicago Tribune*, November 23, 1969, 12.

Wood, Forrest G. *Black Scare: The Racist Response to Emancipation and Reconstruction*. Berkeley: University of California Press, 1968.

Wood, Gordon S. *The Radicalism of the American Revolution*. New York: A. A. Knopf, 1991.

Woodward, C. Vann. *The Strange Career of Jim Crow*. Commemative ed. New York: Oxford University Press, 2002.

Work, Monroe N. "Tuskegee Institute More than an Educational Institution." *Journal of Educational Sociology* 7 (1933): 197–205.

Wray, Matt. *Not Quite White: White Trash and the Boundaries of Whiteness*. Durham, NC: Duke University Press, 2006.

Wright, Charles. *The Messenger*. New York: Farrar, Straus, 1963.

Wurf, Jerry. "The Revolution in Government Employment." *Proceedings of the Academy of Political Science* 30, no. 2, special issue: "Unionization of Municipal Employees" (1970): 134–145.

Yu, Henry. *Thinking Orientals: Migration, Contact, and Exoticism in Modern America*. New York: Oxford University Press, 2001.

Zimring, Carl A. *Cash for Your Trash: Scrap Recycling in America*. New Brunswick, NJ: Rutgers University Press, 2005.

Zimring, Carl A. "Dirty Work: How Hygiene and Xenophobia Marginalized the American Waste Trades, 1870–1930." *Environmental History* 9 (2004): 90–112.

Zimring, Carl A. "Recycling for Profit: The Evolution of the American Scrap Industry." Ph.D diss., Carnegie Mellon University, 2002.

NEWSPAPERS AND OTHER PERIODICALS

American City
American Medical Times
American Nonconformist
Atlantic Monthly
Boston Globe
Chicago Defender
Chicago Tribune
City Club Bulletin
Cosmopolitan
Dallas Morning News
Durham Morning Herald
Ebony
Electric Railway Journal
Fortune
Harper's Weekly
Jewish Advocate
Kingsport Times-News
Memphis Press-Scimitar
Miami Herald
Municipal Journal and Engineer
New York Observer
New York Times
Philadelphia Inquirer
Philadelphia Public Ledger
Pittsburgh Courier
Portland Morning Oregonian
Property Owner's Journal
Scrap Age
Shofar Magazine
Survey
Talking Points Memo
Tri-State Defender
Washington Post
Winston-Salem Journal
Winston-Salem Sentinel

INDEX

Carl A. Zimring is Associate Professor of Sustainability Studies in the Department of Social Science and Cultural Studies at the Pratt Institute. He is the author of *Cash for Your Trash: Scrap Recycling in America* and general editor of the *Encyclopedia of Consumption and Waste: The Social Science of Garbage.*